BSL 54

WORKS ISSUED BY

THE HAKLUYT SOCIETY

THE CABOT VOYAGES
AND BRISTOL DISCOVERY
UNDER HENRY VII

SECOND SERIES
No. CXX

ISSUED FOR 1961

THE
CABOT VOYAGES AND
BRISTOL DISCOVERY
UNDER HENRY VII

BY
JAMES A. WILLIAMSON

WITH
THE CARTOGRAPHY OF THE
VOYAGES

BY R. A. SKELTON

xvi 33L

CAMBRIDGE
Published for the Hakluyt Society
AT THE UNIVERSITY PRESS
1962

THE HAKLUYT SOCIETY

1962

Printed in Great Britain
by Robert MacLehose and Company Limited
The University Press, Glasgow

PREFACE

THE VOYAGES considered in this volume are those made from Bristol in 1480 and 1481, concerning which very little is known save that they took place; the undated discovery of the so-called Isle of Brasil by unknown Bristol men some time before 1496; the expeditions led by John Cabot in 1496–8; those sent forth by the syndicates of Bristol merchants and Azorean promoters in 1501–6, of which syndicates the second was known as the Company Adventurers to the New Found Land; and finally the expedition commanded by Sebastian Cabot in 1509 or 1508–9 and intended for the discovery of the North West Passage.

In 1929 the Argonaut Press published a volume by me upon the Cabot Voyages. It took account of all the evidence I could collect at that time, and expressed some conclusions that have now to be disclaimed or modified in the light of recent discoveries. I have to offer my very sincere thanks to Mr J. E. S. Sawyer, the present proprietor of the Argonaut Press, for his permission to use any material from the 1929 volume, irrespective of his copyright. It will be seen that I have availed myself extensively of this privilege.

In the past thirty years there has been a general increase and clarification of the background knowledge affecting the interpretation of the early oceanic discoveries. How much the men of the time knew, how they understood it, and how widely spread among them the information was, are still in many ways obscure; but they are less obscure than they would have been but for the labours of the students of cartography and of early geographical literature which have borne fruit in the past generation.

In the same period there have been important discoveries of new evidence on the voyages. Professor W. E. C. Harrison discovered in 1930, and Professor D. B. Quinn correctly interpreted, an English document revealing the previously unknown voyage of 1481 as the companion to that of 1480. In 1938–9 Professor Denys Hay, working in the Vatican Library, obtained from a manuscript

v

of Polydore Vergil's *Anglica Historia* a statement on the last voyage and death of John Cabot which did not appear in the printed editions of that work. In 1943 Professor M. Ballesteros-Gaibrois published in the *Revista de Indias* some local documents of Valencia which showed that a Venetian named Johan Caboto Montecalunya resided in the city during the years 1490–3. In 1948 Signor Rodolfo Gallo printed some important legal documents giving details of property transactions of John Cabot in and near Venice in 1482–4, and providing the names of his father, brother and wife. Most recently, exceeding in importance anything on the voyage of 1497 since the revelation of the letters of Pasqualigo and Soncino a century ago, there has appeared the letter of John Day discovered at Simancas by Dr L. A. Vigneras in 1956. This letter not only necessitates a recasting of our ideas on the *Matthew's* voyage, but gives a positive statement that the men of Bristol had previously discovered a part of North America which they identified with the traditional Isle of Brasil. To my former Cabot book I was able to contribute some documents newly obtained from English records. For the present volume I have been unable to glean anything new, except a few additional entries in the Household Books. I have examined without result some classes of documents in the Public Record Office, which I thought might contain something relevant. If they do, it has escaped my search.

In preparing the volume I have been under great obligations to Mr R. A. Skelton, Superintendent of the Map Room in the British Museum and Honorary Secretary of the Hakluyt Society, whose knowledge and judgment of the problems of early maps and geographical lore are unsurpassed, and have helped me in many conversations and in a detailed criticism of the whole writing of the book. In addition, he has applied to the arrangement of the material, and to its references, the standards which he has established for the Society, a system that increases utility to the student. As the reader will see, Mr Skelton has also written directly for the volume a contribution on the maps, which may well have its effect on the controversies that have arisen concerning them

Preface

and will certainly add to the book a stamp of authority which it needs.

My thanks are due also to Professor D. B. Quinn, who has sent me various transcripts and has given great help in obtaining translations. He has also given me good advice on the Record Office documents already referred to; and his standards of accuracy and of judgment in the interpretation of evidence have helped me to keep, as I hope, on the straight path in some important passages.

Signor Rodolfo Gallo and Professor M. Ballesteros-Gaibrois have generously allowed the printing, in English form, of the important Italian and Spanish documents originally discovered by them. My thanks are also due to Dr Geoffrey Marcus for aiding me with his knowledge of the Danish archaeological work on the Greenland colony.

I am indebted to several other scholars for their help or their discoveries on particular topics, and have made my acknowledgements in the explanatory notes to the documents with which they have been concerned. Where no translator is named, the translation is my own or (in some cases) that of the late H. P. Biggar, who generously gave me, long ago, copies of some of his unpublished translations.

Cabot study is never finished. Great parts of the story are still obscure, and even the major outlines are questioned. Evidence is meagre and the reading of some of it uncertain. But advance continues. New documents are found, and growing background knowledge assists their interpretation. It is a living subject.

J. A. WILLIAMSON

December 1960

CONTENTS

INTRODUCTION

DOCUMENTS

BRISTOL AND THE ATLANTIC IN THE FIFTEENTH CENTURY

THE CABOTS TO 1495

Contents

ix

Contents

THE CARTOGRAPHY OF THE VOYAGES
by R. A. Skelton

ILLUSTRATIONS

PLATES

xiii

Illustrations

ACKNOWLEDGEMENTS

Plates I, VI, VIII, X and XI are reproduced by courtesy of the
Trustees of the British Museum. Plates IV, XII and XIII were made
from negatives kindly lent by Dr Armando Cortesão, Coimbra.
Plate II is reproduced by permission of the Academia Real de la
Historia, Madrid; Plate XIV by that of the Huntington Library,
San Marino, California; and Plate VII by that of Ing. R. Haardt,
Globusmuseum, Vienna. Plate V*b*, from a photograph in Crown
Copyright, is reproduced by permission of The Controller of
H.M. Stationery Office. The maps were drawn by Mr G. S.
Holland and Mr G. R. Versey.

SELECT BIBLIOGRAPHY

ALMAGIÀ, ROBERTO, *Commemorazione di Sebastiano Caboto nel IV centenario della morte*, Venezia, 1958.
—— 'Sulle navigazioni de Giovanni Caboto', *Rivista Geografica Italiana*, vol. LXVII (1960).

BALLESTEROS-GAIBROIS, M., 'Juan Caboto en España', *Revista de Indias*, vol. IV (1943), pp. 607–27.

BEAZLEY, SIR C. RAYMOND, *John and Sebastian Cabot*. London, 1898.

BIDDLE, RICHARD, *A Memoir of Sebastian Cabot*. London, 1831.

BIGGAR, H. P., *The Voyages of the Cabots and of the Corte-Reals*. Paris, 1903. [Extracted from *Revue Hispanique*, vol. X.]
—— *The Precursors of Jacques Cartier, 1497–1534*. Ottawa, 1911.

DAVIES, ARTHUR, 'The last voyage of John Cabot and the rock at Grates Cove', *Nature*, vol. CLXXVI (1955), pp. 996–8.

DAWSON, S. E., 'Voyages of the Cabots', *Transactions of the Royal Society of Canada*, vol. XI (1894), pp. 51–112.

GALLO, RODOLFO, 'Intorno a Giovanni Caboto', *Rendiconti Accad. Naz. dei Lincei*, Cl. di Sc. Morali, ser. III, vol. III (1948), pp. 209–20.

GANONG, W. F., 'Crucial maps in the early cartography and place-nomenclature of the Atlantic coast of Canada', *Transactions of the Royal Society of Canada*, ser. III, vol. XXIII (1929).

GASPARINI LEPORACE, TULLIA, *Mostra dei navigatori veneti del Quattrocento e del Cinquecento. Catalogo*. Venezia, 1957.

HARRISSE, HENRY, *The Discovery of North America*. London, 1892.
—— *Jean et Sébastien Cabot*. Paris, 1882.
—— *John Cabot the Discoverer of North America and Sebastian his Son*. London, 1896.

NUNN, G. E., *The Mappemonde of Juan de la Cosa*. Jenkintown, 1934.

Bibliography

PENROSE, BOIES, *Travel and Discovery in the Renaissance, 1420–1620*. Harvard, 1952.

PROWSE, G. R. F., *Cabot's Surveys* [and later monographs, mimeographed]. Toronto, 1931–46.

TARDUCCI, FRANCESCO, *Di Giovanni e Sebastiano Caboto*. Venezia, 1892; English translation, Detroit, 1893.

TORIBIO MEDINA, J., *El veneciano Sebastián Caboto al servicio de España*, Santiago de Chile, 1908.

VIGNERAS, L. A., 'New Light on the 1497 Cabot Voyage to America', *Hispanic American Historical Review*, vol. XXXVI (1956), pp. 503–9.

—— 'The Cape Breton Landfall: 1494 or 1497. Note on a letter from John Day', *Canadian Historical Review*, vol. XXXVIII (1957), pp. 219–28.

WILLIAMSON, J. A., *The Voyages of the Cabots and the English Discovery of North America*. London, Argonaut Press, 1929.

WINSHIP, G. P., *Cabot Bibliography, with an introductory essay on the careers of the Cabots*. London, 1900.

INTRODUCTION

I

KNOWLEDGE OF THE ATLANTIC
IN THE FIFTEENTH CENTURY

IN THE fifteenth century there was an increasing European consciousness of the Atlantic as an ocean containing valuable undiscovered islands, and bounded by a farther continental shore which must be that of Eastern Asia. These ideas had been growing among entirely independent groups of people, of whom some had little knowledge of the others.

There were the students of classical geography, professional scholars and nearly all churchmen, who wrote for one another and generally betrayed little interest in the achievements of actual discoverers. There were the mariners of the Western European ports to whose minds the legendary stories of Atlantic islands carried an impression of lost realities awaiting rediscovery. There were the men of the north who knew that their ancestors had sailed westwards to Iceland and Greenland, which their colonists still occupied, and to lands in lower latitudes to the south-west. There were Englishmen, fishermen who sailed yearly to the Iceland coast, and Bristol merchants who traded regularly with Iceland and perhaps occasionally with Greenland, and began to make experimental voyages towards finding the shadowy western coasts where fishing might be good. There were Portuguese who discovered the Azores and the nearer African islands, and who traded with England and particularly with Bristol; and Castilians, their rivals in the Canaries and on the African trading coast. In most of these enterprises there were Italians and Flemings serving as individuals, and for a time Frenchmen as a group seeking to colonize the Canaries. Finally, there were two all-European lines of thought that indirectly stimulated Atlantic enterprise: the hope that in the non-Moslem parts of Asia allies might be found against

3

the conquering Turk; and the mercantile ambition inspired by the great land-travellers of the thirteenth century who brought to European knowledge the hitherto unknown cities and coasts of Eastern Asia.

The mapping of the world and methods of charting and navigation made steady progress in the latter half of the Middle Ages, but it was left to the fifteenth century to produce the one implement without which all Atlantic knowledge must have remained speculative—the ship in which to cross the ocean and come home again. The weatherly three-masted ship of the culminating century, able to make good a course within seven or even six points of the wind, was something that previous generations had not possessed. The earlier single-masted cog could no doubt have made Columbus's passage to the Caribbean, but it is also likely that she would never have come back.

The leading concept of the classical geographers, that the earth is a sphere with climates in zones of decreasing warmth from the equator to the poles, persisted through the Middle Ages and was increasingly prominent towards their close. There were flat-earth dissidents from this doctrine, but they were never preponderant and had disappeared by the fifteenth century. The fathers of the Christian Church for the most part allowed the spherical earth, and their succeeding commentators elaborated its details. In doing so they produced system and definition rather than new theory. They harmonized physical geography with Christian doctrine, whose discipline led them to perpetuate errors that might otherwise not have attained prominence. They were much concerned with the proportions of land and water on the earth's surface and with the question of the antipodes to the southward of the equatorial zone. On the first head they exaggerated the proportion of dry land and diminished that of the ocean. On the second they argued that the sun's heat rendered the equator impassable by human beings, with the consequence that the antipodean regions were unattainable and could not be inhabited by the stock of Adam. Bede in the eighth century affirmed the spherical earth, as

4

did Roger Bacon and Albertus Magnus in the thirteenth, when also Vincent of Beauvais made an encyclopaedic collection of geography in his *Speculum Mundi*. The academic scholars of the Middle Ages first salvaged such fragments of classical learning as had not perished in Western Europe, and later, by contact with learned Arabs who had preserved much more which might otherwise have been lost, recovered important works from the eastern or Byzantine half of the ancient Empire. By the early fifteenth century much astronomical work of value to explorers had come into the limited circulation of the learned world. At that juncture the rediscovery of some late copies of the maps attributed to Ptolemy of Alexandria provided a stimulus to persons who had never before seen maps of so practical and veritable a nature, and in fifty years it spread effectively among the secular scholars who grew prominent as a class in the later fifteenth century.

Cardinal Pierre d'Ailly, who wrote early in that century, is important less for the substance of his work than for its fortune after his death. For it came into print in the second half of the century, and so helped the scholars' learning to make contact with the minds of Columbus and other men of action. The substance was not original or new. In its remarks on the land-and-water question, and by consequence on the breadth of the Atlantic, d'Ailly's *Imago Mundi* was a repetition of Bacon's thirteenth-century *Opus Majus*, which itself was, in this respect, a recension of the early fathers of the Church and of one or two Arab authorities who drew upon Greek works which had not then returned to Western Europe. The achievements of medieval explorers, and of Marco Polo the greatest of them, do not appear in the *Imago Mundi*, which was a revival of classical knowledge current a thousand years before. The Ptolemaic maps were rediscovered only while d'Ailly was already at work.

The maps had an enormous influence, for they were copied in manuscript volumes and were printed in several editions from 1477, and they shaped the geographical mind of the last generation of the century. Ptolemy's Asia indeed extended no farther east than Malaya, but by that time the work of Marco Polo was increasing its circulation and yielding a rich description of China and the eastern archipelago. Marco Polo, although he influenced cartographers in the fourteenth century, made less impression on the academic geographers; but already there was a lively interest in unknown lands, as the partly fictitious *Travels* of Sir John Mandeville indicate. In the fifteenth century the manuscript copies of Marco Polo multiplied, and the work was also printed long before the century's close. The general result was to build up in the minds of some merchants, scholars, travellers and seamen the conception of the Atlantic ocean as a link between Western Europe and Eastern Asia, the two ends of the tripartite land-mass known to Europeans and consisting of the three contiguous continents of Europe, Africa and Asia. The number of individuals who thought deeply of this concept was probably few, but its existence among educated men ensured that when the leaders in action explained their plans it was to hearers who understood what they were talking of. The principle of the westward passage from Europe to Asia was conceded, although, say in 1480–90, there was still much doubt and disbelief that it would be practically possible. The unbelievers were in fact justified, for it is certain that no expedition at that time could have made the voyage from Europe west to China across an open ocean in which no large land intervened.

The work of Marco Polo attained its full influence in the second half of the fifteenth century. Not only did it bring the wealth of China and the commerce of its seas into European consciousness, but it described Japan in exciting terms. Marco had seen China for himself, but he had not seen Japan, which he reported very inaccurately by hearsay gathered from the Chinese. He mentioned no latitudes, but he gave the impression that it was a large island lying a good deal to the south of what we know is the true position, and some 1500 miles from the coast of China. The cartographers created a tradition of an oblong island, its main axis running north and south, placed partly within the tropics. Marco said that it was extraordinarily rich with gold and pearls. To the south of Cipango and extending towards China was a great archipelago of spice-bearing islands. Such was Japan or Cipango, the richest land of Asia and the nearest to Western Europe. Marco Polo was the first European to write of it. To the men of Cardinal d'Ailly's world, the churchmen-scholars of the fourteenth and early fifteenth centuries, Marco, an unlearned merchant-traveller, was unimportant. But the expanding mind of the fifteenth century found his writings supremely interesting.

The condition of Atlantic knowledge and doctrine in the last quarter of the century is illustrated by the Toscanelli correspondence[1] and the globe of Martin Behaim. The first shows that in 1474 there was living in Florence a physician who applied his mind to the westward voyage. He was Paolo Toscanelli, who some time before had been visited by Fernão Martins, a canon of Lisbon travelling in Italy. Martins listened to Toscanelli's ideas on the westward passage and reported them to Afonso V of Portugal, who asked him to get a written statement. Toscanelli complied with the Portuguese request in a letter dated June 1474, accompanied by a map. His statement amounted to this, that the great city of Quinsay in China would be found in the latitude of Lisbon at a westward distance of 5000 sea miles. But on this voyage, by deviating from the direct course, it would be possible to refresh at the island of Antillia, about 1500 miles from Europe, and at Cipango, about 3500 miles. The Portuguese evidently found such a project unattractive and did not follow up the information; but a few years later Christopher Columbus got wind of it and wrote to Toscanelli. He replied by sending to Columbus a copy of the

[1] The genuineness of the Toscanelli letters was vigorously attacked at the beginning of our present century by Henry Vignaud, particularly in his *Toscanelli and Columbus* (London, 1902). His contention was that the Toscanelli correspondence was forged after the return of Columbus in 1493 in order to support what Vignaud said was a novel claim by Columbus to have sailed with Asia as his objective. After sixty years it is evident that the majority of Columbian scholars do not allow that Vignaud made good his case, and consider on the contrary that the letters are genuine.

letter and map which he had previously sent to Lisbon. None of the originals of these documents has been preserved, but Ferdinand Columbus had in his possession copies of the letters sent to his father by Toscanelli, and included them in his history of his father's life. The map is lost, although reconstructions have been attempted.

The importance of all this to our present subject is that it shows the learned making contact with the men of action. There is no reason to believe that Toscanelli kept his conclusions secret: he was ready to impart them to anyone interested. There were probably other men discussing the same ideas, which could have been already familiar in Italian geographical circles. The Toscanelli plan was typical rather than exceptional. It shows us the acceptance by a new generation of learned men of the discoveries of Marco Polo; the addition of eastern China and Japan and the Archipelago to Ptolemy's Asia, greatly extending its longitude and bringing it nearer to Europe; and the entry of one who was to be a great explorer into the calculation of 'Can it be done?'

The globe of Martin Behaim gives graphic form to the new concepts. Behaim was a German from Nuremberg who travelled to Portugal, displayed some knowledge of geography, and was admitted to the official circle which advised on oceanic projects. He married in the Azores and perhaps took part in an unsuccessful voyage to seek for new lands west of them. He returned to Nuremberg, and there in 1492 constructed the globe which has perpetuated his memory. It is the oldest terrestrial globe now surviving, and owes some of its importance to that, and to the fact that it was completed in the year in which Columbus first crossed the Atlantic. Its outlines are possibly based on a printed world-map by Henricus Martellus, *c.* 1489, and convey a general impression of contemporary thought. It shows Antillia just within the tropic zone and south of the westernmost Azores, Cipango stretching from about 30° N down to 8° N, and Marco Polo's Quinsay in the Chinese province of Mangi almost on the tropic line. All this was in accordance with Columbus's ideas, except that he reduced the east-west distances and so made his project look more feasible. For the Atlantic problem the interest of the Behaim globe is that it expresses a view held by a large school of thought. Neither Columbus nor John Cabot ever saw this globe, but its Atlantic is in broad principle their Atlantic.

In the sixth and following centuries there was navigation of the northern waters by Irish seafarers, including monks and hermits who sought islands whereon to live a solitary life. Their discoveries were among the Scottish islands and north to Iceland. Their records are legends with a substratum of truth, composed mainly from the spiritual aspect and without much basis in geography. For this reason it became possible in the later Middle Ages to transfer the islands concerned from the North to the Atlantic west of Europe, and even farther south. Some thirteenth-century maps showed St Brandan's Islands roughly in the position of the Canaries. From the mid-fourteenth century nautical charts laid down a chain of islands on the meridian of Madeira and running north from about the latitude of Tangier to that of Finisterre. Each island bears a particular traditional name, and below the group there is generally written *Insule Sancti Brandani*. This may indicate a fourteenth-century discovery of the eastern Azores; and the 'false Azores', so located, remained on the charts to the end of the fifteenth century. At the western edge of the charts, from 1424 onwards, cartographers drew the large oblong island of Antillia, extending north and south like Marco Polo's Cipango. Antillia was wholly a creation of the map-makers, who commonly identified it with the legendary island of the Seven Cities, supposed to have been colonized by refugees fleeing from the Moslem conquest of the Peninsula in the eighth century.[1] A Portuguese crew were said to have found the Seven Cities towards the middle of the fifteenth century, and to have landed and conversed with the inhabitants. The discovery, if it really took place, was possibly an early sighting of one of the Azores, which, how-

[1] I owe these statements on the islands to the kindness of Mr R. A. Skelton.

9

ever, were uninhabited until the fifteenth-century Portuguese began to colonize them. It was a persistent cartographers' belief that not far west of Ireland lay the Island of Brasil, which is marked in various fifteenth-century maps and generally placed close to the Irish coast. It appears as an island of the St Brandan's type, not nearly so extensive as Antillia or Cipango.

The lively belief in so many imaginary islands, coupled with the actual discoveries of the Canaries, Cape Verdes and Azores (whose nine units were revealed between 1431 and 1460), caused the Portuguese ocean seamen to be alert for new finds. It was easy even for experienced men to mistake a cloud-formation for land and to report a discovery that might seem worth following up. The Portuguese kings generally rewarded a discoverer with the captaincy of any island he might find and colonize, with sufficient privileges to make his enterprise worth while. In the last decades of the century the Portuguese were intent upon the opening of the seaway round Africa to Southern Asia; and there is no clear evidence that their westward enterprises were directed to Asia as an ultimate goal. They knew of the concept but did not adopt it. Toscanelli sent the plan to Lisbon in 1474. Columbus put it to King John II in 1484 and was rejected. The reason was scientific: the best calculations of longitudes— and those of Columbus were not the best—made the oceanic distance between Europe and Asia too great for an attempt to be practicable.

In the ninth century adventurers from Norway found their way to Iceland and began to colonize it, dispossessing the Irish settlers who were already there. In about 985 Icelandic ships sighted Greenland, and Eric the Red led a party of colonists to occupy it. There were two main settlements, the East and the West, both lying west of Cape Farewell, the southern point of Greenland. The east side of Greenland, nearest to Iceland, was not colonized owing to the permanent obstruction of its coast by icefields. In the East and West settlements the Norsemen found fiords extending deep into the land and surrounded by pastures capable of maintaining sheep and cattle. It would seem that the edge of Greenland's permanent ice-cover did not extend so far south as now; and in the colonized area the conditions are said to have been in some respects more attractive than those of Iceland. At its best the Greenland colony had perhaps 3500 inhabitants, as evidenced by the remaining traces of farm buildings and churches.

The Greenland colony is more important in the story of Atlantic discovery than used to be supposed. It has long been known from Icelandic sagas that from the beginning of the eleventh century ships sailing for Greenland passed south of it and reached the American coast. The accounts specify three regions, Helluland or Stony Land, somewhere in present Labrador; Markland or Wooded Land, southern Labrador and Newfoundland; and Wineland the Good, farther south but not conclusively identified. Fridtjof Nansen, the Artic explorer and historian, was sceptical of the Wineland story, which he considered full of mythical or impossible elements. He classed it rather with the building-up of imaginary lands west of the Atlantic islands by the Portuguese, a Norse contribution to a common form of self-deception.[1] Most other historians have accepted Wineland, but there has been little agreement on its whereabouts. An Icelandic geography of the early fifteenth century stated: 'South from Greenland is Helluland, next to it is Markland, thence it is not far to Wineland the Good, which some men think is connected with Africa.'[2] About Markland there is no doubt. It is well attested that Icelanders and Greenlanders went there for timber, certainly far into the fourteenth century, and possibly later. For our purpose the sum of the evidence is that Greenland was a known and accurately located country, and Markland was well known to exist and its timber helps to place its latitude south of Greenland's, while Wineland was a still more southerly possibility.

[1] Fridtjof Nansen, *In Northern Mists* (London, 1911), ch. IX.
[2] Cited by G. M. Gathorne Hardy, *The Norse Discoverers of America* (Oxford, 1921), pp. 257–8.

The Cabot Voyages and Bristol Discovery

Together, by the implications of the sagas, Helluland, Markland and Wineland formed the coast of a continent bounding the north Atlantic.

Modern research, chiefly archaeological, indicates that Greenland was not a forgotten country in the fifteenth century. Danish archaeologists believe firmly that the colony continued alive, though decaying, until the latter half of that century, and did not die out, as was formerly thought, a hundred years earlier. Some go so far as to say that a remnant was probably still extant when the great period of Atlantic discovery set in with Columbus and Cabot. The evidence of burials shows, if we may trust their dating, that the Greenlanders had some contact with Europe in the late fifteenth century, since articles datable to that period have been found in the graves. But the contact became ever more casual and precarious. The Greenland exports were of no great economic importance, a few hides, narwhal ivory, and the white falcons much prized by European sportsmen. For these the colony received tools, weapons and grain. The Greenland trade was a Norwegian royal monopoly. The Scandinavian north had a bad time in the fourteenth century, being hard hit by the Black Death, and thenceforward the Hanseatic League became in effect the controllers of its commerce. The royal ships ceased to sail with any regularity to Greenland. Rome still appointed bishops, but none actually went to his diocese after 1386. By the late fifteenth century Greenland, though not forgotten, was so far out of touch that in the 1470's the Danish king Christian I, bethinking himself of his distant province, sent the two captains Pining and Pothorst to look it up in what was virtually a voyage of exploration.[1] What they achieved is unknown, but no reunion resulted. The occasional Greenland contacts which archaeology claims to have taken place may well have been accidental, by Hanseatic and English vessels driven off their course on voyages to Iceland. The Western settlement disintegrated first, the Eastern continuing in a moribund state until the close of the century. The burials examined

[1] Sofus Larsen, *The Discovery of North America* (London, 1925).

12

were mostly of young people, and few of the dead had passed middle age.[1]

In the early fifteenth century fishermen from the eastern ports of England began to sail to Iceland for cod. The men of Bristol did the like, and Bristol merchants developed a trade in Icelandic products. A point of some interest, and one at present unsettled, is the course taken by the Bristol ships, whether northwards through the Irish Sea, or round the west of Ireland with Galway as a port of call or refuge. A vague record of Columbus's early life states that in 1477 he sailed to Iceland, and another that he once visited Galway. It may have been in a Bristol ship. The fact that Bristol merchants were trading with Iceland opens up a cardinal question. These merchants, men of open minds and broad views, as some were to prove themselves, had opportunities of learning about Greenland and the American lands beyond. Did they in fact do so? It is a question of likelihood, for there is no direct evidence.

[1] It is difficult for the outside observer to make an unqualified statement about the survival of the Greenland colony. The archaeologists are positive that it endured until the second half of the fifteenth century. The chief finds were made in 1921 at a cemetery at Herjolfsnes where the soil had become permanently frozen and had thus preserved the clothing buried with the corpses. There were some round flat-crowned caps with the sides fairly high: 'Any period might have designed them, but we recognize them as a head covering that was very popular in the fifteenth century, whereas caps from earlier times are different. . . . There remains one cap about which there cannot be much discussion. It is 25 to 30 cm. high, rather conical, standing steeply up from the forehead but widening out at the back of the neck. It is one of the high caps shown us on the paintings of Dirk Bout, Memling and other Flemish painters, worn in the time of Louis XI and Charles the Bold, the latter half of the fifteenth century.' Furthermore: 'There are fragments of dresses with quite close folds sewn at the waist, one of these also with a V-shaped neck opening, and these two are fashion details belonging to the later part of the fifteenth century.' The quotations are from Poul Nørlund, *Viking Settlers in Greenland* (Cambridge, 1936), p. 125. Dr Nørlund considered the tall cap to have been probably an imported article, and thus to be evidence of a visit of North European shipping. The above, and especially the tall cap, is almost convincing. But is it impossible that such things were made at an earlier date? Dr Geoffrey Marcus quotes for me a passage from Mr C. L. Vebaek, a Danish authority, written in 1958, which gives the date of the disappearance of the East settlement as most probably at the beginning of the sixteenth century. I am greatly indebted for the help of Dr Marcus, whose knowledge of the Scandinavian languages has enabled him to keep abreast of this question.

13

These things were living knowledge among a restricted class in Iceland who preserved and copied the sagas. But the story of lands to the west and south, and their traditional names, must have been current in vague form among the illiterate people of the ports and coast with whom the English inevitably had dealings. We do not know if the Bristol men had any intellectual contact with the few who knew the history recorded in the sagas, but it seems very probable that they heard of Markland and Wineland and perhaps of western fisheries which the Icelanders themselves had no need to exploit. It was misty and uncertain, but it would stimulate adventurous thought. Map-makers in continental Europe knew of the existence of Greenland. A map of the north by Claudius Clavus in a manuscript Ptolemy of 1427 shows the eastern half of Greenland with the name Gronlandia. A later map by Clavus, extant in a copy made about 1467, has both coasts of Greenland with a number of place-names, most of which have been shown to be fabricated. It is easier to establish the existence of such knowledge than to be sure of the extent to which it was spread. We have no evidence that it existed among men of maritime pursuits in Bristol or London, but there were geographical manuscripts in English monasteries in the fourteenth and fifteenth centuries; and a merchant's office, such as that of William Canynges of Bristol, can have collected information from various sources.

The truly discovered Atlantic islands, north of the Cape Verdes, were all open to English trade. There was among some Englishmen a chart-knowledge of the islands. Andrea Bianco, a Venetian seaman, made or at least signed an Atlantic chart in London in 1448. William Worcestre, a man with Bristol connections, saw a chart of the islands about 1480 and wrote comments on their positions. By the Treaty of Alcaçovas in 1479, a settlement of Spanish-Portuguese disputes, the Canaries fell to Spain and Madeira to Portugal. The Portuguese title to the Azores had not been challenged. The Canaries were inhabited by warlike aborigines whose resistance was hard to overcome. By about 1490 the Spaniards were in general possession. They welcomed adventurers of other nations, and it is on record that Englishmen took part in the conquest and received grants of land.[1] There is thus a strong probability of some English trade: it was allowed by Spain under the terms of the Treaty of Medina del Campo in 1489. In 1480, as appears from a customs record, Bristol merchants were shipping goods direct to Madeira, although in a Breton ship. In 1486 there is an entry of a Portuguese ship arriving direct from Madeira with sugar and bowstaves.[2] That there was more trade than this is indicated by two considerations, first that the majority of the Bristol customs records for these years are missing, and second, that much trade with Madeira and the Canaries may have been carried on by Englishmen from Lisbon and Seville, since at both ports there were English merchant colonies. As for the Azores, there is no record of English trade at this period; but no record does not prove the negative, and by 1500 we have sure evidence of the presence in Bristol of Azoreans of sufficient standing to be associated with leading Bristol merchants in grants of privileges from the Crown. The reign of Edward IV is badly documented, but it has come to light that in 1481–2 there was a well-advanced project for Englishmen to open a trade with North Africa, a plan which the Portuguese were able to check by diplomatic protest.[3] In 1488 again, there was in England a fugitive Portuguese nobleman, the Count of Penamacor, advocating a similar project, but Henry VII did not allow it.[4]

From these indications it is apparent that English merchants, and particularly those of Bristol, were in the 1480's and 90's sailing in the temperate latitudes of the North Atlantic and forming projects for commercial expansion. They were at least acquainted with the position of the Azores, a thousand miles out from Europe, and

[1] E. G. R. Taylor (ed.), *A Brief Summe of Geographie* (Hakluyt Society, 1932), p. xxi.

[2] Document 5.

[3] D. B. Quinn, 'Edward IV and Exploration', *Mariner's Mirror*, vol. XXI (1935), pp. 275–84.

[4] J. W. Blake (ed.), *Europeans in West Africa* (Hakluyt Society, 1942), vol. II, pp. 287–8.

may possibly have visited those islands. They were in contact with Portuguese ocean mariners whose minds were set upon the discovery of western islands yet unknown and upon the acquisition of colonizing rights from the Portuguese Crown.[1]

There lies in all this an important stimulus to English enterprise. On its nature one point is clear. The Portuguese were seeking desirable islands, but not a westward passage to Asia. Their government had considered that proposition, and had rejected it as impracticable owing to the length of voyage involved. It had committed itself to reaching the Indian Ocean by circumnavigating Africa. There was a limit, moral rather than physical, to the length of a passage across open ocean without sight of land. Columbus in 1492 reached that limit with his 3000 miles passage from the Canaries to the Bahamas. He was a commander of strong personality, and yet he narrowly escaped a mutiny that would have cut short his voyage before he made his landfall. Neither he nor any other leader would have got a crew of those days to sail the 5000 miles that Toscanelli had stated as the westward distance to China.[2] Toscanelli indeed had indicated Antillia and Cipango as refreshing places, but they were hearsay islands which no one had yet located. Columbus could get his attempt sanctioned only by making an unscientific reduction of the distance involved and by gaining the favour of Queen Isabella, whose mind, like his own, was mystical rather than mathematical.

There is one more factor to be mentioned here, the direct impact of Columbus in his suppliant period upon English thought. Three well-informed Spanish writers, Las Casas, Ferdinand Columbus, and the historian Oviedo, each of whom wrote from his own independent sources of information, state that Chris-

[1] See, in general, S. E. Morison, *Portuguese Voyages to America in the Fifteenth Century* (Harvard, 1940).

[2] Bartolomeu Dias discovered and rounded South Africa in 1487–8, but his track lay close to the African coast, at which he stopped and landed in several places. His mutiny occurred when he was on the threshold of the entirely new waters of the Indian Ocean. The success of Columbus in 1492 overthrew the psychological barrier to long ocean passages.

topher, while waiting for Spanish acceptance of his proposals, sent his brother Bartholomew to open the same enterprise to Henry VII. Bartholomew was captured and robbed by Easterling pirates and the completion of his journey long delayed. But he was in London in 1488-9, laying before Henry and his councillors the plans and illustrative maps of Christopher's project. By one account Henry was considering the matter with no great haste when Christopher Columbus was at length able to close with the Spanish sovereigns. By another, Henry refused to entertain the proposal. The latter is more likely to be correct, because Bartholomew went over to France, where he was when Christopher set sail in 1492. There is not a scrap of documentary evidence, English or Spanish, about this mission of Bartholomew Columbus; but the authority of the writers above named obliges us to believe that it took place.[1] It shows that by 1490 the idea of the westward passage to Asia was known to Henry VII and his advisers, and that it was not taken up. The reluctance may or may not have been due to geographical scepticism. Henry had many other great affairs, economic and political, to claim his attention, and a war with France in prospect over the disposal of Brittany; and it may be that he considered the proposal a good one but the time not opportune. Whether the affair was a council secret, or whether it was talked about outside, we have no means of knowing. In London, even in commercial circles, there would at that time have been few to whom a far-fetched novel idea such as this would have been attractive, for their minds were not prepared. There is no evidence on which to base an inference that Bristol knew anything about it.

We may sum up these probings into the knowledge and outlook of the Bristol merchants towards the year 1490. They shared the Portuguese knowledge of the Atlantic islands already discovered. They were trading certainly with Madeira, probably with the Canaries, possibly with the Azores. They knew of an English project for trading in Africa. They were already making voyages for the discovery of land west of the British Isles, as will be shown

[1] Document 13.

in the following pages. These statements are well evidenced. By their intercourse with Iceland they had, in strong probability, learned of the existence of Greenland, which they may even have visited, and Markland, and of the belief in Wineland the Good in a temperate western region; and they may have heard of good fishing on those western coasts. These statements are probabilities lacking documentary proof, which amounts only to the fact that the Bristol men did business in Iceland. There is no direct evidence that the academic geography with its promise of the westward route to Asia had reached their minds, or that they had heard of the discoveries of Marco Polo; although there may have been some inkling of both those influences. There were certainly no English versions of Cardinal d'Ailly and Marco Polo, and we must leave to our own imaginative judgment the question whether English merchants were likely to be practised readers of Latin or other foreign tongues, or to obtain the relevant manuscripts or books. In fact, we just do not know. There is, however, one ray of illumination: in the winter of 1497-8 an English merchant, John Day, was in possession of a copy of Marco Polo which he had obtained for a Spanish correspondent who was probably Christopher Columbus.[1] This was after the way to Asia had become a public topic on the return of John Cabot from his first discovery. From this single and late instance it would be going too far to deduce a general English interest in such works. The facts, as we do know them, point to a strong objective interest in Atlantic discovery, not reinforced by any of the wider knowledge that inspired Columbus and, as we shall see, his contemporary John Cabot.

[1] Document 25.

II

PRE-CABOTIAN EXPEDITIONS FROM BRISTOL

THERE IS no doubt, as will be shown, that from 1480, if not earlier, the merchants of Bristol were making voyages for the discovery of unknown lands to the westward of the British Isles; and we have now good reason to suppose that John Cabot, formerly thought to have lived many years at Bristol before he made his American voyages, did not come to England until 1495 or possibly 1494. This is the inference to be drawn from certain Spanish documents first made public in 1943, which will be considered in subsequent pages of this book. The period of the pre-Cabotian voyages from Bristol is therefore approximately from 1480 to 1494 or 1495. We have here to consider the evidence that bears upon them.

It has long been known that there was a voyage of exploration in 1480. The authority for it is a passage in the *Itinerary* of William Worcestre, a Latin MS preserved at Corpus Christi College, Cambridge.[1] It states briefly that John Jay the younger, and others for whose names a blank space is left, equipped a ship of 80 tons at Bristol. On 15 July 1480 she set sail from the Kingrode to look for the Island of Brasil to the west of Ireland. Her commander was 'Thloyde', the most expert master mariner of England, a man who appears in the customs records as John Lloyd. He did not find any new land, and after nine weeks (mis-stated as months in the MS) had returned to an Irish port by September 18. They were driven back, says the account, by rough weather, to repair the needs of the ship and crew. Professor E. M. Carus-Wilson has discovered an administrative document which is very possibly connected with

[1] Document 6.

19

this voyage.[1] It is a licence for Thomas Croft, Collector of Customs, and for William Spencer, Robert Straunge and William de la Fount, merchants of Bristol, to trade for three years to any parts with any except staple goods, despite any statute to the contrary, with two or three ships of 60 tons or under. The date of issue is 18 June 1480.

It will be noted that William Worcestre gave the name of only one promoter, John Jay, who was not one of those licenced. If there is any connection between the voyage and the licence, John Jay may have been a sub-partner, and probably there were others. In the mercantile syndicates of the ensuing period we frequently find the system of a few named partners receiving official recognition and each lessening his risk by admitting the investments of sub-partners under his name. It is quite possible that this and other voyages of discovery may have been financed by the greater part of mercantile Bristol. William Worcestre naturally mentioned Jay because he was related to the Jay family and presumably had his information from them. He knew that there were other promoters but had not learnt their names. The discrepancy in tonnage —Worcestre's 80 tons and the 60-ton limit of the licence—is not important. Tonnage ratings were only approximate and were often loosely stated.

Late medieval maps show the Island of Brasil as a small island of some conventional outline, a circle or a half-moon or twin half-moons, lying close to the west coast of Ireland. Its position is such that it would certainly have been discovered by ships going to Galway. There is no such island, unless we take account of the Aran Islands, lying in sight of one another and of the mainland at the entrance of Galway Bay. To those navigating the Irish coast there could never have been any mystery about them, or need for expeditions to discover them. The map-makers' Brasil may have arisen from reports of the Porcupine Bank, a shallow area some 140 miles out into the Atlantic. Shoal depths alter the appearance

[1] E. M. Carus-Wilson, *The Overseas Trade of Bristol in the later Middle Ages* (Bristol Record Society, 1936), pp. 157–8.

of the sea and would be noted by ship-masters, who would have taken soundings and embodied them in the rutters.[1] Hence the cartographers may have concluded that some land must be near, and their Isle of Brasil could have been the result. The coast dwellers of western Ireland shared the belief, which continued into the nineteenth century; although by that time it had become mythical rather than rational, as evidenced by its elaboration that the land could be seen once every seven years.

The cartographers' Brasil is misleading to students of the discoveries, since the Brasil which the explorers were seeking was something different. The Brasil in the minds of the Bristol merchants was a land worth expensive efforts in discovery, lying a long way out westwards in the Atlantic. The scanty records name only Brasil, but one may suspect that Antillia also may have been in contemplation. John Lloyd did not need sixty days' sailing to fail to find an island nestling close to the Irish coast. We must believe that Lloyd pushed out as far as he could into the ocean in search of something worth having. How far he got we cannot tell: July was late in the year for a successful westbound passage of the Atlantic.

The Portuguese believed that there was a large land north-west of the Azores. In 1452, according to a story that reached the ears of Columbus, a ship from Fayal tried to find it but was beaten back by contrary winds; and then her navigators changed course and sailed north of east to the latitude of Cape Clear in Ireland, where the smoothness of the water in a strong westerly wind made them think that there must be an unseen land to the westward. But this story has very likely been modified in transmission, and the persons concerned may have told it differently. Las Casas, who records the 1452 story, has another which is of interest to our investigation. An old sailor told Columbus that

---

[1] The depths are about twice as great as those on the great bank off Newfoundland. Some thirty years ago a fragment of Roman pottery was brought up in the net of a Cardiff trawler on the Porcupine Bank (*Journal of Roman Studies*, vol. XXIV (1934), p. 220).

21

while on a voyage to Ireland he and his shipmates had seen a land which others also believed to exist, which they imagined was a point of Tartary projecting that way from the east. But, says Las Casas, 'I believe truly it was that which we now call the Baccalaos'.[1] The Baccalaos, when Las Casas wrote, meant Newfoundland and the adjacent coasts. 'Projecting from the east' may indicate Greenland, but there are instances in which the North American lands are described as being in the east by people who thought of them as the coasts of eastern Asia. Las Casas evidently took the reference in this sense. Columbus thought it worth while to record this tale as evidence of western land to be reached by a ship from Europe.

The Portuguese mariners may themselves have gone to Iceland and there have heard of American lands south-west of Greenland, or they may have had such information from English merchants of Bristol. When we remember that Portuguese were regularly trading in Bristol, and Bristolians in Lisbon, we may validly assume that there was an exchange of ideas between men with a common interest in the farther Atlantic. This, with the English westward search already begun, may have its bearing on a Portuguese undertaking of 1486, when Fernão Dulmo (Ferdinand van Olm, a Flemish settler in Terceira) and Afonso do Estreito of Madeira obtained a grant from John II for discovery and colonization of a great island or mainland thought to be that of the Seven Cities. The location is not given, but can only have been to the west or north-west. No result of the venture is recorded. Either it never sailed or it was unsuccessful.[2]

The Bristol men received a good deal of sea-lore from the Portuguese and Spaniards, as they almost certainly did from the men of Iceland. The sea air of the late fifteenth century was laden with stories of lost or unknown lands across the ocean. The Brasil of Bristol minds was something more distant than the little Irish island of the maps.

The next English transaction, in 1481, supports this interpreta-

[1] Document 3.   [2] Morison, pp. 44–8.

22

tion.[1] Not content with the failure of 1480, the Bristol men sent out another expedition, and this time employed two ships. We have no account of the voyage, but know that it took place because Thomas Croft, who was one-eighth owner of the ships, was subsequently accused of engaging in trade while holding office as collector of customs. The ships were the *George* and the *Trinity*. They sailed on 6 July 1481 'to serch and fynde a certain Isle called the Isle of Brasile'. That is all. We do not know where they went or when they returned, but the *Trinity* at least did return, being found in the customs accounts two years later. Croft had shipped 40 bushels of salt in each of the vessels, which caused him to be charged with trading. He explained that the salt was not for sale but 'for the reparacion and sustentacion of the said shippes', and was acquitted. Fishing may have been intended. The stockfish technique required only light salting followed by a thorough drying in the wind, which had to be carried out on shore. The 40 bushels were valued at 20 shillings.

So, as so often, we are baffled on the destination and purpose of this expedition of 1481. Where was the Island of Brasil thought to be? Where was the fishing, if any, to be done? Was there any success in discovery? There is not a hint.

Ten years elapse before we reach any further evidence of the quest, years in which much or nothing may have happened. In 1498, when John Cabot had come home from his first American voyage and had just set out on his second, a Spanish representative in London made a report to Ferdinand and Isabella.[2] He was Pedro de Ayala, and in the course of his letter he said: 'For the last seven years the people of Bristol have equipped two, three [and] four caravels to go in search of the Island of Brasil and the Seven Cities according to the fancy of this Genoese.' The Genoese was Cabot, as the context shows. If the seven years are literally true they carry us back to 1491 as the beginning of the series of expeditions of which Ayala had heard. It is impossible to say whether the figure

---

[1] Document 7. See also Quinn's article cited above, p. 15, n. 3.
[2] Document 37.

is literally true or just an approximate number, but the doubt is sufficient to put us on our guard against giving 1491 as the clearly established date of a new series of Bristol voyages. That there was such a series is evident, but it may well have begun a little before or after 1491. Ayala had been the envoy of the Spanish sovereigns to Scotland, and had only recently come to England. Nothing in his letters suggests that he had himself been to Bristol. If he is right in saying that from two to four ships had been sent out yearly for several years, we have an indication that something promising had been discovered, for it is hardly credible that the merchants concerned would have spent their money at that rate on a series of failures. But Ayala had not heard that they had discovered anything. On the contrary, he implied that they had not, because he went on to say that last year, 1497, sure proof had been brought to the King that they had found land. This refers to John Cabot's voyage, which was by that time an exciting topic in London. On the whole it does not seem that Ayala knew with any exactness what had been going on at Bristol. The relevant passage in his letter, although short, raises several puzzling questions. To obtain a just impression it is not sufficient to analyse its several statements, and it should be carefully read as a whole.[1]

There are two, possibly three, indications that a discovery of North America took place in 1494. The most circumstantial is unfortunately the least convincing as evidence of the date.[2] In 1843 a copy of a printed world-map came to light in private possession in Bavaria, and next year it was bought by the French government and lodged in the Bibliothèque Nationale. It is therefore often referred to as the Paris Map. The map was printed in 1544, and the typography of the inscriptions has been judged to be not Spanish but more likely that of the Netherlands. It carries a number of descriptive legends, separately printed and pasted on, and they are in two languages, Latin and Spanish. The Spanish

[1] See the introductory note to Document 37, on the ciphering and deciphering of the text.
[2] Document 21.

text was written in Spain, and the Latin version was a translation from it, made very likely for the publishers in the Netherlands. The Eighth Legend may be thought to refer most nearly to the Cape Breton region of North America. It says: 'This land was discovered by John Cabot the Venetian and Sebastian Cabot his son, in the year of the birth of our Saviour Jesus Christ 1494, on the 24th of June in the morning, to which they gave the name Land First Seen, and to a large island near the said land they gave the name Saint John, because it had been discovered on the same day. . . .' The Legend itself yields no exact location, but the words Prima Tierra Vista are inscribed on the map as running northwards from Cape Breton across the St Lawrence estuary. The Legend goes on to a description of the people, animals and fish of the coast, gathered from later information. In the Spanish version the date is expressed in Roman style: M.CCCC.XCIIII. In the Latin version it is in Arabic numerals: 1494.

In view of what is known of John Cabot's voyage of 1497, it is extremely unlikely that he made this discovery in 1494; for if he did, he said not a word about it in London, where he described his 1497 achievement as something new. If he had been to North America three years earlier he successfully concealed the fact, and there seems to be no reason why he should have done so. It is therefore necessary to conclude that the date on the Paris Map is wrong, and that it should read 1497. The Paris copy of the map is the only one now surviving. But it had a fairly wide circulation, and we find evidence of copies possessed in England, and a presumption that there was more than one edition, with a subsequent alteration of the crucial date to 1497. The error could have arisen in a very simple manner. The number four was rendered in Roman numerals by four strokes, as it is on our more conservative clock-faces today: IIII. If the penmanship was careless the first two strokes of what the writer intended to be VII might have been imperfectly closed at the bottom, and the printer could have read the number as IIII. If the Latin version was translated from the Spanish, its Arabic 1494 would follow. The Spanish text was

25

written in Spain, and very likely Sebastian Cabot, then Pilot-Major at Seville, had something to do with it; but he would not have been able to correct the printer's proofs in the Netherlands. The outcome of all this is that we must reject the Paris Map as testimony to a Cabot discovery in 1494. On a discovery by anyone else the map betrays no knowledge at all and is irrelevant.

Among the merchants active at Bristol in the 1490's were Robert Thorne and Hugh Elyot. The son of this Robert Thorne, also named Robert, was in Seville in 1527, when he wrote to Edward Lee, the English ambassador in Spain, a memorial on a project for exploration. Three years later he and Roger Barlow wrote *The Declaration of the Indies* for the eye of Henry VIII. In the course of the letter to Lee he remarked: 'This Inclynation or desire of [discover]ing I inherited of my father, which with an [other] Merchant of Brystow named hughe Elliot [were] the discoverers of the Newfound Landes, of the wh[ich] there is no doubt, (as now plainly appeareth) yf [the] mariners wolde then have been ruled and followed the[ir] Pilots mynde, the Land of the Indians from wh[ence] all the Gold commeth had bene ours: for all is one Coast, as by the Carde appeareth, and is afores[aid].'[1] In Seville in 1527 the Golden Land of the Indians could mean Mexico and, possibly, the coasts to the south of it, from which treasure had been coming in after the recent conquest by Cortes. The younger Thorne thus claimed that his father and Elyot had discovered the main coast of America, afterwards learned to be continuous with that of Mexico, and that the refusal of their men had prevented them from following it. The younger Thorne, in the versions of his writing which we now possess, gives no date for his father's discovery. Here it should be mentioned that the word 'discoverer' as then used did not invariably mean the first finder of a strange land, although that was its usual application: it might mean one who

---

[1] Document 15. This quotation is from the Cotton MSS version (Cotton MS Vit. E vii), with a somewhat different emphasis from that of Hakluyt's printed versions.

made a fuller examination of a land already known to exist, who discovered, in the sense of uncovering, the facts about it. The lack of a date makes it possible that the statement refers to a pre-Cabotian voyage by Thorne and Elyot, or that they accompanied John Cabot in 1497 or 1498, or that they led one of the subsequent expeditions to America.

It is just possible, however, that Robert Thorne the younger, in writing to Edward Lee, did indicate a date, perhaps in the margin of his manuscript, and that the date was 1494. Thorne's original manuscript is lost, but we have four sixteenth-century versions of it, differing verbally from one another. Thorne died in London in 1532, leaving his manuscripts to his friend Emanuel Lucar, who in due course transmitted them to his son Cyprian Lucar. The earliest copy derived from these originals is at Hatfield House (MS 29). Professor E. G. R. Taylor has shown, by comparison of spelling, phrasing, handwriting and watermarks, that this copy was made in 1532-9, and was a copy of a copy, and not of the original. She does not consider that it is the most accurate version, although the earliest.[1] Cyprian Lucar lent his copy to Dr John Dee in 1577, and Dee employed a writer to transcribe the letter to Lee and the Declaration of the Indies. This copy is preserved in B.M., Cotton MS Vitellius E vii, ff. 329-45, with some words lost by burning of the MS. There is another copy of this date in B.M., Lansdowne MS 100, ff. 65-80b. In comparing these the present writer thought that for the short passage now under discussion it was not so good as the Cotton copy, but Professor Taylor thinks that over all the Lansdowne is the best surviving version. Finally, Richard Hakluyt had a copy, not now extant, from which he printed Thorne's writings in *Divers Voyages*, 1582, with variations from the known manuscripts, and again in *Principal Navigations*, first edition 1589, and second edition 1598-1600, each time with new variations. The upshot of all this is that we have no strict version of what Thorne actually wrote, and that allowance must be made for copyists' errors and editors' amendments. Elizabethan

[1] Taylor (ed.), *A Briefe Summe of Geographie*, pp. XXVI–XXVII.

27

copyists were a careless lot, and Dee's man in two separate places left out a whole line of the matter, as can be seen by comparing his with the other versions; while the omission of a word from Hakluyt's copy has saddled the unfortunate Robert Thorne, from that day almost to this, with a ridiculous statement that he did not make. And if the copyists were careless, their employers were no less so.

In 1577, therefore, Dr Dee was in possession of the then un-published manuscripts of Robert Thorne the younger. Next year he wrote a statement of the Queen's title by right of discovery to North America.[1] The discoveries he advanced were as follows: (1) Madoc, a Welsh prince, made a colony in America in the twelfth century; (2) 'Circa An. 1494. Mr Robert Thorn his father, and Mr Eliot of Bristow, discovered Newfound Land'; (3) Brandan discovered western lands in the sixth century; (4) 'Circa An. 1497. Sebastian Caboto, sent by King Henry the Seventh, did discover from Newfound Land so far ... to Laborador'; (5) in 1576 and 1577 Martin Frobisher discovered the broken lands 'sowth of Laborador'. Omitting consideration of the confusion between John and Sebastian Cabot in (4), which does not concern the present purpose, we are left with the fact that Dee believed that there had been two discoveries of North America, the Cabot achievement of 1497, and a previous one by Thorne and Elyot in 1494. Dee had the correct Cabot date, 1497, although he applied to it the wrong Cabot voyage. Whence did he obtain the Thorne and Elyot date 1494? He had evidently no information about the identity of the explorers save that supplied by the younger Thorne, who did not mention his father's Christian name. He referred to him as 'my father'; and Dee also did not know the Christian name, but spoke of 'Mr Robert Thorn his father'. And yet Dee produced a date which is lacking in the existing versions of the Thorne writings. At first sight it looks as though he had it from the Paris Map. But the map attributed the 1494 discovery to the Cabots. It may possibly be that Dee, having independent

[1] Document 14.

knowledge that the Cabot date was 1497, was moved to attribute the Paris Map's date to Thorne and Elyot, in other words, correcting the map statement not, as we do, by saying that its date was wrong, but by saying that its explorers' names were wrong. It is not a very likely explanation, but at that we must leave it. As the evidence stands, Dee's statement offers only feeble evidence of a discovery in 1494.

Some time before 1829 Craven Ord, an archivist in the State Paper Office, made a transcript of entries in certain Household Books of Henry VII.[1] To two of these entries on John Cabot's 1497 discovery he appended notes of his own to the effect that Newfoundland had been discovered in 1494. There is a faint possibility that Ord had seen some evidence that cannot now be traced. But it seems more likely that he had examined Dee's map of the Atlantic, the first item in the catalogue of the Cotton collection in the British Museum, and had read on the back of it Dee's statement on Thorne and Elyot in 1494. This would account for Craven Ord's notes, although he does not mention the names of Thorne, Elyot or Cabot. His notes cannot be considered as of any evidential value on a 1494 discovery.

The evidence so far discussed in this chapter shows that from 1480, if not earlier, the merchants of Bristol were intent on the discovery of unknown land in the Atlantic, and that in the 1490's their efforts were intensified. The land sought was named the Island of Brasil, although Ayala added to it the Island of the Seven Cities. We find no suggestion that there was any idea of reaching Asia. The hints pointing to a discovery in 1494 prove on analysis to be of slight value. On the contrary, the evidence so far quoted gives no ground for stating positively that there was a discovery at any time. Nevertheless there was.

In 1956 the research of Dr L. A. Vigneras in the Spanish archives at Simancas revealed a letter[2] written by an Englishman named John Day in Andalusia in the winter of 1497-8, addressed

[1] The transcript is now Add.MS 7099 in the British Museum. See Document 26.
[2] Document 25.

29

to a Spanish notable who was most likely Columbus himself. Its purpose was to give particulars of John Cabot's voyage in 1497, and in the course of a description of the land Cabot had explored, John Day remarked: 'It is considered certain that the Cape of the said land was found and discovered in the past by the men from Bristol who found Brasil, as your lordship knows. It was called the Island of Brasil, and it is assumed and believed to be the mainland that the men from Bristol found.' So here is proof, as positive as any proof of this period ever is, that the men of Bristol discovered North America some time before John Cabot's voyage of 1497.

An important question is, how long before? Day's letter is in Spanish, either of his writing or translated from his English in order to be intelligible to its recipient. It was probably translated, for those who have examined it with knowledge are of opinion that the Spanish is that of a native Spaniard and that the hand looks like that of a scrivener. The text says that it was *en otros tiempos* that the Bristol discovery was made. The majority of Spanish scholars, questioned by Dr Vigneras on the implication of this phrase, have answered that it probably means 'a long time ago', a generation perhaps: a minority, however, hold that it may refer to some quite recent date. We have to remember also that the thought behind the words was English, which the translator— Day or another—expressed in Spanish as nearly as he could. If the thought was 'in time past', the contemporary equivalent of our 'formerly', the translation would naturally make it *en otros tiempos*, but it would not actually intend any suggestion of how long ago. The phrase therefore gives no clue to the date of the Bristol discovery. Something else may give an indication, Ayala's statement that for seven years past (from 1498) the Bristol men had been sending out two, three or four small ships a year. His letter does not suggest literal precision, and we may dilute it to 'for several years past'. Even so, it is testimony to sustained activity in the 1490's, and the multiplicity of ships suggests that something valuable had been discovered. The whole statement, coupled with what we otherwise know, suggests that the discovery was in the early 1490's. But, for all we know to the contrary, there could have been a discovery in the early 1480's, perhaps by the expedition of 1481; but that is speculation without evidence.

From when we pass to where: the location of the Bristol discovery. There is an indication in John Day's letter, but the analysis and deduction necessary to clarify it would have to be performed over again in discussing John Cabot's discovery in 1497, for the two topics are not separable. It seems best therefore to leave this question of the locality of the Bristol discovery to the chapter in which the first Cabot voyage is considered, and meanwhile to state provisionally that the Bristol men probably discovered Newfoundland, where they would find good facilities for the production of stockfish and would profitably employ the shipping mentioned by Ayala.

It is possible to give two interpretations to John Day's statement. To the present enquirer it seems most likely, the collateral evidence considered, that the 'Island of Brasil' came into permanent relation with Bristol and that voyages were successively made to it. But the evidence can be read in another sense, namely, that Brasil had been discovered long ago and subsequently lost, and that the voyages noted by Ayala were attempts to rediscover it, fruitless until John Cabot succeeded in 1497. The evidence can so be read, but there are some considerations against so reading it. Mariners who had found a western coast, not by chance but by deliberate purpose, as the record of 1480 and 1481 makes clear, would have known the compass courses that led them to it and home again, and would have made an approximate estimate of their latitude on arrival. It does not seem likely that such a discovery, of a large country and not a tiny island speck, could have been 'lost' in spite of annual efforts to recover it. Some voyages may have been fruitless, as we know at least two were, in 1480 and 1496, owing to stress of weather. But we must regard the Island of Brasil as a certainty and not a fading possibility in Bristol at the time when John Cabot came there. On the other hand we shall see from the Cabot story that the earlier discovery was apparently not known to many people in London in 1497, although John Day did know of it, and the King and his councillors must have known. The probable explanation is that until Cabot obtained his letters patent for a grandiose plan of western discovery and came home to announce that he had found the way to Asia, few men outside Bristol were in the least interested in a new fishery worked from that port. To mercantile London the cod fishery meant Iceland and the regular activities of a dozen east-coast ports. It needed the promise of Cathay and Cipango and the spice trade to awaken interest in the West.

Note to pp. 29–32. These pages were not written as a rejoinder to Professor D. B. Quinn's 'The Argument for the English Discovery of America between 1480 and 1494', *Geographical Journal*, September, 1961. Before that date my chapter was with the printer, and it is unaltered. Professor Quinn and I have agreed and differed independently, and, I am glad to say, have mainly agreed.

III

THE CABOTS TO 1495

THE DATE of John Cabot's birth is not even approximately known. He first appears in historical record at Venice during the term of office of the Doge Nicolo Tron (9 November 1471 to 28 July 1473). At some date in that period he was granted the privilege of Venetian citizenship, having previously been an alien resident in the republic. A Senate entry of 28 March 1476 confirms the grant. A condition of naturalization was that the applicant should have been domiciled in Venice for at least fifteen years. Documents preserved in the archives of Venice and first published in 1948[1] show John Cabot in the years 1482-4 engaged in some complicated property transactions in or near Venice. His wife was named Mattea, and she was a Venetian. His father, deceased, had been a merchant named Egidius or Giulio Caboto, and John had a brother Piero. At the close of 1484 John Cabot was mentioned as the father of two or more sons. In all contemporary references in Italian his Christian name appears as Zuan or one of its variants.

His nationality before he became a Venetian is not known with absolute certainty, but the trend of the evidence is that he was a Genoese. This was stated in 1498 by Pedro de Ayala, his contemporary in London, who wrote that he was 'another Genoese like Columbus'. It was also stated by John's son Sebastian, although we have no direct evidence of it in his own words. It is fairly safe, however, to assume that Sebastian, in his old age in England, was the originator of a statement repeated by four English chroniclers from 1559 onwards, to the effect that his father was a Genoese. The chroniclers copied one another, and their words do not constitute four separate testimonies, but one.[2]

---

[1] Document 11.

[2] The chroniclers are Lanquet (1559), Grafton (1569), Holinshed (1577) and Stow (1580). Stow worked from a document in his possession which may have been a source different from that of the others; but for the particular statement of the nationality he may have copied.

Against this there are records of a Caboto family dwelling at Gaëta in the kingdom of Naples until nearly the middle of the fifteenth century, and ceasing to be traceable there after 1443, eighteen years before the latest date at which John Cabot could have moved to Venice.[1] This suggests a Gaëtan origin, but certainly does not prove it, for there were also persons surnamed Caboto in Genoese territory. In the mid-nineteenth century Rawdon Brown, an English archivist working in Venice, wrote manuscript notes to the effect that he had discovered 'what he considers documentary evidence of John Cabot's English origin'.[2] Whatever Rawdon Brown may have found has been searched for by later students but never found by them; and he himself did not produce any allusion to it in his subsequent *Calendar of Venetian State Papers* covering this period. His assertion that John Cabot was of English birth is undoubtedly a mistake. There are other indications that Brown was inaccurate and that his accounts of the contents of documents are not always to be trusted. The Bristol customs show a Richard Cavot commanding a ship of that port in the reign of Henry VI, and persons named John Corbet, John de Savot, and John Chavet doing business there in 1483–6; but these are resemblances proving nothing. There was also a Chabot family well known in France. The historical Cabots' name was spelt in a large variety of ways during its owners' lifetimes, and our agreed English form is itself a mis-spelling of what Italian writers prefer to render as Caboto. Perhaps the conclusive argument against John Cabot's having been an Englishman is that his son Sebastian betrayed no knowledge of the fact; although it would have been very useful to Sebastian in his later years to be able to call himself an Englishman's son. We may conclude by saying that John Cabot was certainly an Italian and most likely a Genoese.

---

[1] Roberto Almagià, *Commemorazione di Sebastiano Caboto* . . . (Venezia, 1958), pp. 37–8.
[2] Document 9. See also Document 10 for some contemporary names resembling Cabot occurring in the Bristol customs accounts.

To clear the way for a reconstruction of John Cabot's early history it is important to establish the date and place of birth of his son Sebastian. The date cannot be fixed to a definite year, but it can be assigned to a narrow period. The documents published by Signor Rodolfo Gallo in 1948 show that in 1484 John Cabot had two or more sons (*dei figli*).[1] The patent granted by Henry VII in 1496 names three sons of John Cabot in this order: Lewis, Sebastian, Sancio, from which it may be inferred that Sebastian was the second-born. By this evidence Sebastian was born in or before 1484, the date of the document which refers to the sons. Spain provides evidence of Sebastian's age at a later period of his life. On the last day of 1536 he was called as a witness in a lawsuit and gave his age as *de mas de 50 anos*, or somewhat over fifty, which would place his birth somewhat before 1486. In April 1538 he was again a witness in court, and the documents have two independent entries of his age: one represents him as saying that he was about fifty-eight, or born about 1480, and the other about fifty, or born about 1488. One figure is evidently a clerical error. Lastly, in October 1543 he appeared once more as a witness and said that he was about sixty, or born about 1483.[2] The obvious criticism is that we must reject both the 1538 ages, the one as too high, the other too low and probably an understatement by the witness himself. The Italian and Spanish evidence taken together indicates that Sebastian Cabot was born not later than 1484 and not a great deal earlier; and the Italian documents show that he was born in or near Venice, where his parents were then living.

There exists a variety of statements on Sebastian Cabot's nationality, and therefore his birthplace; for by the custom of the time a man was a national of the country in which he was born, irrespective of the nationality of his father. A patent of 1505, whereby Henry VII granted Sebastian a pension, describes him as

[1] Document 11.
[2] The legal references are from J. Toribio Medina, *El Veneciano Sebastián Caboto al servicio de España* (Santiago de Chile, 1908), vol. I, p. 10.

a Venetian.[1] This was undoubtedly on the grantee's own information or with his concurrence, and it was a point on which accuracy was important, since a mis-description would provide a quibble on which the grant might be invalidated. In 1512, when Sebastian was taken into the Spanish service, the documents describe him as an Englishman; but this was the impression of Spanish officials who may have assumed it without verification, since he had come to Spain with the English army serving there as King Ferdinand's allies against France.[2] Thenceforward for thirty-six years, and in continental Europe for much longer, every allusion to Sebastian Cabot's nationality makes him a Venetian, and that undoubtedly was his own assertion. Peter Martyr of Anghiera in 1515 describes him as a Venetian by birth, but taken by his parents to England while yet a child. The information came from Cabot, who was a personal friend of Martyr at that time. The anonymous 'Mantuan Gentleman' declared some time before 1550 that Sebastian was a Venetian citizen. Ramusio the Venetian historian referred to him in 1556 as 'Signor Sebastian Cabot our Venetian'. Gomara the Spanish historian calls him in 1552 'Sebastian Cabot the Venetian'. Galvão the Portuguese refers in 1563 to 'a Venetian named Sebastian Cabot'. This looks a fairly good consensus, although it must be borne in mind that Gomara and Galvão very likely took their description from Peter Martyr. At least, none of them believed that he was an Englishman. More weighty than these literary references is the official report of Gasparo Contarini, the Venetian ambassador in Spain in 1522, who quotes Sebastian as saying: 'My lord ambassador, to tell you the whole truth, I was born at Venice, but was brought up in England.'[3]

If this were all, Sebastian Cabot's Venetian nationality would be hardly disputable. But in 1548 he quitted his post as Pilot-Major in Spain and returned to England. It was a flight and not an authorized departure, and in due course Charles V requested that his servant should be sent back. To this the Council of Edward VI replied that as Sebastian was an Englishman they had no legal

[1] Document 51.   [2] Documents 68 and 69.   [3] Document 70.

power to send him back against his will.[1] He himself was the author of this new claim to English nationality, whose utility was obvious. The geographer Richard Eden, who knew him at this stage of his career, wrote: 'Sebastian Cabot told me that he was born in Bristol and that at four years old he was carried with his father to Venice, and so returned again into England with his father after certain years, whereby he was thought to have been born in Venice.' When Mary Tudor came to the throne in 1553 and a period of close alliance with Spain set in, the danger to Sebastian Cabot of return under duress was increased.[2] There is no doubt that he maintained his claim to be of English birth and secured its general acceptance in England. For a generation English writers continued to assert that he was born in Bristol. What may be the first English author's statement to the contrary does not occur until 1596, when Charles Fitz-Geffrey wrote in his poem *The English Captains*:

> Honour of England, brave Sebastian,
> Mirror of Britain's magnanimity,
> Although by birth a right Venetian,
> Yet for thy valour, art, and constancy,
> Due unto England from thy infancy;
> Venice, thou claimst his birth, England his art,
> Now judge thyself, which hath the better part.

By Fitz-Geffrey's time Peter Martyr's *Decades* were available in an English translation, and most likely provided the basis of his statement. Richard Eden had read the Latin *Decades*, for he was their translator, which no doubt caused him to question old Cabot and so elicit the ingenious Bristol-Venice-Bristol explanation, which is not at all likely to be true.

John Cabot's employments during his Venetian period included those of a merchant or a merchant's factor. This was stated by

---

[1] The documents in this matter are given by C. R. Beazley, *John and Sebastian Cabot* (London, 1898), pp. 170–2.

[2] In September 1553 Charles V wrote to the Queen to ask her to give Captain Cabota leave to visit him. *Cal. S. P. Foreign* 1553–8.

Raimondo de Soncino, who spoke with him in London in 1497,[1] and also in one of the Venetian documents of the period about 1483-4. Soncino wrote that Cabot had been as far as Mecca in pursuit of the spice trade, and had questioned those who came thither with the caravans, to ascertain the Far Eastern origin of the spices; and that this had prompted Cabot's conception of a short voyage across the Atlantic to reach Eastern Asia.

The slight outline available of John Cabot's life yields no proof of his presence in England before 1495. There are however two distinct grounds for argument that he may have been living at Bristol for some years before that date. One is the old-age claim of Sebastian Cabot to have been an Englishman born. This has been dealt with above, and the effect of the evidence is that Sebastian was born in Venice in the early 1480's, and therefore that his father was not resident in Bristol at that period. The Venetian records go further, and show John Cabot in 1484 and the previous years as concerned in detail with property near Venice, and by implication a Venetian resident.[2]

The other ground for arguing his presence in Bristol is more serious, for it turns upon the interpretation we are to make of the words in Pedro de Ayala's dispatch from London on 25 July 1498.[3] Ayala said: 'I have seen the map made by the discoverer, who is another Genoese like Columbus, who has been in Seville and at Lisbon seeking to obtain persons to aid him in this discovery. For the last seven years the people of Bristol have equipped two, three [and] four caravels to go in search of the Island of Brasil and the Seven Cities in accordance with the idea [*con la fantasia*] of this Genoese.' For our present purpose the crucial phrase is *con la fantasia*. Does it mean that Cabot has been for several years promoting the search, or that the search, having already gone on for several years, is what Cabot is now promoting? After premising that Ayala, when he wrote the perhaps ill-considered phrase, had no prescience that it would one day be used for argument in a historical controversy, we must answer that it can mean either.

[1] Document 24. [2] Document 11. [3] Document 37.

38

The Cabots to 1495

To one with only a limited knowledge of Spanish, *con la fantasia* in its context seems a perfect example of ambiguity. But a Spanish scholar believes that if Ayala had meant that Cabot was the instigator of *all* the voyages he would have written *por la fantasia* and not *con*.[1] The attendant circumstances should be considered. The Bristol men were looking for Brasil as early as 1480, long before Cabot could have come on the scene, so that their original inspiration was not Cabot's. In the early 1490's, by Ayala's testimony, they were intensifying their efforts, and by John Day's evidence they had already discovered a main land in the west some time before 1497; and Day certainly does not imply that Cabot had a hand in that, but rather the contrary. Then, citing Ayala again, we learn that Cabot had been in Lisbon and also in Seville seeking support. Ayala does not say when this took place, but the inference from the context is that it was fairly recent. Thus, taking all into a proportional consideration, it may be concluded that on the evidence so far considered there is a possibility that Cabot had been in England since about 1491; and a perhaps greater possibility that he had not been in England before 1495 when, as will be shown, his appearance was quite clearly reported. The evidence we have next to consider tends to favour the later date.

In 1943 Professor M. Ballesteros-Gaibrois published three documents which he had extracted from the archives of Valencia.[2] The documents show that as early as 1490 a certain Venetian named John Cabot Montecalunya (*Johan caboto montecalunya venesiu*) was resident in the port of Valencia, and that in 1492 he proposed certain harbour improvements and offered to take charge of the constructional work entailed. He was sufficiently skilled in map-making to draw the explanatory plans of his project. The local officials brought this to the notice of King Ferdinand, who was then at Barcelona. In September and again in November 1492 Cabot had interviews with the King and explained his ideas. The

---

[1] M. Ballesteros-Gaibrois, 'Juan Caboto en España', *Revista de Indias*, vol. IV (1943), pp. 607–27.
[2] Document 12.

King approved and ordered that the work should be undertaken, but local difficulties were too strong, and nothing came of it. This conclusion became evident in February 1493. In the document of that date Cabot is not mentioned, but it is reasonable to believe that he was still in Valencia, since he was unlikely to have left before the decision was reached. There we lose sight of him, but that is of course no indication that he left immediately afterwards.

The question arising is that of identity. Was John Cabot Montecalunya the historical John Cabot? Montecalunya looks like a place-name, but all efforts to trace it or anything like it in Italy and Spain have so far failed. Enquirers have hit upon no explanation of the word on geographical or any other grounds. Apart from this mystifying word the identification looks reasonably probable. The John Cabot of Valencia was a Venetian, so far interested in maritime affairs as to have ideas on harbour improvement, able to illustrate his ideas by plans of his own drawing, and of sufficient knowledge and personality to make it worth while for King Ferdinand to see him—much the same sort of man as we shall find in 1497 talking of projects to Henry VII. That he was a Venetian is also in favour of the identification for, although there were other Cabots in Gaëta and round Genoa, the historical Cabot family is the only one so far reported from Venice. In the present writer's opinion the Cabot identity is very probable but not absolutely certain. It cannot yet be used as a confirmed fact in building up the story of John Cabot's life—and yet there is much that dovetails with that story.

Valencia and Barcelona in the spring of 1493! Before March was out the news came through that a Spanish squadron led by Christopher Columbus had reached the islands and even the main of Asia, and that its leader had returned first to Lisbon, then to Palos and Seville, and was bidden to attend the sovereigns at Barcelona. In early April he appeared, passing through Valencia city and on by the coast road eastwards. All Valencia, like all other places on the route, turned out to see the show, the great Admiral richly clad, his servants and seamen, the captured natives from

Hispaniola, the gold ornaments and the parrots that they bore. By the 20th he was at Court, welcomed and honoured like an equal by the King and Queen, the man who had sailed to Asia in thirty-four days from the Canaries, who had proved the geographers wrong about the ocean's breadth, and himself, mystically guided against all learning, right. So much is known about those germinal weeks of 1493.

What of the Venetian John Cabot, known in Valencia as Montecalunya? Did he gaze with the rest and then go home and think of harbour works and whatever business yielded him his bread? Or was he the man who had bought spices at Alexandria and followed the pilgrim horde to Mecca and questioned Arabs about the farther East? The man who had read his Marco Polo and knew from it the civilization of Quinsay and the rule of Kublai Khan, the great ships of China, and the riches they carried in their holds. Did this man follow on to Barcelona and there, mingling in the throng of a medieval court, behold the reception and even hear the tale: 'I, Christo Ferens, have been in the land of the Great Khan from which the spices come. The people are loving and gentle and fit to be Christians. They are docile and will make good slaves. The distance is not half what the mathematicians would have it.' It was a good tale, believed by its teller and his royal auditors. But Cabot (the right Cabot), if he was there, could have had his doubts: the childish simpletons on show, as naked when caught as Adam and Eve, paraded as the men of imperial Cathay, the lack in the explorer's report of all things necessary to that great land, the ships, the cities, the pulsing trade, the Khan's officers ruling provinces like Christendom's kingdoms, the city walls, the massed populations, the organized wealth. Cabot could have seen through it, though the sovereigns did not: Columbus had not reached Cathay, he had stopped at half-way islands. That, as will be shown, is implicit in the project that Cabot was to present in England before three years had passed. We may doubt whether it all flashed upon him at the first return of Columbus, but he had worked it out by the time he stood before the English King.

Cabot, as Ayala tells us, went to Seville and Lisbon to seek support. He may have done so before Columbus sailed. If so, he would have found Columbus in possession of what strings there were to pull in Spain, and at Lisbon the government had already decided against the westward project. It is perhaps more likely that Cabot made these approaches after Columbus had come home successful. He could have pointed out, what several Spaniards had noted, that the discoveries of Columbus did not correspond with Marco Polo's descriptions, and, what the geographers had insisted, that Columbus had not gone far enough. But this, if in fact Cabot did urge it, could not win him recognition. The Spanish sovereigns had publicly accepted Columbus's contentions, and to exploit his discoveries was now the official policy. If there was to be any extension westward Columbus by his privileged rights would be in command of it. In Lisbon the government of John II was thoroughly alarmed, especially by the papal bulls that Spain so easily obtained from Alexander VI in the summer of 1493, which not only gave the westward expansion solely to Spain but could also be interpreted as blocking the way to India round the Cape. But for Portugal this problem was firstly a matter of diplomacy, and if a western expedition became necessary she had good leaders of her own available, and geographers who understood the conditions as well as Cabot himself. There was no need for Portugal to commit her fortunes to a foreigner. Thus Cabot, whether before or after the Columbian triumph of 1493, had no success in Spain or Portugal. The Valencian documents show that Cabot Montecalunya had speech with King Ferdinand in the autumn of 1492. They give not a hint that he spoke of western discovery. This is in order, for he would not have had the chance to do so. He was admitted to the royal presence to explain a harbour project and would not have been allowed to diverge into other matters. The path to the King's ear had to be opened by the appropriate officials, and those of Valencia dealt only with local business.

Cabot was determined to lead an expedition to Cathay, and

there remained one more chance, in England. Here we have some facts, but we have not the requisite dates, and so a narrative cannot be established. In Lisbon and Seville there were English merchant colonies, and their Bristol members at least were committed to Atlantic discovery. They were probably aware of the Norsemen's Markland and the story of Wineland the Good, in other words, that a large land existed in approximately English latitudes in the western ocean. Be that as it may, they did certainly find a land, as the John Day letter proves, at some date before 1497, *en otros tiempos* from 1497, whatever that may mean. They had been looking for this land as early as 1480, and may have found it in the ensuing decade. They were sending numerous ships westward in the 1490's, which argues that they had then found the land. However, we have not the date, and can only say that the Bristol discovery was made before the mid-1490's.

This Bristol discovery, as already noted, made no great noise in the world. It was not accompanied by any recognition or favour from the English kings, Edward IV, Richard III, Henry VII, whichever may have been contemporary with it. There were, so far as we know, no money rewards to successful captains, no letters patent conferring monopoly of the new enterprise. There can be little doubt that Henry VII knew of it. He had a keen eye for maritime progress and a personal acquaintance with the merchants of Bristol, which he visited in 1486 and again in 1496.[1] The derivable impression is that the America discovered by the Bristolians offered no prospect of spectacular profits, but simply a good fishery unhampered by the bothering disputes that continually cropped up in Iceland. Its users, not wishing to attract competitors, did not advertise it, and their enterprise excited little attention in London. That, we must suppose,[2] was the maximum extent and importance of the Bristol discovery, 'The Isle of Brasil', before John Cabot came on the scene.

That he made contact with the Bristol leaders is clear enough. When and where, whether in Seville, Lisbon or Bristol, are un-

---

[1] See below, p. 54.   [2] I emphasize 'suppose': there is no direct evidence.

The Cabot Voyages and Bristol Discovery

known. But by the close of 1495—the first date we can give—John Cabot had joined the English enterprise and was in England seeking to transform the English discovery into a world-shaking revolution of inter-continental trade.

One must still insist on the limitation imposed by evidence. To say that Cabot had come to England by 1495 is not to say that he came in 1495. He may have come earlier. If our Cabot was John Cabot Montecalunya, he was not in England from 1490 to the early months of 1493. His Seville and Lisbon attempts must have taken up some time, and the most likely period for them is that preceding his recorded presence in England towards the end of 1495. We cannot reasonably suppose that he could have gone to Spain and Portugal and carried on negotiations after that date, for his activities are too well accounted for. Moreover, having found backers in England, he had no need to look elsewhere.

IV

THE PROJECT OF JOHN CABOT

THE INSPIRATION of John Cabot was in effect that of Columbus, to reach the wealthy parts of Eastern Asia by a westward voyage from Europe. Columbus mingled Christian missionary fervour with zest for the expansion of empire and the profits of trade. Of Cabot we hear nothing of religious enthusiasm, but only of a single-minded desire to divert and monopolize the oriental trade. But what we do hear is the report of others, and there is not a word of his own writing to testify the mood in which he framed his plan. His reporters may have been selective in their statements, as they had reason to be; for in 1497-8 they were dazzled by a brilliant economic prospect. Some priests did accompany the second expedition.

The idea of a westward passage to Asia was by this time familiar to geographers and to some merchants and seamen. It was not even yet common to all educated men, as we may judge from the letter of Raimondo de Soncino, the Milanese ambassador in London, written on 18 December 1497.[1] Here, more than four years after the first return of Columbus, the writer gives an impression that the concept was new to him, and that he had been converted to it by Cabot's evident ability: 'He [Cabot] tells all his this in such a way, and makes everything so plain, that I also feel compelled to believe him.' And Soncino evidently did not credit his ducal master Lodovico il Moro with any greater knowledge, for he laboriously explained how the spices were produced in the Far East and came through many hands to Europeans in the Near East, and how the roundness of the earth would make a westward voyage a short cut to the countries of production. Neither a great man like the Duke of Milan nor a man of the world like his

[1] Document 24.

ambassador in London had knowledge of the travels of Marco Polo, for Soncino reports as a novelty Cabot's talk 'of an island which he calls Cipango', where the jewels and spices have their origin. For Soncino and his master Cipango was Cabot's notion, and a new one to them. Henry VII knew better, for he had listened to Bartholomew Columbus and must have had reports of the Columbus claims from Englishmen in Spain. Public opinion in London, however, even among the intelligent middle classes, was still densely ignorant, not from lack of opportunity, since there were Londoners in Spain, but rather from lack of any spontaneous interest. Men heard no doubt of the Spanish voyages, but idly let them pass as of no account in their lives.

Active as Bristol had been in the search for lands worth exploiting, there is no evidence that on the big subject of trade with Asia it was any more enlightened than London. There is not a hint that any Bristol man had read of Zaitun or Quinsay, Cambalu or Cipango. They had devoted their time and money to the quest for the islands, Brasil and the Seven Cities, goals of the Portuguese Atlantic captains, localized no doubt in a hazy fashion by the tradition that somewhere over westward between 45 and 60 degrees of latitude or, as they would have put it, between a rhumb south-west and two rhumbs north-west from Bristol, lay Markland and Wineland the Good. A portion of this they found, and used so quietly that London knew little about it. And of Asia? No trace whatsoever in any English talk before John Cabot came on the scene. To all appearance Bristol merchants, having heard in Seville about Columbus, were not interested.[1] To us it may seem incredible, because we know all that has followed. But we should remember that the Columbian discoveries, after the first triumph in 1493, became very unpopular in Spain itself and were in some danger of being abandoned. Englishmen in Seville witnessed the glorious return in the spring of 1493 and the enthusiasm of the

---

[1] I would emphasize that this is as far as the evidence now goes. But any writing on these matters must be but an interim report, for there are discoveries of evidence still to be made, and as yet we have very little.

second sailing in the autumn. Thereafter they saw only ruined men straggling back from the Indies with maledictions on the hell to which Columbus had lured them.

Cabot knew, among the first, that Columbus had not reached Asia. He learned that the Bristol men had found a coast in the west, in about their own latitude. It occurred to him that this might be the north-east corner of Asia, projecting more towards Europe than the tropical region, and brought nearer still in mileage by the narrowing of every degree of longitude as one moved from the equator towards the pole. He was a map-maker, but the plane method of projection would not show this to full advantage to eyes unaccustomed to maps of large areas. He was also a globe-maker. The globe would show what he meant, and we know that he made one. The new land of the Bristol men was not certain to be the corner of Asia, but it was worth investigating. The course thither was known, and anything that would shorten the open-water distance of a long voyage must be taken advantage of. Cabot's plan was to pick up the new land and follow it. If its coast trended south-west it would bring him to Cipango and the rich tropical part of the Great Khan's empire. These would be in Columbus's latitudes, but they would be far beyond Columbus in longitude. Columbus had not gone far enough, and his Indies positively did not meet the specification of Marco Polo's Asia.

That these were Cabot's plans in 1497 we have ample proof. That they were his plans before ever he set sail we can infer from the wording of the letters patent that he obtained from Henry VII. He made contact with the merchants of Bristol, whose backing with ships and money was essential.[1] He travelled to Bristol. A rental of 1498–9 shows him to have been tenant of a house in St Nicholas Street at a rent of 40 shillings a year.[2] He employed the arguments which had failed him in Seville and Lisbon. The Bristol

---

[1] With ships may be included crews. The history of long expeditions into the unknown shows that men in the Tudor period did not readily volunteer for them, and that pressure had often to be used. Local leaders of good repute could raise a crew where a stranger might fail.

[2] Document 30.

men were open to conviction, for they had experience of a 2000 miles ocean passage. To double the distance by coasting on along a continental shore seemed feasible. The rewards of success would be very great. All the spice import of England then came in through Southampton, the English port used by the Flanders galleys of Venice. Although Southampton was not a great place, the spice import made it rich, and its customs receipts were second only to London's. The new route would transfer Southampton's monopoly to Bristol. It would do more, for the long transit of the existing route and the stranglehold upon it of the Arabs of the Middle East, coupled with the profits of the Venetian distributors in Europe, made all the eastern wares extremely expensive to the consumer; and a simple direct sea-supply would confer upon its exploiters the monopoly of the trade for all Christendom. This was to be proved within a decade by the Portuguese, who opened the sea passage round the Cape and soon knocked out the whole racket of the caravans, the Arabs and the Levantine Venetians. The Portuguese monopoly followed for the next century, but it would not have lasted two years if Cabot had been right in his geographical premises.

On 21 January 1496 Gonsalez de Puebla, the Spanish ambassador in England, wrote to the Spanish sovereigns a letter that has not been preserved. On March 28 they replied: '. . . In regard to what you say of the arrival there of one like Columbus for the purpose of inducing the King of England to enter upon another undertaking like that of the Indies, without prejudice to Spain or to Portugal, if the King aids him as he has us, the Indies will be well rid of the man [i.e. nothing will be done]'. The sovereigns go on to say that they consider this to be a French attempt to divert Henry from fulfilling his obligations to them. It is impossible, they add, that this should be without prejudice to Spain or Portugal, since no such English undertaking can be without harm to both the Iberian powers. Here it should be noted that Spain and Portugal were now in amity on the oceanic question. Their sharp dispute of 1493 had been ended by a final papal bull dividing the

Atlantic area of operations between them, and in 1494 by the Treaty of Tordesillas they had agreed to shift the Pope's line of partition to a meridian 370 leagues west of the Azores or the Cape Verde Islands.

From the above letter it follows that Cabot had come to England and had in all probability made arrangements with the Bristol merchants. He had next approached the King, who in turn had then mentioned the matter to Puebla, all before January 21. This brings Cabot to England certainly before the close of 1495. He may have been in Bristol some time earlier, but his appearance in London was reported by Puebla as recent.

The same lapse of time is implied by a business that had been proceeding concurrently. On 5 March 1496 Henry VII granted letters patent for a new enterprise to John Cabot and his sons. Some patents relating to routine business were in stereotyped form and may not have taken long to complete, although even for them there was a ritual procedure shared among several officials. But a patent for a new and large undertaking involving big questions of economic and foreign policy was a different matter. The petitioners had first to agree on their proposals and put them into shape. They had then to open an approach to the King, who with some of his councillors considered the project in principle and did not hastily arrive at a decision. We may assume with confidence that at this stage there was at least one long interview between the King and John Cabot, with elaboration of facts and arguments, and production of maps, and a general hammering-out of the design; for Henry was no rubber-stamp monarch, but the personal director of policy. Having passed this stage and received the royal approval in principle, the proposition had then to take shape in the detail of legal language, first at the hands of the petitioners' lawyers and then under the criticism of those of the Crown. Here there was hard bargaining and a scrutiny of every phrase and word. The result was a legal instrument as perfect as trained minds could make it, devoid of ambiguity, meaning exactly what it said, no more and no less. If we moderns find obscurities in such

E   49   W.C.V.

documents it is only because we are not conversant with the thought and language of the fifteenth-century law. They had no obscurities for those who devised them. There will be two more major patents of the same type to be considered in this book, and the opportunity has been taken here to explain their nature. The legally drawn version was remitted to the King for final approval, and delivered to the beneficiaries, usually but not always after being copied on the rolls in the care of the Lord Chancellor. There were fees payable at every stage to officials, down to the chafewax who warmed the wax for the impression of the great seal. The fee for enrolment was a large one, and patentees did not always pay it, taking the risk that if they lost their precious document there was no official copy from which it could be reissued. All this process, terminating on 5 March 1496, we must regard as having been initiated at least some weeks before, and therefore as proof of John Cabot's arrival before the end of 1495.

The formal record of the petition for the grant bears the same date, March 5, as the patent itself. The petition is in English and spells the Cabot names as 'John Cabotto, Citezen of Venice, Lewes, Sebastyan and Soncio, his sonnys'. The patent, in Latin, is granted to the above-named Cabots and to their heirs and deputies. This disposes of an argument often advanced on the birth-date of Sebastian Cabot, whereby it is contended that he must have been over twenty-one in 1496 to qualify for inclusion in the grant. It is quite invalid, for the grant is to his heirs also; and if he had been old enough to have any in that year they would certainly have been infants. Moreover by this reasoning it would have been impossible to include any minor son of John Cabot in the family privileges, which does not make sense. The rights were in fact heritable in perpetuity; but by the prerogative they were always revocable at the King's pleasure. That they were still theoretically arguable in 1550 is shown by the fact that Sebastian Cabot obtained a reissue of the patent in that year, certified to be a true copy of the enrolment of 1496. It will be noted that the rights were to be exercised not only by the Cabots but by their deputies.

These may include the Bristol merchants known by other evidence to have been associated with them.

The grantees are given authority to use five ships of any tonnage they may choose and to sail to all parts of 'the eastern, western and northern sea', to discover and investigate 'whatsoever islands, countries, regions or provinces of heathens and infidels, in whatsoever part of the world placed, which before this time were unknown to all Christians'. This is an apparent but not a real ambiguity. Cabot may cross the ocean with a limitation of latitude, not to the southward. But having done so and found new land, he may follow it to any part of the world, to any latitude or longitude, provided that it is land hitherto unknown to Christians. Here is the essence not only of Cabot's plan of exploration, but also of the King's policy towards Spain and Portugal. Cabot crosses the Atlantic in English latitudes, picks up the coast he knows to be there and assumes to be the north-east projection of Asia, and follows that coast, which he believes will trend southwestwards to the rich regions of which he has learned from Marco Polo, a country all unknown to Christians, or at least to any Christians now living. It is a clearly implied contention that Columbus has not reached Asia and that his Indies are only partway there: if Cabot carries out this voyage he will not fall foul of the Christians in Hispaniola.

Henry VII must have given deep thought to this matter, a first-class question of policy without precedent in past history. His solution was that he would respect Spanish rights to what Spain had actually discovered, and even to monopoly of the sea route that led to it. But he would not recognize in advance any Spanish right to prospective discoveries not yet accomplished: if the English could get first into these prospective regions, theirs was to be the right in them. Viewed from the standpoint of 1496 it was a fair and just proposition. We of today are so indoctrinated by the mighty map of the ensuing Spanish Empire that we find it hard to see what Henry saw: a geographical concept not the peculiar invention of any one man or country, a Spanish attempt which seemed substantially to have failed, a new and better solution offered to himself, and a commonsense proposal that each should take and enjoy what he could find. He made no concealment of his purpose. From the outset he talked of it to Puebla; and at a later stage he allowed public exposition of Cabot's plans and listened to Ayala's arguments against them.

Spain of course thought otherwise. She was imbued with the idea of prescriptive right by fifty years' knowledge of Portugal's doings on the African coast. Portugal had been fortified by papal bulls. Spain had obtained such bulls in 1493. Spain and Portugal had then settled their dispute of overlap and divided the prescriptive rights, assumed to be their joint world-monopoly, by the treaty of 1494. Henry VII was a pious son of the Church, obedient to its decree in any matter of religion. In political matters he did not admit the right of the Pope to order his decisions. Neither in practice did anyone else, and the bulls of partition were not binding on Henry VII. It is just possible that in 1496 he did not know of their existence. How far such bulls were published seems to be an unsettled question. Copies were sent to those to whom they were addressed, in this case the Spanish sovereigns, who could communicate them at their discretion to others. Whether they or the Pope had sent them to the English king is unknown. Admiral Morison says that no trace of their communication has been found in the archives of any European state but Portugal.[1] The Treaty of Tordesillas bound only its signatories.

The rest of the Cabot patent deals with the mechanism of the business. The new discoveries were to be occupied in the King's name, the patentees being his vassals. One-fifth of the net profits were to be paid to the King. The grantees were to be exempt from paying customs on the goods brought home, and they were bound to bring goods solely into the port of Bristol. No other subjects of the King were to resort to the new discoveries without licence from the grantees, under pain of forfeiture of ship and goods. All subjects of the King were commanded to render assistance to the

[1] S. E. Morison, *Admiral of the Ocean Sea*, p. 379.

grantees in fitting out ships and buying stores and victuals. Only one of the above clauses needs comment, that on exemption from customs inward. It did not mean exemption from all duties, for the subsidy, otherwise known as tunnage and poundage, was also payable. On such goods as were likely to be brought from the new discoveries, Englishmen paid no custom and 1s. in the £ subsidy; while foreigners paid 3d. in the £ custom and 1s. subsidy. Duties on wine and woollen cloth imports were considerably higher, but these were not likely to arise in the early stages. In practice therefore the Cabots received an exemption of 3d. in the £. The subsidy, four times as great, was not remitted.

We may conclude by noticing a very wide implication of the patent. It was at that time accepted as a fundamental law of Christendom that all Christians were in a state of war with all infidels. This was the justification of the permission to 'conquer, occupy and possess' any non-Christian territories that might be found. It also justified the enslavement of infidels which Portugal had long been practising in Africa and which Columbus began as a matter of course in the Antilles. If one had the military right to kill a man, one was behaving mercifully by merely enslaving him, especially as in the process his soul might be saved from damnation. Columbus, a humane man, was quite at ease on the question of slavery. Queen Isabella took a more liberal view. She regarded the Indians as her subjects, not her enemies, and as potential if not actual Christians. She therefore, as sovereign of Castile, forbade the enslavement of the Indians, although her commands were seldom effective.

V

THE VOYAGE OF 1497

IT IS now known, and was unknown before the discovery of John Day's letter, that John Cabot led an expedition in pursuit of his plans in 1496. It was to this that Day referred in the following brief statement: 'Since your lordship wants information relating to the first voyage, here is what happened: he [Cabot] went with one ship, his crew confused him,[1] he was short of food and ran into bad weather, and he decided to turn back.' It was an unlucky attempt at the westward passage, similar to that of John Lloyd in 1480. Day does not give the date, but it was presumably after the issue of the patent, and so can only have been 1496. The King was in Bristol on August 12,[2] and it would be interesting to know whether Cabot had returned by then.

Before considering the voyage of 1497 a review of the evidence will be useful. The contemporary narrative and descriptive pieces are four in number. The first in order of date is a letter written from London on 23 August 1497 by Lorenzo Pasqualigo, a Venetian merchant, to his family in Venice.[3] The part relating to Cabot is a brief objective statement of the principal facts collected by the writer during the fortnight which had elapsed since the return of John Cabot to London. It has no controversial colouring, and its crisp and definite sentences yield an impression that confidence may be placed in its writer as an accurate observer. Next day, August 24, a correspondent of the Duke of Milan wrote from London a letter containing a very brief statement on the voyage.[4] The writer, whose name is not recorded, either was less fully informed than Pasqualigo or did not consider the matter impor-

---

[1] . . . la gente que llevaba le desconcerto'. This might mean: 'he had a disagreement with his crew'.
[2] An entry in the Household Book (P.R.O., E 101. 414. 6) shows that the King was there on that date.   [3] Document 22.   [4] Document 23.

tant; but his statement does embody a small independent contribution to the story. Nearly four months later, on 18 December 1497, Raimondo de Soncino, ambassador of the Duke of Milan in London, wrote a dispatch to his master with explanatory and critical remarks, as well as narrative details of the voyage.[1] Soncino writes as an impartial observer of a public event, with a faint suggestion of amused tolerance, which is at least a guarantee that he is not distorting his account through enthusiasm. He brings an intelligent but fresh mind to the geographical matters involved, for it is fairly evident that he has not previously been interested in them. His letter adds certain details on the events of the voyage to that of Pasqualigo, but is mainly important for its exposition of the motives of the explorer, the intentions of the King, and the excited optimism prevailing in London. Soncino had become a personal acquaintance of Cabot, and had derived information from private talk with him as well as from his public statements.

The fourth main document is newly discovered.[2] It is an undated letter written in Andalusia by John Day to a Spanish notable not named but addressed as 'The most magnificent and most worthy Lord the Lord Grand Admiral'. Dr L. A. Vigneras, who brought this letter to light in 1956, considers that there were only two persons who could have been so addressed, the hereditary Grand Admiral of Castile, who was a court dignitary and is not known to have been concerned in oceanic affairs; and Columbus himself, who was in Spain at the material time. The contents of the letter indicate that its addressee was deeply interested in western discovery and in books relating to geography. It is therefore fairly certain that he was Christopher Columbus. On internal evidence the letter can be dated between December 1497 and the early spring of 1498; for it mentions John Cabot's pension from Henry VII and is clearly anterior to the fitting-out of the expedition of 1498. Only one certain piece of information about John Day beyond that derivable from the letter has so far been dis-

[1] Document 24.   [2] Document 25; Pl. V*a*.

55

covered.[1] The letter implies that he was a merchant who had recently come from England and was in touch with those who had information about the Cabot venture. It was not his first correspondence with 'the Grand Admiral', but was an answer to a letter from that person, which itself followed up an interview with or a letter from Day. They may have been in fairly frequent communication. Day expresses his willingness to be of service, although not to the extent of revealing anything that could be prejudicial to the King of England, and asks that in return the great man will give information to him. He sends a copy of Marco Polo, which may mean a manuscript or a printed edition, and had meant to send but has mislaid one of *Inventio Fortunata*, a book on northern geography written in the fourteenth century, of which no example is now known to exist.

A chronicle of Bristol and national events written in or after 1565 by one Maurice Toby gave a brief notice to the voyage of 1497.[2] It said that in the civic year from 15 September 1496 to 14 September 1497 'the land of America' was found by the merchants of Bristol in the ship *Matthew*; and it mentioned three dates, May 2, June 24 and August 6 as those respectively of the departure, the first landfall, and the return. The chronicle, subsequently known as the Fust MS, was accidentally burnt in 1860, but an extract of the above passage had previously been made and

---

[1] Dr Vigneras has very kindly sent me particulars of a document concerning John Day, dated 20 December 1500, which he has discovered in the Archivo General de Simancas, Cédulas de la Camara, leg 4, f. 252, 2. It relates to a cargo of lead to be handed over to 'Roberto Espexforte yngles' in the name of 'Juan Day yngles', to replace a similar quantity of lead belonging to Day which has been requisitioned at Malaga. Another document shows that the requisitioning had taken place in November 1499. In English records there are John Days, none of them certainly relevant. A possible is 'Maister John Dey, clerke' who in 1495 owned property in London (L. Lyell (ed.), *Acts of Court of the Mercers' Company* (Cambridge, 1936), p. 243). This man may have been the John Dey, clerk, who was granted in 1500 the custody of the lands and marriage of Thomas Newnham, a minor, and had the same confirmed in 1509 (*Letters and Papers, Henry VIII*, vol. 1 ed. 2, No. 257.75). In February and November 1499 John Dey is shown concerned with Richard Empson and others in a transfer of land (*Cal. of Close Rolls, 1485–1500*, Nos. 1085, 1170).

[2] Document 19.

was printed in the *Encyclopaedia Britannica* of 1876. The loss of the original permits a doubt of the literal accuracy of the copy, since experience shows that transcribers have often made mistakes. In this case there were two transcribers involved, Maurice Toby working from his Bristol material now lost, and the person who copied the extract before the loss of his chronicle. The chronicle was a historical form surviving from medieval times, purporting to give entries compiled in each successive year. But the chronicles of this period were all written up long after the events and based upon materials that may not have been in chronicle form at all. Consequently there can be no objection to Toby's work on the ground that it names 'the land of America', a name not existing in 1497, for it was the natural word for the compiler to use in 1565. Toby is the primary authority for the three dates and the ship's name, all of which receive partial corroboration from sources which, except that for June 24, could not have been known to him. We must conclude that he represents a genuine documentary authority.

The three letter-writers, Pasqualigo, Soncino and Day, represent a good class of evidence, but not the highest class, since they wrote through their individual minds, each producing his own selection and emphasis of facts. But there exists a better class of evidence than this, that of the administrative document, written without any motive of establishing or perverting the truth about the voyage, but for a quite different purpose, usually that of financial record. To this class belong certain entries in the Household Books, written to account for the spending of money from the privy purse, but incidentally throwing light on the voyage; and some documents on the payment of the pension which the King granted to John Cabot. These documents give unconscious testimony, since their writers had not in mind that they were giving evidence on the advance of Atlantic exploration. This sort of evidence is of perfect credibility so far as it goes, but its scope is very limited.

The Eighth Legend on the Paris Map has already been noticed

in dealing with the possibility that 1494 was the date of the original discovery.[1] With the date corrected, as it should be, to 1497, this becomes a testimony to John Cabot's first successful voyage. It tells us that the landfall was made on June 24 and that an adjacent island was discovered on the same day and named St John. It says that the discovery was made by John Cabot and his son Sebastian. The position of the words Prima Tierra Vista on the map indicates that Cape Breton was the approximate locality of the event; but too much can be made of this, since we do not know whether the draughtsman had any precise instructions from Sebastian Cabot or whether he inserted the words on his own responsibility. The Seventeenth Legend ascribes the authorship of the whole production to Sebastian Cabot. This can hardly have been entirely true. As we shall see at a later stage, he claimed to have discovered the North West Passage in the reign of Henry VII; yet the outlines of that region are so drawn in the map as to preclude the possibility of the Passage. Again, in the Argentine region of South America, the river courses, which he himself had followed in 1528–30, are so erroneously shown that he could not honestly have drawn them. The general execution of the map is of an inferior quality, the Spanish legends were either written by an ill-educated person or barbarously treated by the Flemish or German printers, and the Latin versions are even worse.[2] It looks as though the whole thing was a money-making venture with little regard for excellence, and that Sebastian Cabot did little more than lend his eminent name to it.[3] Yet with all this the Eighth Legend does contain some valuable statements about the voyage of 1497, namely, that the senior leader was John Cabot (an unusual ascription in the mid-sixteenth century, when few writers

[1] Document 21.
[2] These criticisms are drawn from the careful study of the map made by Beazley, ch. XIII–XV. He prints in English translation the texts of all the legends, with the variations between the Spanish and Latin versions.
[3] On 11 March 1541 an agreement was signed in Seville between Sebastian Cabot on the one hand, and Lazarus of Nuremberg and Gabriel Mizel (or Wizel) on the other, for the printing of a world map in Germany (Almagia 1958, p. 58).

had even heard of him), that the date of the landfall was June 24, and that its place was apparently near Cape Breton. This information could have been contributed, perhaps orally, by Sebastian to the Spanish writer of the legends. This printed map was a popular publication which sold well. It or its later edition were to be seen in many merchants' houses in England and no doubt in other countries. Its testimony to Cabot history is enveloped in an aura of unreliability. We should remember, however, that the American discovery was a very small and incidental part of its purpose, which was to give a general view of the geography of the whole world.[1]

Finally, there is the evidence of contemporary or nearly contemporary maps. Of these, the nearest to the events and the only one that clearly makes a statement on the English discoveries is that drawn by the Spanish pilot Juan de la Cosa in the year 1500 (Pls. I, II; Fig. 2). The meaning of that statement has provoked enormous controversy. There is no agreed interpretation of it, but there are varying contentions, differing radically from one another, on the identity of the stretch of coastline which La Cosa allots to the English. When we add the number of voyages of which La Cosa could have had information, two by John Cabot in 1497 and 1498, and possibly those made earlier by the Bristol discoverers, we see that as *narrative* testimony to what occurred in 1497 alone the La Cosa map is a very weak authority. What it does give is the state of knowledge achieved, in its author's estimation, by 1500; and it does this dimly and disputably. As

[1] The following notes are by Mr R. A. Skelton: 'I think you are quite right in doubting Cabot's authorship; and the suggestion by some writers that the map was copied from the Spanish *padrón real* is absurd. It is true that it shows the results of some recent Spanish explorations (e.g. Ulloa in California 1540 and Orellana's descent of the Amazon 1542), but these were also known in Portugal. The general outlines of the Paris Map are copied from some world-chart of Dieppe type (cf. Desliens 1541), i.e. indirectly derived from a Portuguese original, with the outlines of north-eastern North America modified (as in the Dieppe maps) to accommodate Cartier's discoveries. The Paris Map, printed, with Spanish legends, was presumably intended primarily for the Spanish market (the Latin legends point to the expectation of sales in other countries also); how Sebastian's personal information got on to the map is a matter for guess. That it is there, and to be treated as primary evidence, cannot reasonably be disputed.' See below, p. 299.

regards the narrative of 1497 later maps are weaker still and virtually irrelevant, for new voyages supervened in rapid succession before they were made. The maps do record the advance of geographical knowledge, which was what the cartographers intended, and we cannot blame them for not recording the events that produced the knowledge. The maps therefore rank low as evidence of actions, for they will not meet the tests which must be applied to historical documents before we can base confident statements of narrative upon them.

John Cabot, having failed in his first attempt in 1496, made a new one in 1497. The patent permitted him to sail the eastern, western and northern sea, in practice the waters not yet explored by the Spaniards and Portuguese. 'Eastern' may appear unnecessary. The explanation is that he was seeking Eastern Asia, and although his direction would be westward he would arrive in the eastern seas if successful. It was not his intention to make a trading voyage or even to push as far as the trading regions of Asia. He was going simply to make a reconnaissance, to find out if the land already known was continental and if its general trend was southwestwards towards the tropics where the rich part of Asia would be found. The exploitation was to be left to a subsequent expedition equipped for trade. What the pre-1497 discoverers had found seems not to have been extensively examined. John Day says that they called it the Island of Brasil, but now believed it to be part of the continent. If they were using it as a fishing coast their lack of further enterprise is paralleled by that of the multitude of European fishermen who afterwards used Newfoundland without clearing up its geography, so that to the end of the sixteenth century Newfoundland was believed by some to be an archipelago. Fishermen quickly developed a seasonal routine that left no time for geographical research. The Bristol pioneers must, however, have worked out a course to their discovery and have known its approximate latitude.

Cabot took one fairly small ship with a total company of eighteen according to Soncino, or of twenty according to Day.

These included two or more Bristol merchants, their names un-
recorded, and two friends of Cabot, a Burgundian and a Genoese.
This left about twelve to fourteen for the master and crew. Young
Sebastian Cabot, aged about fifteen, may have been with them,
but there is no reason to suppose it, other than the statement on
the Paris Map. The ship's name was certainly the *Matthew*.
Maurice Toby states it, and there is some corroboration. The
Bristol customs records give the names of the ships using the port.
In the book for 1492–3 there is no record of the *Matthew*. There-
after the books are missing until 1503–4, and the record of that
year contains several mentions of 'navicula vocata le Mathewe de
Bristow'.[1] Navicula means a ship of the smaller sort such as in the
Tudor period was called a bark. Day states that Cabot's ship was
of fifty tons, which accords fairly well with the figure estimated for
the working crew. The customs book implies that there was no
Bristol ship named the *Matthew* in 1492–3, in which case she was
recently built or acquired in 1497. The Italian documents published in 1948 by Signor Gallo[2] show that John Cabot's wife was
named Mattea, and we know that she was with him at Bristol. It
looks as though he had the naming of the ship. The name indeed
may have been *Mattea*, anglicized by the Bristolians, who had no
English feminine form of the word. It is pleasant to think of John
Cabot's compliment to his wife, perhaps the only wife of a great
explorer to see her name borne by her husband's ship.[3]

The date of sailing is discrepantly given as May 2 in our version
of Toby's chronicle and as 'towards the end of May' in John Day's
letter. Day further states that they 'must have been on the way
35 days before sighting land', which, counting back from June 24,
gives May 20 as the starting date. It is likely that there is an error of
transcription in the published extract from the Fust MS, and that
by the best probability the sailing date was about May 20. On the
other hand Pasqualigo, a good witness, says that the whole voyage

[1] Document 20.   [2] Document 11.

[3] In a list of Bristol ships in January 1513 appears the *New Matthew* (*Letters and
Papers, Henry VIII*, vol. I, ed. 2, No. 1577).

occupied three months, which taken literally would imply a start about May 8.

The *Matthew* sailed past southern Ireland and then turned north to a parallel on which Cabot made the greater part of his westward passage. Before completing it he came into an area where the variation of the compass, as could be checked by sight of the pole star, amounted to two points or $22\frac{1}{2}$ degrees westward. At that time there was an eastward variation in Europe, and the line of no variation passed through the Atlantic not far west of the Azores. Cabot, as we now know, was not the first to sail into the North American waters, and by John Day's letter we gather that the variation did not perturb him. He had the advantage of knowing the conditions from his Bristolian predecessors. It was those unknown men who first worked out the course from the British Isles to the north-east corner of America. One of the factors was the southward set of the Labrador current as the coast was neared, not accurately detectable but empirically absorbed into the solution.[1] Cabot had with him Bristol merchants who either had made the 'Brasil' passage themselves or were instructed by those who had. Who were they? There is no record of their names, but one thinks of Robert Thorne and Hugh Elyot who, as the former's son afterwards wrote, 'were the discoverers of the New Found Land'. The Bristol men, as we see from Toby's Chronicle and the phrase of the younger Thorne, considered themselves to have been the discoverers. The part of Cabot, with whom they were now in alliance, was to be the extension of the discovery from that of a fishing coast to that of the spice trade with tropical Asia, in which he was a specialist. Day states that for most of the outward passage the wind was east-north-east and the sea smooth, but that two or three days before sighting land they ran into bad weather which lasted a day. During part of this sailing they had, unknown to themselves, the eastward set of the Gulf Stream Drift, about one mile an hour, against them, but even so the passage was long if in reality the wind was continuously fair. The Elizabethan

[1] See Fig. I.

Edward Hayes, who collected details on the Newfoundland voyage, said that up to the end of May the outward passage was commonly performed in twenty-two days or less and that in June the winds began to turn contrary.[1] Present-day weather-maps do not suggest the extent of contrast implied by Hayes and reveal a less clear-cut situation, with a fair amount of westerly wind even in the spring.[2] Their figures are averages based upon many observations. It was always possible for the lucky navigator to get through with a mainly fair wind and beat the average. It must also be considered that the modern observations are taken more than four centuries later and that there may have been climatic changes. There is good reason to believe that the Greenland ice-cap has shown some changes, which may have had some influence on the winds.

Cabot made his landfall on June 24, a date furnished by the Paris Map and Toby's Chronicle. The accuracy of the map's evidence is in general somewhat suspect, but in this particular we may regard the fact as having been furnished by Sebastian Cabot, since in 1544 he was almost the only man in Spanish circles in a position to know it. Bristol men no doubt treasured this date— St John the Baptist's Day—and it was through them that Maurice Toby had it. It is not likely that he copied the Paris Map, for his other details are not in it. The Island of St John, discovered and named on the day of the landfall, cannot be identified, since we do not know that it really was an island, nor do we know the exact locality of the landfall. Its existence rests upon the Eighth Legend, which also says that the land was seen in the morning and that Cabot named it Prima Tierra Vista. This looks like genuine recollection or tradition from Sebastian's Bristol days. He had seen his father's maps, which are now lost, and as a boy he may even have

[1] Document 34.
[2] But it may be observed that north-east winds are said to be of frequent occurrence, principally during the forty or fifty days after the two equinoxes, when a direct westerly course may be shaped (A. B. Becher, *Navigation of the Atlantic Ocean*, ed. 5 (1892), p. 145). In 1497 the spring equinox was in the first week of April.

been present at the great event. But the Legend goes on to give details of the natives, their costumes and customs, and the animals of the new land. These things, as we know quite positively from other evidence, cannot have been observed in 1497, and belong to later experience. This does not imply that the whole Legend was a fake. It was more probably a muddle: its writer got some details from Sebastian Cabot and abridged them and mixed them up.

Near the point of the landfall Cabot went on shore and cere-moniously took possession, erecting a cross and the banners of Henry VII, the Pope, and St Mark of Venice. Pasqualigo, a Venetian, mentions the banner of St Mark but not that of the Pope: Day mentions the Pope's banner but not that of St Mark. With his small landing party, a dozen or so men being available, Cabot did not seek to gain touch with the inhabitants and did not venture more than a bowshot from the shore. The explorers saw no people, but found evidence that men were there, a track lead-ing inland, a burnt-out fire, notched or felled trees, snares for game, and a carved stick like a netting-needle. There were tall trees suitable for masts, other woodland growth, and rich grass. The weather was fine and hot, so that it appeared to be a land where brasil-wood might grow and silkworms be bred. But it must have been awesome, there in the heat and silence, surrounded by the great trees and undergrowth, and watched, as they might guess, by hidden hostile men. Personal danger apart, the leaders could not afford to risk an ambush with their discovery un-reported. They withdrew to the beach, filled water-casks at some spring or brook, and re-embarked. Pasqualigo puts it simply: 'Being in doubt, he returned to his ship.'

Cabot, as John Day expressly states, did not land again in the whole course of the discovery. He coasted eastwards and took a month in doing so. Save that Pasqualigo reported that the coasting covered 300 leagues, there is no evidence of the distance to the point whence Cabot took his departure for England. We do not know how close he kept to the land, what winds he had, or what stoppages he made. At night he may have anchored or hove to, as

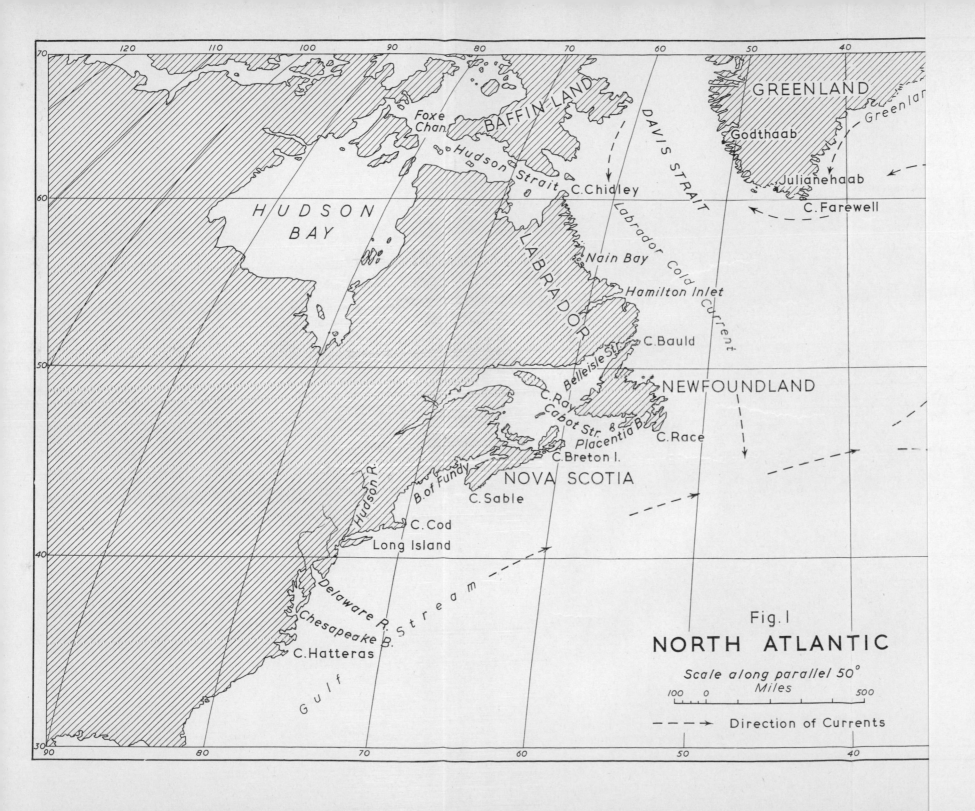

Fig.I

NORTH ATLANTIC

Scale along parallel 50°

Miles

100   0   500

- - - → Direction of Currents

Columbus often did on a strange coast. He was evidently close in at some points, but they may have been exceptional. He had an impression that there were fields and might be villages. At one place there was a forest that looked beautiful. At another the voyagers saw two forms running on the shore, but could not tell whether they were men or animals. In the coastal waters there were quantities of fish. John Day sent his Spanish correspondent a 'copy' of the land found, containing names of capes and islands, but it has not been preserved with his letter.[1] La Cosa's map has a score of place-names, not all capes and islands, and not all certainly derived from this voyage. Day alludes to the Island of the Seven Cities, whose southernmost part, he says, is west of Bordeaux River, as included in the discovery; and the southern part of Nova Scotia might stand very well for that of the Seven Cities as depicted in the traditional form. Day goes on to state that the easternmost cape is 1800 miles west of Dursey Head in Ireland, an assertion that, as will be seen, arouses a considerable difficulty of interpretation. Pasqualigo says that the land is distant 700 leagues, presumably from Bristol, which agrees approximately with Day's 600 leagues from Ireland. These are the evidences for the month's coasting, and we shall later have to try to assess what they amount to.

Of the passage home Day told his Spanish correspondent that it took fifteen days from the easternmost cape 'of the mainland' to Europe, with a fair wind and good weather all the way. But it ended with a landfall on the coast of Brittany, from which they had to sail round the Land's End to Bristol. The mistaken course was against Cabot's judgment and was due to his companions, who insisted that he had been heading too far north. This mistake makes it certain that on the homeward track they did not sight Dursey Head, which Day uses as a chart reference-point for latitude. The *Matthew* was certainly back at Bristol about August 6, the date given by Toby, since Cabot had an interview with the King in London on or before the 10th, a date established by

---

[1] The copy (*la copia de la tierra*) may have been a written description, but was more probably a copy of the chart made by Cabot as he went along.

an entry in the Household Book. The fifteen-day passage from continent to continent is probably a record among the few dated voyages of the ensuing century. Jacques Cartier in 1536 made one of seventeen days to St Malo, and thus could easily have sighted the Breton coast a day earlier. In 1597 the *Hopewell* of London, probably foul and deeply laden, reached English soundings from Newfoundland in twenty-two days. Cabot's recorded time may seem a little too good.

After leaving the main American coast Cabot saw two islands but did not stop to investigate them. If he came from Cape Breton these may have been St Pierre and Miquelon or projecting points of the Avalon Peninsula of Newfoundland appearing as islands. If he had already left Cape Race there is nothing by which they may be accounted for. This information is from Pasqualigo's letter, and when it was first translated into English in 1837 the rendering was that 'he saw two islands to starboard', which he could only have done if he had been coming from the northward down the east coast of Newfoundland. But 'to starboard' was one of Rawdon Brown's inaccuracies, and H. P. Biggar gave the original Italian and a correct translation in his book of 1911: it contains no words meaning 'to starboard'. Biggar's correction discounted certain interpretations that had been made concerning Cabot's landfall and the location of his coasting, and shows what care is necessary in getting as near to the original text of records as is possible.

We have now to consider the very difficult question of the coasts visited by Cabot in the *Matthew* in 1497. Many and various interpretations of the evidence have been made, so mutually contradictory that most of them must be fallacious. It has been argued: (i) that Cabot made his landfall in southern Labrador and thence coasted southwards to Cape Race, the south-eastern point of Newfoundland; (ii) that he passed through the Strait of Belle Isle into the Gulf of St Lawrence, and that his prolonged coasting was of the northern shore of that Gulf; (iii) that he entered the Gulf past Cape Breton Island, sailed westward until he sighted the

Gaspé peninsula, and thence turned eastward to and along the south coast of Newfoundland; (iv) that he made his landfall near Cape Breton and went on along the south-western shore of Nova Scotia; (v) that he made his landfall in Nova Scotia, and thence coasted back north-eastwards to Cape Breton, sighting on the homeward passage the southern points of Newfoundland and mistaking them for islands. There are minor variations of these themes, with the result that no two investigators are completely in agreement.

The problem should be kept strictly objective, yet it tends to become subjective. Some yield to the fascination of maps, wildly incorrect maps as they obviously are, and strive to extract from them secrets which for the most part they do not contain. The Cabotian map-scholar has too often allowed his mind to become permeated with the idea that the early sixteenth-century maps were designed primarily to give information about John Cabot, whereas in fact the cartographers may have known little or nothing about his voyage and may not even have heard his name. This is a form of self-deception unrecognized by its victim and increasing its influence as his mind becomes more absorbed in the study. His minutely detailed scholarship becomes ever more admirable, while his judgment of the broad implications of evidence decays. Those who have read much in the Cabot literature of the past century will not be at a loss for examples. Then there are those who allow themselves to form a prejudice, a conviction that there is not evidence to clinch, such as that the shore first discovered, Prima Tierra Vista, 'must have been' in Newfoundland, or in Nova Scotia, and warp their thinking to this end; or a personal animosity such as Henry Harrisse conceived for Sebastian Cabot, who became for him an unmitigated villain and the liar who plunged John Cabot's story into the obscurity that covers it. Such are the snares that beset the Cabot student. He must be alert to keep the critical, even sceptical, mind and see the evidence for what it is truly worth.

Taking the written evidence for the landfall and coasting, and leaving to separate consideration the La Cosa map, we may assemble statements drawn from Pasqualigo, the letter-writer of August 24, Soncino and Day, who were all witnesses to John Cabot's statements after his arrival in London in 1497. Pasqualigo said that the land was the country of the Grand Khan and was 700 leagues distant from England, and that Cabot had coasted for 300 leagues, and that on the way back he saw two islands. The writer of a letter to the Duke of Milan on August 24 said that Cabot had found two very large and fertile new islands and had also discovered the Seven Cities 400 leagues from England. Soncino wrote on December 18 that Cabot had reached a part of Asia, a mainland, with a climate suitable for brasil wood and silk. Day said that most of the discovery was made after turning back from the first landfall, near which place Cabot made his only landing; that the southernmost part of the Seven Cities was west of Bordeaux River (a method of indicating its latitude by reference to a chart of Western Europe); that Cabot spent about one month in exploring the coast, and took his departure homewards from the Cape nearest to Ireland, 1800 miles west of Dursey Head; and that the aforesaid cape was that discovered in the past by men of Bristol who had called it the Island of Brasil, although it was now believed to be part of the main continent. Soncino and Day both spoke of the abundance of codfish on the new coast. The Eighth Legend, coupled with the name Prima Tierra Vista, implied, not very conclusively, that the landfall was in the neighbourhood of Cape Breton.

Day's statements are the most detailed, but they raise new uncertainties. He indicates two latitudes by reference to those yielded by a chart of the western coasts of Europe (cf. Pls. XII, XIII). Such charts as survive from that time are not minutely accurate, and we may, for caution's sake, suppose a possible error of at least one degree either way in Day's locations of Bordeaux River and Dursey Head. He probably meant the mouth of the Bordeaux River, which is in 45° 35′ N. Bordeaux itself is in 44° 50′. Dursey Head is in 51° 34′. The latitudes recorded by Cabot from the other side of the Atlantic were subject to greater error, because they were observed from on board a ship which even in fine weather gave an unsteady platform from which to use a quadrant or an astrolabe. Such instruments were at their best when handled on firm land. Latitudes on Cabot's voyage were almost certainly observed by the Pole Star, and there was no opportunity for that on the occasion of his single landing. Day's evidence therefore is that the south end of the Seven Cities was approximately, and with a wide margin of error, in latitude $45\frac{1}{2}°$; and that the cape of departure homeward was, with a similar margin, in $51\frac{1}{2}°$. These two indications yield, for the lower latitude, the south-western end of Nova Scotia, somewhere near Cape Sable; and for the higher, the northern point of Newfoundland. One of these two latitudes must be grossly in error, because between them they demand an improbable or even impossible amount of coasting to have been performed in a month. Moreover the coasting would involve turning the salient of Cape Race in south-eastern Newfoundland, of which change of course Day gives not a hint, and neither, as we shall see, does the La Cosa map. Day certainly implies that Cabot sailed back, in a general easterly direction, from his first landfall to his cape of departure. That being so, we are obliged to find the big error in the statement that the cape was 'west of Dursey Head'; for it looks as though the cape from which Cabot sailed for England was either Cape Breton or Cape Race. In favour of Cape Breton is that it allows the sighting of the two islands or supposed islands on the way home, whereas east of Cape Race there are no islands. On the whole the evidence so far traced points to Cape Breton as the eastern end of Cabot's coasting; but it is vague and uncertain evidence and the conclusion is not a proven fact. Cape Breton does not stand as well as Cape Race for the Isle of Brasil discovered in earlier years.

Pasqualigo stated that Cabot coasted for 300 leagues, and he is the only witness to give an estimate of the distance covered. He had the figure at first or second hand from Cabot or someone who sailed with him, and we cannot regard it as incontrovertibly established; in fact, in Cabot's own mind his coasting distance cannot have been exactly measured. The 300 leagues has in the past been much doubted, chiefly on the ground that he had not the time for it. But in point of fact he had, for, as we now know, he took a month over it, in fine weather, with a midsummer length of day. Allowing for progress only in daylight, nine hundred miles would average thirty miles a day made good, at a speed over the ground of no more than two knots for a fifteen hours day. No days were wasted in landings, after the first, and the mileage was possible even with some head winds. The nine hundred miles indeed could have been exceeded. It is notable, by the way, that none of the accounts of early American coastings makes mention of fog. If there had been much we should probably hear of it. The coasting ended at 'the cape nearest Ireland'. It began farther west. It may be instructive to apply the assumed nine hundred miles to each of three possible terminals, Cape Bauld the northern point of Newfoundland, Cape Race its south-eastern point, and Cape Breton, and to see which approximate starting-point for the coasting each would yield. It must be borne in mind that such a calculation involves some arbitrary treatment of the facts and cannot be regarded as exact; for 'coasting' may have more than one meaning, a careful following of the intricacies of the coast, a straight course from one salient point to the next, or even a prolongation of a given course without land in sight in the hope of picking up the coast again farther on. The state of the atmosphere would be an important factor in any of these procedures. Our application of the supposed coasting distance to the modern map cannot therefore yield any exact result, and is useful only as providing suggestions.

The suggestions work out as follows. Nine hundred miles back from northern Newfoundland ('west of Dursey Head'), in straight lines joining the salient points, takes us round Cape Race to the neighbourhood of Cape Breton. The same distance west from Cape Race leads to somewhere near Portland, Maine. From Cape Breton it goes down the American coast somewhat beyond Long Island. Theoretically then, the landfall, from which the homeward coasting began, could have been at Cape Breton, or in Maine, or beyond Long Island. Practically, any of these would have involved much more than nine hundred miles of coasting, since Cabot could not have sailed on a straight line between salients, out of sight of land, unless he knew where the next salient was. We have therefore to rule out anything as far as Long Island as beyond probability: from that locality, keeping reasonable touch with the coast, Cabot could hardly have reached Cape Breton, let alone Cape Race, in a month.

A landfall somewhere in Maine is a more attractive proposition. Cabot's object was to find the continent of Asia and to see enough of it to make sure that it was the continent, and his method was to strike as far west as possible and then to follow the continental coast back towards Europe. So much we have on good evidence. He knew the approximate location of the Isle of Brasil already discovered, and he hoped for something west and south of that to fit his Asiatic theory. There was no need therefore for him to make for 'Brasil' on the outward passage. He may have deliber-ately missed it and passed on westwards, through open water, with the continent, as he believed, lying beyond the northern horizon. Then, having bitten off as much as he could chew (for what was only intended to be a summer's voyage), he turned northward, closed the land, and began to follow it back homewards, finding it fairly adjacent to 'Brasil', and 'assuming and believing' that they were all one land. The above, it must be emphasized, is only a speculative explanation of what may have taken place. It would not have been advanced at all but that it is not inconsistent with any of the known facts. It could have been what happened, and that is all. We cannot know the detailed plan in Cabot's mind, or what waters the *Matthew* really sailed.

That Cabot did make a landfall on the coast of Maine is a supposition arising from the tenor of John Day's letter. He speaks of the Island of the Seven Cities as included in the discovery, but he does not say that it was the locality at which the discovery began. Amid all the uncertainties there is something amounting to

The Cabot Voyages and Bristol Discovery

a strong probability, and it is that the Seven Cities of John Day's letter was Nova Scotia. The southern half of that country is of the size and outline which had long been attributed to the legendary island, and the Bordeaux latitude cited by Day cuts the Nova Scotian coastline. By one reading of Day's letter it might appear that the coasting began somewhere west of the Seven Cities and encountered them in its course; and this, as we shall see, is in a dim way supported by the La Cosa map. In modern terms, it began in Maine and rounded Cape Sable in Nova Scotia. Where it ended, whether at Cape Breton or Cape Race, is indeterminable on the written evidence: it depends on what could be done in a month. But it looks as though Day's 'cape of the mainland nearest to Ireland' was one of those two, and that to put it in the latitude of Dursey Head was a mistake. The Maine landfall, as we have seen, is a supposition. If it is not true, Nova Scotia takes its place. Only that 'copy of the land' which Day sent to Columbus could settle the matter, and it is lost.

The only surviving map which indubitably gives evidence on the discovery of 1497 is that made by Juan de la Cosa in 1500. It does quite certainly give evidence on English discoveries made up to that date, for it marks a portion of the North American coast with English flags and verbally attributes discovery to the English. If only it were a good map we should have our problems elucidated. But it is far from good, and gives only disputable answers to questions on the locality and extent of the discoveries. La Cosa as a cartographer was not in the same class as the Portuguese map-makers who were shortly to extend their attention to North America. It was natural that he should not be, for they had behind them more than half-a-century's experience of mapping new discoveries on the African coast, whereas the Spaniards were comparative beginners. The La Cosa map has been aptly described as 'a primitive', somewhat weak as a scientific record; and commentators should beware of trying to get out of it what was never put in. Since its emergence into modern light in 1832, when it was found among the stock of a Paris antique shop, it has been the

72

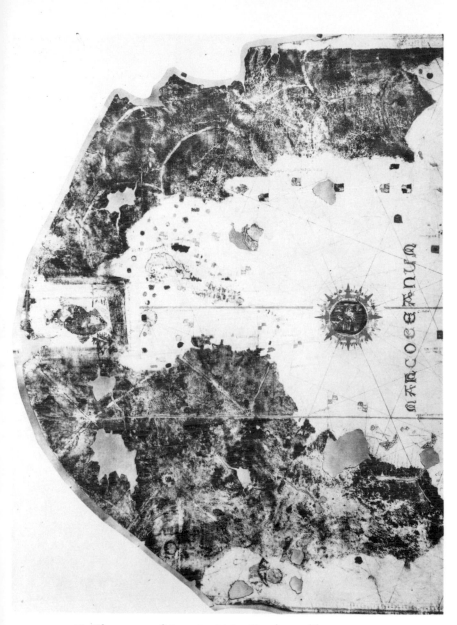

II. The coasts of America in La Cosa's world map, 1500

subject of enormous interest and controversy, and every work dealing with Spanish, Portuguese and English western discoveries has had to take account of it. There are several surviving Portuguese and Italian maps of slightly later date. No English maps survive, except in so far as the ghosts of them haunt the La Cosa design, as there is reason to believe they do.

The La Cosa is a large map showing the old world as well as the new.[1] It depicts them in markedly different styles. Eastern Asia is ruled off by the right edge of the map not far beyond the mouths of the Ganges. The unknown hinterland of America is likewise bounded by the curved left edge of the map. Whether Asia and our America are to be regarded as continuous or separate is a question that the method of representation does not answer. It is possible that La Cosa was doubtful, and so avoided a pronouncement. One may believe from the general appearance of the Asiatic part of the map that it was copied from one that gave a wider eastern extension, which La Cosa cut off. To have included the China coast as Martin Behaim had done eight years before would have been to raise the question, what then is the western continent across the Atlantic? And the answer would have had political implications which the cartographer was unwilling to face. Another question left unanswered is that of the continuity of North and South America. No one knew whether they were joined or whether there was a strait between them. La Cosa neatly evades committing himself by inserting a framed picture of St Christopher in the critical region.

In 1953 Mr G. R. Crone first drew attention to the fact that the map is actually a combination of two separate maps, one of the old world, the other of the new, joined at a meridian passing through the Atlantic; and that the two are on different scales, that of the western part being considerably larger.[2] From this there

---

[1] A technical description is not attempted here, but is available in works on the cartography of the period. Our reproduction of the whole map (Pl. I) is taken from that of Jomard, which shows most clearly the general outlines, although it is untrustworthy in detail. Pl. II shows the present state of the map.

[2] G. R. Crone, *Maps and their Makers* (London, 1953), pp. 84–5.

The Cabot Voyages and Bristol Discovery

follows a conclusion pertinent to our present subject. There are various parallels shown on the map, including the equator and the tropic of Cancer. Measurements from these two yield approximately correct latitudes for places on the coasts of Northern Africa and Western Europe. These parallels are continued straight across into the New World portion of the map; but there, owing to the difference of scale, no valid latitudes can be obtained by measuring north and south from them. In other words, the fact that the English coast of North America is shown on the latitude of southern Ireland does not really indicate that La Cosa considered it to be in approximately 52°. There is an aberration which, through the presence of unknown factors, cannot be exactly allowed for. Similarly there is a very noticeable apparent error in the location of the Spanish West Indies. Cuba and Hispaniola are shown well to the north of the tropic of Cancer, and Columbus's landfall in 1492 is about on the latitude of Gibraltar, thus making nonsense of the courses recorded in Columbus's journal. Juan de la Cosa the cartographer was not the man of that name who sailed with Columbus on his first voyage, but he did accompany Columbus on his second, which reached Hispaniola and Cuba, and he must have been well acquainted with the compass courses needed for the West Indian navigation. The fact that he completely disregarded them in constructing his map shows that no calculations of American latitudes can be made on his authority. The map was not, even in its author's intention, an exact geographical statement.[1]

Another distortion lay in the orientation of new coastlines. These were commonly laid down from magnetic bearings, not from true; and where a map covered a large area like the Atlantic, with different variation in its different parts, there was considerable apparent displacement in the coastlines, each being drawn in accordance with the variation in its own region. In La Cosa's map

[1] This revised view of the nature of the map invalidates arguments, such as my own in 1929, based on the reasons for La Cosa's errors of latitude. I then assumed that the errors were intentional and that considerations of policy accounted for them. I do not now believe this.

74

the English part of North America is oriented on a variation which John Day tells us was about two points, or 22°½ W. This variation is also implied in the oblique scale of Pedro Reinel's map (Kunstmann I).[1]

Many of the inscriptions scattered along the coasts are words which seem to be Spanish but in fact are not recognizable words of any language, and remain meaningless. This gives rise to the suspicion that the map as we have it is not the original but a copy, made by a person who failed to decipher the place-names and merely drew them to the best of his ability. Some of the words on the English coast of America are of this unintelligible sort, although some are clear enough. There are other maps of the early period which are copies of lost originals and exhibit the same faults in the inscriptions. Indeed, any map of a large area of the world was ultimately a copy, since it had been compiled from pilots' charts and explorers' surveys of the different coast-lines. The late W. F. Ganong pointed out that, since the successive copies were apparently drawn freehand by eye and not by instrument, there was a progressive degeneration from the originals, capes and bays being smoothed into straighter lines. One may see this tendency in operation when a lecturer draws a freehand map upon a blackboard. Consequently the coast which La Cosa shows as of English discovery was undoubtedly much more accidented than the map suggests. Add to this that Cabot's survey of 1497 could have made no claim to thoroughness, for that was not his purpose. All he aimed at was to ascertain the general direction of a long coastline.

The late George E. Nunn was dissatisfied with the dating of the La Cosa map. From various indications he concluded that, even granting 1500 as the date of the original, the copy we have was altered later, not long before the death of La Cosa in 1510. He published a short study to this effect.[2] If this conclusion were justified as it concerned the coast of North America, it would

---

[1] See below, p. 313; and Pl. XII.
[2] George E. Nunn, *The Mappemonde of Juan de la Cosa* (Jenkintown, 1934).

dilute the map's value as a record of the Cabot expeditions, since there were several more English voyages in the years following 1500, whose results might have contributed to the drawing of the map as we have it. One of Nunn's contentions against the early date is that the map shows Cuba as an island. Columbus contended that Cuba was a large promontory of the Asiatic continent, and the first recorded circumnavigation of Cuba did not take place until 1508. But there are conceivable reasons why La Cosa could have judged in 1500 that Cuba was an island. One is that he had coasted southern Cuba with Columbus in 1494, very nearly reaching its western end before turning back. Sign-communication with the natives may have given him the impression that the end of the land was not far away. Some of the company evidently thought so, and Columbus would not have it. He compelled every man to declare that Cuba was part of the continent. La Cosa submitted with the rest, although he may not have believed it. There is another possible reason why La Cosa could have known in 1500 that Cuba was an island. Nunn claimed to have searched the records of all known voyages in support of his contentions; but there was one voyage of which he could not search the records, for there are none, and that is the English voyage of 1498. If the English had got so far southwards as to sight Cuba they could have acquired knowledge of its insularity. The insular Cuba appears in La Cosa's map, and does not disprove that it was drawn in 1500. Further, the map does not show the results of Columbus's last voyage in 1502–4, which revealed much of the coastline veiled by La Cosa's vignette.

There is another large reason for adhering to the date of 1500, which after all is inscribed upon the map itself. It is that the author had knowledge of the return of Vasco da Gama in 1499, for he draws Portuguese ships on the track across the Indian Ocean. But he was evidently not informed of the geographical discoveries made in the voyage, the lie of the East African coast and the shape of India. These in the La Cosa map are of the erroneous pre-Gama outline, whereas in maps from 1502 onwards they begin to take their true proportions. It was only in 1500 that a Spaniard could have known just so much and so little.

After this introduction to the La Cosa map we may proceed to its evidence on the Cabot voyage of 1497. The map shows a North American continent stretching continuously from a high northern latitude to one on a level with Cuba, where it is interrupted by the vignette of the saint already mentioned. Up in the north there is an east-pointing cape on the level of Iceland, and this is generally considered to represent Greenland and its Cape Farewell, wrongly oriented. A broad bay or bight carries the coast southwards to the next promontory, on the level of southern Ireland. This stands for the west Greenland coast carried right across Davis Strait, whose existence was then unknown, and continued down the coast of our present Labrador and Newfoundland. At this second promontory begins the English coast, running westwards, quite plainly marked as a coast of English discovery. There are no place-names on the coasts to the north of it.

The English coast runs east-and-west and must be supposed to be oriented on its compass bearings. Five English flags are planted along it. The western third of the coast has no place-names but a general title written across the adjacent sea, *mar descubierto por inglese*. The names have produced a great variety of readings, for some are extremely doubtful, and the map has deteriorated in the hundred and thirty years since it was first known. Some of the earlier readings are probably better than those that can now be made. On the hinterland of the coastline there was formerly visible a fragment of inscription naming the Seven Cities, apparently in Spanish, and an inconclusive vestige of it is still detectable. In 1929 W. F. Ganong, having compared all the previous readings, made what at that date was considered to be the most probable list. Ganong worked from some good reproductions, but not from the original map itself. More recently, in 1951, a facsimile atlas entitled *Mapas Españoles de América* was published at Madrid by the Real Academia de la Historia, and for

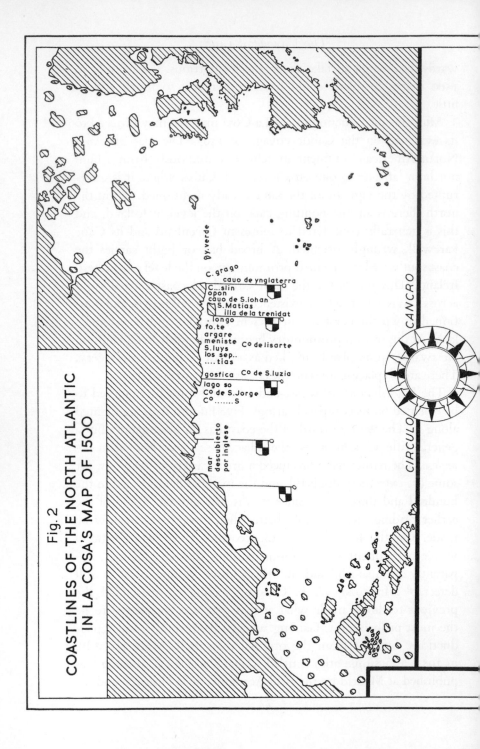

Fig. 2
COASTLINES OF THE NORTH ATLANTIC
IN LA COSA'S MAP OF 1500

ßy. verde
C. grago
cauo de ynglaterra
C...slin
apon
cauo de S.iohan
S.Matias
illa de la trenidat
. longo
fo.te
argare
meniste
S.luys
los sep..
....tias
Co de lisarte
gosfica
lago so
Co de S.luzia
Co de S.Jorge
Co.......S

mar
descubierto
por inglese

CANCRO
CIRCULO

the La Cosa reproduction Admiral J. F. Guillén y Tato, working from the original with scientific aids such as infra-red rays, produced a list of the names as they could thus be deciphered. The two lists are given below, the names running from east to west:[1]

Ganong's list	*Guillén's list*
y. berde or verde	y: verde
s: grigor	C: grago
cauo de ynglaterra	cauo de ynglaterra
c. fastanatre	c . . . slin
agron	opon
cauo de s. iohan	cauo de s iohan
s. nicolas	S Matias
isla de la trenidat	illa de la trenidat
ro. longo	. longo
forte	fo.te
argare	. . . . . .
meniste	meniste
co. de lisarte	C° de lisarte
s: luzia	s. luys
jusquei or insquei	los sep . .
requilea or r. conilia	. . . tias
co. de s. luzia	C°: de S luzia
ansto or austo	gosfica
lago fori	lago so . . .
co. de S: jorge	C° de S: Jorge
cauo descubierto	C° . . . . s
mar descubierta por inglese	mar descubierto por inglese

The English meanings of some of the names are clear enough, but attempts to interpret the more obscure ones have failed to yield agreement, although *Cabo de Lisarte* is generally held to indicate a cape resembling the Lizard on the coast of Cornwall. The problem of fitting the coast to the modern map has produced

[1] Ganong gave his list as from west to east, but the order is here reversed for better comparison with Guillén's. In Fig. 2 (herewith) the names have been given in the forms of Guillén's list, which, as a document standing up to strict criticism, is by far the best available.

79

divergent answers. The solutions which make it the coast of southern Labrador with eastern Newfoundland, or a region inside the St Lawrence estuary, seem to be precluded when one looks at La Cosa's North America as a whole. The orientation rules out Labrador-Newfoundland. The northern shore of the St Lawrence estuary might serve as the English coast, but that it would have been impossible for Cabot to have made his landfall towards the western end of it without seeing any land to the southward, and then to have coasted eastwards and out, presumably by the Strait of Belle Isle, also without seeing any land to seaward. For La Cosa clearly shows an ocean coast facing southward by compass bearing and with no other lands offshore save a few small islands close in. His English coast can only be somewhere between Cape Race and Maine. He apparently draws it in too high a latitude as compared with the British Isles, but that is owing to the difference in scale between the eastern and western sides of his Atlantic: as we have seen, he was not trying to make any exact statements of American latitudes.

Ganong found reason to believe that the coasting of 1497 began at the westernmost flag and worked back eastwards, ending at Cavo de Ynglaterra, where the easternmost flag is placed. John Day's letter has confirmed the direction, which we can now say positively was from west to east. But nothing has confirmed Ganong's belief that the 1497 coasting began at the westernmost flag, for this rests on an assumption that the flagged coast represents the results of the 1497 expedition and nothing else. Ganong further assumed that the five flags each marked the locations of landings by Cabot, although we now know from Day that he landed only once. The flags are La Cosa's, not Cabot's. Ganong relied a good deal on these landings in his identifications of the places named by La Cosa; and his identifications break down into guesswork. Nevertheless his overall analysis, apart from the details, is, to the present writer's view, by far the best reasoned, and when he is guessing he says so, and does not offer supposition as fact.

The information that La Cosa certainly had, and additionally may have had, for his drawing of the North American coast, is as follows. He certainly had two cartographical statements by Cabot, available in the winter of 1497–8. One was Cabot's general view of the geography of the western Atlantic, embodied in a world-map and a globe which he exhibited in London.[1] We can say with confidence that a copy of the map was sent to Spain: John Day spoke of supplying it at the beginning of 1498, but had not had time to make a good copy; and Ayala a few months later believed that his government had received a copy, and if not, he had one ready to send.[2] The other cartographical statement by Cabot was 'the copy of the land which has been found', which Day did send to Columbus. This we may take to be the primary chart of the coast actually explored, and the foundation of La Cosa's detailed drawing, at least of the named part, of the English coast. It may equally have been a written description of the coasting. It gave, as Day noted, the names of the capes and the islands and the point of the first landfall; and several English names are visible in Spanish guise in La Cosa's map. What Day may have sent was not the original chart but a copy, or even a copy of a copy, and the process of degeneration of the outline, to which Ganong drew attention, had begun before ever the Spaniards saw it.

La Cosa himself did not work on this material until about the middle of 1500, because in 1499 he had been away with Alonso de Ojeda on a discovery of what was afterwards called the Spanish Main of South America. By the date of his return there had been time for additional information to have come from England, information of further discovery made by the Cabot expedition of 1498. We do not know, and can only guess, what that discovery was; but whatever it may have been, there was no reason why La Cosa should not have incorporated it in his map of 1500. The map makes a distinction: the 'named coast', that is, the part covered by the detailed place-names, is not so long as the 'flagged coast', of which it forms the eastern two-thirds. The western third, inscribed

[1] Document 24.   [2] Document 37.

'Sea discovered by the English',[1] has no place-names on the shore. The suggestion that these two distinct sections of the English coast came from two different sources of information is fairly strong; and if there were two sources the second can only be dated to 1498–9. But here we stray into the gaping gulf of supposition based upon supposition and had best draw back. All that can positively be said is that it is not certain that the whole of La Cosa's English coast is based upon the discovery of 1497.

The identification of the coastline of 1497 as a whole (apart from the details) has produced a vast amount of speculation, some of which is now discounted by the two features of La Cosa's delineation which have only recently received much attention, the uncertainty of the scale and the amount of compass variation on which it was plotted. To these we have to add the new statements of fact in Day's letter, and they are of governing importance. The written evidence, already analysed, coincides with the La Cosa map evidence in placing the discovery on a coast facing roughly south (by compass) across the open ocean.

The Seven Cities were evidently accepted in London as part of the discovery of 1497. They were mentioned with a wrong location in the letter of August 24, again by John Day, and by Ayala in the following year; and Day's latitude, if it is approximately correct, shows that Nova Scotia was the Seven Cities. La Cosa inscribed the name on the mainland of his English coast. In spite of its traditional description as an island, contemporaries were prepared to think of it as continental. The eastward end of Cabot's coasting, as we have seen, was probably either Cape Breton or Cape Race. La Cosa names it *Cavo de Ynglaterra*. Day says that 'the cape of the said land was found and discovered in the past by the men from Bristol who found Brasil, as your Lordship knows.

[1] This is the translation of *mar descubierto por inglese* that has become traditional with commentators. It is possibly what La Cosa meant, and the omission of the final 's' may be accidental. It should be noted, however, that the actual translation of the inscription as we have it is 'Sea discovered by the Englishman', as if La Cosa had some individual commander in mind. If the inscription relates to 1498 the commander may or may not have been Cabot.

It was called the Island of Brasil, and it is assumed and believed to be the mainland that the men from Bristol found'. The best interpretation of this is that Brasil when found was thought to be an island, but is now strongly surmised to be part of the mainland newly discovered by Cabot. This would make the Island of Brasil Newfoundland and 'the cape of the said land' Cape Race. But La Cosa is in conflict with this identification of the cape; for he shows an island, Ysla Verde, to the east of his Cavo de Ynglaterra, and there is no island east of Cape Race. Working from La Cosa alone we should make his *Cavo de Ynglaterra* Cape Breton and his *Ysla Verde* the Avalon Peninsula of Newfoundland. The discrepancy between Day and La Cosa appears to be insoluble, and we cannot say whether Cape Breton or Cape Race was the terminal point of Cabot's coasting. The position of *Prima Tierra Vista* on the Paris Map of 1544 favours Cape Breton as the landfall; and if this is true Cape Breton could not have been the point of departure on the ocean passage homewards. But the authenticity of the placing of *Prima Tierra Vista* remains suspect. We do not know if Sebastian Cabot gave precise instructions to the cartographer, or if he saw the finished map before it was engraved. What does come out of the investigation is that the Bristol men's Brasil was Newfoundland (although probably not the whole of it), and that Cabot's discovery included the southern shores of Nova Scotia. All the foregoing discussion, however, rests on the substantial accuracy of Pasqualigo's 300 leagues of coasting; and we do not know that he was accurate. It is possible that the whole discovery was on a smaller scale, the southern shore of Newfoundland, for example, with the Burin peninsula serving for the Seven Cities, and no more than the Avalon Peninsula for the Island of Brasil. Such an interpretation is not so likely, in the present writer's opinion, as that already discussed, and would involve further difficulty with Day's latitudes. But all the evidence is unsatisfactory, because none of those who gave it knew exactly what they were talking about in terms of the ascertained facts as observable in the modern map.

VI

JOHN CABOT:
BETWEEN THE TWO VOYAGES, 1497-8

AT THE beginning of August 1497, probably on the 6th, the date given in Toby's Bristol chronicle, Cabot came back to Bristol; and he was at court reporting to the King on or before the 10th, a date fixed by the entry in the Household Book of the bestowal of £10 upon 'hym that found the new isle'.[1] The word isle may represent the clerk's erroneous impression of what had been found, or it may be an allusion to the Seven Cities. The whole affair immediately became public and attracted a great deal of attention. Its early phase is recorded in the letter of Lorenzo Pasqualigo, written on August 23.[2] It says that 'that Venetian of ours who went with a small ship from Bristol to find new islands has come back and says he has discovered main land'. The phrasing appears to indicate that Pasqualigo had previously written on the departure of Cabot in the spring, but this letter has not come to light. Pasqualigo says quite positively that the main land discovered is that of Asia, 'the territory of the Grand Khan'. The King is much pleased and has promised him ten armed ships next spring, and all the prisoners. The King has also given him money, and he is now with his Venetian wife and sons at Bristol. His name is Zuam Talbot.[3] He receives vast honour, is called the Great Admiral, and dresses in silk. The English run after him like mad, and so do our own rogues. The rest of the letter contains the details already quoted about the voyage itself. So far goes Pasqualigo in a pretty sound preliminary report made in thirteen days.

Not so good was the letter written next day by the unknown correspondent of the Duke of Milan. Some months ago, it says,

[1] Document 26.   [2] Document 22.
[3] Zuam was a Venetian form of Giovanni.

the King sent out a Venetian mariner skilled in discovering new islands, who has returned after discovering two large and fertile new islands; and he has also discovered the Seven Cities 400 leagues to the westward of England. This is poor reporting, but it does contain the first mention of the Seven Cities as one of the results of the discovery. The '400 leagues' may be the writer's error or a bad estimate on the part of someone else, for there is no land at that distance. After that, with Cabot at Bristol, and the King otherwise engaged, we hear no more for close on four months.

The year 1497 was one of crisis for Henry VII. At midsummer, while Cabot was on the American coast, the pretender Perkin Warbeck was in Scotland, where James IV took up his cause and declared war on his behalf. Henry levied taxation for defence, whereupon the people of Cornwall rose in revolt, saying that they would not pay for a Scottish war. They marched up to London, where Henry routed them at Blackheath and sent them home, all but three ringleaders, with his pardon. This clemency did not produce peace, for the Cornishmen had been beaten by force of numbers and merely went home determined to try again. Hearing of these things, Warbeck went southwards to an Irish port, and thence sailed for Cornwall, while James IV crossed the Border and besieged Norham Castle. Warbeck landed in Cornwall in the third week of August, while London was showing its first enthusiasm for Cabot and Cathay. A new and more formidable rebellion began in the West Country, where Exeter was hard pressed and nearly lost by the King. Henry had to leave London to deal with this, and the Earl of Surrey faced the Scots on the Border; and a fleet was mobilized for service on the east coast. September saw the royal forces relieve Exeter and crush the revolt; and Perkin Warbeck was captured and confessed to being an impostor. But the making of a thorough settlement detained the King for some time in the West, and he did not return to London until November 27. Peace with Scotland was signed on December 5.

These events account for a long suspension of the Cabot business, which did not resume activity until December. The war expenses may have made the King's contribution to the expedition of the following year less liberal than he had first intended.

The state of European politics was also relevant to English schemes of expansion, and must be briefly outlined. Since 1495 French and Spaniards had been in rivalry for the control of Italy, and both sides courted Henry VII, who intended to hold the balance rather than join in the fight. In 1496 he grudgingly became a member of Ferdinand's Holy League for the expulsion of the French from Italy, but only on condition that he should not take part in the war. But, on his own terms, Henry desired friendship with Ferdinand and Isabella, for he saw great advantage in the marriage of his son Arthur with their daughter Catherine. The children were then too young, but the negotiations for the match were being pursued, and some hard bargaining resulted. In 1497-8 also Henry was full of zest for the oceanic discovery and the wealth which Cabot promised. Spain strongly disapproved, but wanted Henry as a belligerent against France. Ferdinand sent Pedro de Ayala to Scotland to mediate the Anglo-Scottish peace and free Henry's hands for Spanish service. Having effected the peace, Ayala took up residence in London with a watching brief for his sovereigns' interests. Puebla, the permanent ambassador, remained also, but was not fully trusted by the sovereigns, who suspected that he was more Henry's servant than theirs. They kept him very short of money, and the Household Books show that Henry gave him presents.

The diplomatic situation as it affected Cabot was therefore that Henry was not greatly afraid of Spanish disapproval, although he was not at all desirous of a real breach with the sovereigns. He proceeded to give a brilliant display of diplomatic ability whereby when time was ripe he achieved the Spanish marriage without having to fight for Spain, and also gained a free hand to probe the possibilities of oceanic discovery.

In December 1497 Henry found leisure to attend to Cabot's business. On the 13th he granted Cabot an annual pension of £20, payable by instalments at Michaelmas and Easter out of the Bristol customs, and beginning from the Feast of the Annunciation (March 25) in 1497. There was a hitch in the administrative mechanism, and payment was delayed until a further warrant was issued to ensure it on 22 February 1498.[1] A payment of 8 January 1498 'to a Venetian in reward 66s. 8d.'[2] may well have been to John Cabot on account of the delay in his pension.

Meanwhile the project was elaborated, and its development took administrative shape. The King allowed free discussion before the court and the foreign ambassadors. One of these was Raimondo de Soncino, ambassador of the Duke of Milan. On December 18 he wrote to the Duke an account of what might almost have been a public lecture by Cabot, illustrated by a map and a globe of his own construction.[3] Pasqualigo in August had said that Cabot claimed to have been in the land of the Grand Khan. The title was derived from Marco Polo's travels as that of the Mongol sovereign of the greater part of Asia. It was still used by Europeans of the fifteenth century, who were apparently ignorant that the Mongol Empire had disintegrated and that the revived Chinese Empire was one of its successors. Soncino opens his letter with the news that 'His Majesty here has gained a part of Asia without a stroke of the sword'. Later he says that the new land is in the East, far beyond the country of the Tanais, which means that of the Don and the Black Sea. He says also that over against its coast will be found the island of Cipango (Japan) in tropical latitudes, and that the expected result will be the foundation of an English spice trade. These statements leave no doubt whatever that Cabot's discovery was claimed to be Eastern Asia.

It is to be noted that John Day's letter[4] does not say this, making no reference at all to Asia or to any commercial consequences of the discovery. But the Day letter is a follow-up of a previous communication either by speech or writing. This is proved by its phrase 'as I told your Lordship', and implied by the way in which

[1] Documents 27 and 28.	[2] Document 26.
[3] Document 24.	[4] Document 25.

it speaks of a map that has evidently been promised, and of the books desired by 'the Lord Grand Admiral', who, it is virtually certain, was Columbus. Now, in this letter which we have, John Day had no need to mention the Asiatic objective. It would have been an obvious thing to mention, as it was for Pasqualigo and Soncino, in the opening letter or conversation. 'What is he looking for?' would have been the great man's first question. The existing letter takes it as stated.

Returning to Soncino, we find an account of the discovery as it now stands in December, and is to be developed. The Bristol men are eloquent on the fishery, which can be made to render the English demand independent of Iceland. Cabot himself emphasizes the spice trade. He will work along the coast from the place at which he touched until he reaches the island of Cipango in the equinoctial region, 'where he believes that all the spices of the world have their origin, as well as the jewels'. Here Cabot was relying on Marco Polo, whose exaggerated account of Japan was his greatest error.[1] Marco had also mentioned the numerous islands of South East Asia, among which in fact the spices were produced. Cabot must have read this, since he had read the description of Japan, and he probably spoke of it; but his hearers concentrated the whole upon the one name of Cipango.

It is clear then that in his next expedition Cabot intended to work westwards and southwards from his new land along the continental coast until he came to the tropics. It is also clear that he claimed this destination to be westward of the Spanish Indies, for by the terms of the patent he was debarred from intruding in them. His map and globe must have showed this, but they are lost. There are surviving maps which show this interpretation: the Spanish Indies in mid-ocean, and west of them Cipango, and farther west the main Asiatic continent.[2] We have evidence that a

[1] Document 32.
[2] As in the Contarini-Rosselli world map of 1506 (Pl. VIII) and the Ruysch map of 1508. There is ground for believing that both of these published maps were designed a few years earlier than their dates of publication.

copy of Cabot's general map did go to Spain and that it indicated the trend of Cabot's Asiatic coast at least down to the latitude of Cuba. Ayala was highly indignant at the whole geographical argument, which he saw as an attack upon the achievement of Spain: 'Having seen the course they are steering and the length of the voyage', he wrote after the sailing of the 1498 expedition, 'I find that what they have discovered or are in search of is possessed by Your Highnesses, because it is at the cape which fell to Your Highnesses by the convention with Portugal.' What was this cape? The likely answer is that it was Cuba, which Columbus did not admit to be an island. He had not been round its western end, and he was asserting vehemently that it was a great projection of the Asiatic main continent. This was the anchor of his claim that he had truly reached Asia. Cabot did not believe it (and neither did Juan de la Cosa). For Cabot Cuba was only a midway Atlantic island, and the continent lay far to the west. However, the Spanish official view was that Asia had been reached, and Ayala had been briefed to express it to Henry VII: 'I told him [Henry] that I believed the islands [of Cabot's quest] were those found by Your Highnesses, and although I gave him the main reason, he would not have it.' And Ayala ends by saying that Cabot's map is 'exceedingly false'.

Taking all the evidence together, it is indubitable that on his second expedition Cabot was going to make for the tropics from the coast already found; and that coast, as two good witnesses stated, was held to be the part of eastern Asia that existed in temperate latitudes.

Soncino in December outlines the intended course of action. The King will equip ships and will give them all the malefactors, and they will go to 'that country' and form a colony. By this means they hope to make London a more important mart for spices than Alexandria. There is great enthusiasm. Cabot has bestowed an island on the Burgundian who went with him, and another on the Genoese barber. They think of themselves as counts, and the Admiral esteems himself a prince. Some poor

Italian friars will go on the next voyage, with the promise of bishoprics. Soncino himself, as a friend of the Admiral, could have an archbishopric if he chose to go: 'but I have reflected that the benefices which your Excellency reserves for me are safer, and I therefore beg that possession may be given me of those which fall vacant in my absence. . . .' One wonders what happened to the cheerful pluralist and his benefices not two years later, when the French took Milan and the Duke fled, to be ultimately captured and to die in a French prison.

With the new year measures to equip the new exploiting expedition begin to be taken. First we have to consider a clue that leads to nothing. Both Pasqualigo in August and Soncino in December reported that the King had promised a body of prisoners or 'malefactors' to be employed on the labour of founding a colony. We hear nothing more of these prisoners, although some of them may have been transported, and a 'colony' or trading post may possibly have been founded. The trading-factory was a Venetian institution in the Levant. We need not take it for granted that the post was to be in the populous parts of China or Japan. Cabot knew enough from Marco Polo to be aware that when he did impinge upon the rich and well-organized peoples of Asia he would have to behave circumspectly. He might get permission to establish a trading-factory, but he would probably not be able to take the high hand. Thus the confidence with which the convicts were to be shipped before the further conditions were known may point to an intention to form a post on the outlying part of Asia already visited, a half-way house on the trade-route from England to Japan, in some good harbour of what we know as Nova Scotia or New England. Here the goods from a long trading coast might be concentrated to await transit across the Atlantic. Such a post also, in the climate and amidst the fishery described by the voyagers of 1497, might provide victuals for the shipping. To us with our knowledge of what took place in early colonial ventures, this idea may seem wildly optimistic; but such optimism did pervade American projects for a century after Cabot's time. The Elizabethan records are full of it, and the half-way post was always attractive. Two years after Cabot's death we shall find elaborate colonial schemes, probably of that nature. However, of Cabot's own colonial scheme we have no more information.

On 3 February 1498 Cabot received letters patent enabling him to gather his shipping.[1] It was not a comprehensive grant of privileges and in no way superseded the grant of 1496, which continued to be operative. The patent of 1498 empowered John Cabot and his deputies to impress six English ships of not more than 200 tons burden, paying for them at the King's rates. Navy papers of the subsequent period show that the Crown paid 3d. per ton per week for impressed shipping. The grant also permitted Cabot to take with him all such subjects of the Crown, including masters and mariners, as would voluntarily accompany him. This was a general passport necessitated by the laws that prohibited the King's subjects from leaving the realm without his permission. The law was commonly dormant, but could be put in operation at any time by proclamation, and probably had been, owing to the events of the previous summer. The destination is described as 'the land and isles of late found by the said John in our name and by our commandment', a recognition that continent as well as islands had been discovered. The document is a commission to perform an executive act. Perhaps for this reason, it omits mention of Cabot's sons as too young for such authority.

In the event the fleet consisted of one ship equipped by the King and four by the merchants of London and Bristol. This is attested by statements in certain London Chronicles written in or after 1509.[2] They were derivatives from a common source now lost and constitute one testimony in three variant forms. Their effect is that in 1498 a Venetian skilled in geography induced the King to man and victual a ship at Bristol to search for an island which the Venetian knew to be rich and full of great commodities. In this ship some merchants of London adventured 'small stocks', or 'slight merchandises', or 'slight and gross merchandises'. Three or

[1] Document 35.　　　[2] Document 31.

four[1] small ships similarly laden sailed with her out of Bristol, the commander ('conditor of the said fleet') being the said Venetian. The rich island filled with great commodities was evidently Cipango. There is no list of the ships' names, and we do not know if the *Matthew* was one of them.

The fitting-out of the fleet went on in March and early April, 1498. According to Polydore Vergil,[2] the King provided a ship complete with crew and weapons, but not with cargo. It is not altogether likely that this was one of the King's small fighting fleet, but more probable that she was a private merchantman hired for the occasion. Lancelot Thirkill and his partner Thomas Bradley, who were London men, received payments totalling £113 8s. od., for the preparation of Thirkill's ship for a voyage to the New Land. It may be noted that a year's hire at the King's rate for a 200-ton ship would have amounted to £130; and we are told independently that the fleet was provisioned for a year.[3] It is therefore possible that the ship contributed by the King was Thirkill's and that she was just under 200 tons in burden. The detailed payments are as follows: March 22, to Lancelot Thirkill of London upon a prest for his ship going towards the New Island, £20; March 31, delivered to Lancelot Thirkill going towards the New Isle, in prest, £20; April 1, to Thomas Bradley and Lancelot Thirkill, going to the New Isle, £30; April 6, delivered to Thomas Bradley and Lance Thirkill, in full payment of £113 8s. od., £43 8s. od. Two days later there is a payment to one John Cair, 'going to the newe Ile in Rewarde', of 40s.[4] It is fairly evident that Thirkill was going on the voyage in person with his ship, unless by some slackness the clerk who made the entries intended the wording of March 22 to apply to March 31 and April 1 but did not trouble to write it out in full. The ship, whether equipped in the Thames or not, was at Bristol before the beginning of the

---

[1] By other evidence four was the correct number (Document 36).
[2] Document 33.   [3] Document 37.
[4] Document 26. The exact dates of payments may vary by two or three days from the dates recorded.

Atlantic voyage. We have no information on the financing of the four smaller Bristol ships. Although the Bristol men had talked in London of the fishery, it was not for fishing that they sent out these ships, which, as the Chronicles tell us, were laden with the same sorts of merchandise as the King's ship.

The date of sailing from Bristol is not precisely fixed. It was certainly after April 8, when the last Household Book payment was recorded. Fabyan's Chronicle and the Great Chronicle say 'in the beginning of May', and the Vitellian Chronicle, 'in the beginning of Summer', so that we may take early May as the time. As before, we have no names of the Bristol merchants who went. Ayala's letter of July 25 mentions that 'another Friar Buil' had gone in one of the five ships. This is an allusion to a missionary who had accompanied Columbus on his second voyage. We may couple it with Soncino's statement that some Italian friars were to sail with Cabot. Of one of these men we have something more. On 30 June 1498 Agostino de Spinula, a London correspondent of the Duke of Milan, wrote that a letter had arrived for Messer Giovanni Antonio de Carbonariis, who had left recently with five ships that His Majesty had sent to discover new islands.[1] It appears that Messer Giovanni was something more than one of Soncino's 'poor Italian friars'. He was a cleric who had been employed as a royal messenger from Henry VII to the Duke of Milan in 1489.[2] In 1497 Soncino alluded to him as 'the reverend master' whose advice he would take while in England.[3] In 1498 the Duke wrote to Brother Giovanni Antonio de Carbonariis a letter in terms which show the recipient to have been a man of some importance.[4] After his departure with Cabot there is no further mention of him.[5] It may be presumed with fair certainty that Lancelot Thirk-

[1] Document 36. [2] *Cal. S.P. Venice*, vol. 1, No. 947.
[3] *Cal. S.P. Milan*, vol. 1, No. 537. [4] Ibid., No. 562.
[5] Mr David O. True has very kindly notified me of a point that has attracted his attention, the existence of the old place-name Carbonear on the eastern shore of Newfoundland. Its similarity to the unique personal name de Carbonariis is suggestive. It might be supposed that Antonio de Carbonariis was in some way linked with this place in the voyage of 1498, or equally that he was there in the course of some subsequent expedition.

ill, Thomas Bradley and John Cair sailed with Cabot. If so, Thirkill came home, for he appears in a record of 1501.[1] But we do not absolutely know that he sailed: sickness or some other cause might have prevented it.

[1] BM, Add.MS 21480, f. 35b.

VII

THE VOYAGE OF 1498

HISTORIANS AND geographers of continental Europe in the sixteenth century—Spanish, Italian, Portuguese, French and German—wrote between them a number of short notices of the discoveries made by Sebastian Cabot under Henry VII. These notices either gave no date for Sebastian's voyage, or gave mutually contradictory dates, 1496, 1498, 1508, so that no certainty on the point was obtainable from them. During the same century there were no narrative accounts by learned writers of the voyages of John Cabot, with the solitary exception of the Eighth Legend on the Paris Map of 1544, which does not appear to have made any impression on the historians. In England Richard Hakluyt printed in 1582 the text of the letters patent granted in 1496 to John Cabot and his sons, but even this official mention of John did not alter the universal impression on the continent that the only leader of English exploration was Sebastian Cabot. The true facts about John Cabot, known to many people in 1497-8, died completely out of memory. Even the London Chronicles which we have quoted, dating from the early years of the sixteenth century, referred to him only as 'a Venetian', without giving his name. And so, by the middle of the century, the same idea was established in England as on the continent, that Sebastian Cabot was the discoverer of North America. Old Sebastian lived until 1557 and spent the last decade of his life in England. So far as we know, he did nothing to correct the false impression. The only contemporary English writer who knew him, Richard Eden, did not suspect that it was false and so did not tackle him on the point, having apparently no knowledge that John Cabot had commanded expeditions. Eden, with his geographical interest, could hardly have missed seeing the Eighth Legend, and we can only suppose that he did not consider it to be authentic, since for him

95

Sebastian remained the only explorer. The vigilant critical method of modern historians scarcely existed in the sixteenth century. Hakluyt at its close sometimes displayed it, but not always. Most writers adopted statements as they happened to find them, and if the statements were discrepant, used those which suited their prejudices and ignored the others. The prejudice once established in favour of Sebastian Cabot, as the doer of what we now know John did, was destined to a very long life.

The above is a necessary preface to consideration of the voyage of 1498, for the Sebastian prejudice, although now long discredited, has none the less affected the conclusions of historians to our own time. The Sebastian supremacy, if we may so call it, lasted well into the nineteenth century, until it culminated in Richard Biddle's *Memoir of Sebastian Cabot*, published in 1831. Biddle of course knew of the 1496 patent, but he did not infer from it that John Cabot was the leader. He set down John as an elderly merchant who did not go to sea, and constructed the story of discovery on the old lines as the achievement of Sebastian Cabot. Enlightenment began to come soon afterwards. In 1837 Rawdon Brown published Lorenzo Pasqualigo's letter. In the 1860's those of Soncino and Ayala come to light, and various minor pieces of evidence were accumulating. By the 1880's and 90's it was fully realized that a great mistake had been made about Sebastian Cabot, and the outline of his father's work as leader of the 1497 and 1498 expeditions was established. It was only an outline, and hardly even that for 1498 if the strictly contemporary evidence alone was used: all that could be said of that venture was that it set out under the command of John Cabot, with nothing known of its outcome. Yet there existed all the literary evidence produced in the sixteenth century about a voyage attributed to Sebastian Cabot. It was in sum too weighty to be ignored: these writers, some of whom personally knew Sebastian, could not have imagined the story out of nothing. The late nineteenth-century historians accepted the story and fathered it on to the voyages of John Cabot, for which they used it as true evidence. The inevitable corollary was that Sebastian was a shameless liar who had seized the whole credit of his father's deeds for himself and had systematically deceived his contemporaries, the writers of the sixteenth century. This was the burden of Henry Harrisse's book of 1896 on the Cabots. Other investigators of about the same date, while not using such harsh language about Sebastian, nevertheless agreed that the stories of his voyage truly applied to John Cabot. And since there was no contemporary evidence on the course of John's voyage in 1498, they applied the Sebastian evidence to it and produced a circumstantial account of John's discovery amid the ice of the far North West.

It was an illusion, and the nineteenth-century men had set up a prejudice as great as the old one which they had overthrown, the prejudice against Sebastian Cabot following the earlier one in his favour. There were difficulties in the application of the Sebastian stories to John in 1498. John sailed with five ships and meant to go south-west to the tropics of Asia. Sebastian sailed with two ships and went in search of a north-west passage round America, an America which John in 1498 did not know to exist. This ought to have given pause to historians of this school, but it did not: their interpretation possessed them and excluded judgment. A casual statement by Peter Martyr, one of those who personally knew Sebastian, was overlooked; and in it he had said that Sebastian's discovery took place in 1508. Before Harrisse wrote his final book a Venetian state paper was published (in 1892), wherein a servant of the republic reported that Sebastian sailed in the life-time of Henry VII but returned to find him dead—and thus that the date of the voyage was 1509 or 1508-9. These things led inevitably to a second enlightenment. In 1900 G. P. Winship marshalled the evidence and concluded that all the Sebastian stories related to an entirely different voyage from those of John Cabot, a voyage veritably led by Sebastian, and that its date was 1508-9.

It follows then that our present task, the elucidation of John Cabot's voyage of 1498, must be approached without citation of the evidences for the north-west voyage of Sebastian Cabot, which evidences have no relevance to the subject. Another tangle needs also to be cleared. A Portuguese captain named João Fernandes, a *llabrador* or small land-owner from the Azores, was at Bristol by the close of 1500 and became a member of a syndicate which obtained a patent for discovery from Henry VII early in 1501. Some inscriptions on early maps reveal that Greenland was named, certainly from 1503, Terra de Labrador, because information on its geography was given to the English by a *llabrador* from the Azores. This man is reasonably to be identified with João Fernandes. We shall be more fully concerned with him on a later page.[1] Here it is sufficient to say that there is no evidence that Fernandes made a voyage of discovery to Greenland or anywhere else before the year 1500. Pedro de Ayala, as we have seen, reported in July 1498 that John Cabot had been in Lisbon and Seville seeking support for his projects of discovery. Ayala gave no date for these proceedings. In 1903 H. P. Biggar published an account of the Cabot voyages.[2] He rejected Winship's re-assessment and, in the older style, applied the stories of Sebastian Cabot's north-western discovery to the elucidation of John Cabot's proceedings in 1498. He thus took John Cabot to Greenland and Davis Strait in contradiction to John's expressed intention, reported by Soncino, of going to his new land and thence south-westward to the tropics. Biggar accounted for this change of plan by assuming that John Cabot went to Lisbon in the winter of 1497–8 and there met João Fernandes, who convinced him that a voyage northwards up the Greenland coast was the best means of reaching tropical Asia. It is hard to express disbelief in the conclusions of a man of Biggar's great learning, but the facts must be faced. There is no evidence or likelihood that John Cabot went to Lisbon—and Seville—in the winter of 1497–8. He had plenty of backing in England and needed no support elsewhere. He was busy with preparations for his next voyage from Bristol. Henry

[1] See below, p. 116, and Ch. VIII *passim*.
[2] H. P. Biggar, *Voyages of the Cabots and of the Corte-Reals* (Paris, 1903).

VII would not have paid him a pension if he was flitting over to the Peninsula with the idea of transferring his project to Spain or Portugal. If he had gone to those countries while still proposing to sail in English service, the authorities there would have found reasons for detaining him and putting a stop to his plans: it was a risk he would have been foolish to take. There is no evidence either for any meeting between John Cabot and Fernandes at this or any other time.

Some other commentators of the pre-Winship period had stated, on the authority of the Sebastian Cabot narratives, that John Cabot in 1498 was seeking a north-west passage to Asia. This involved a serious confusion of thought, for such a passage could have been considered only if it was realized that the continent due west across the Atlantic was not Asia; and no one had the least inkling of that before the voyage of 1498. In the winter of 1497-8, the interval between the voyages, John Cabot was quite certain that Asia faced him across the Atlantic. The Sebastian Cabot narratives do indicate a voyage to the north-west, and that alone is proof that they do not relate to the voyage of 1498. In that year John Cabot, as we see by clear and direct evidence, set out to go west and south. Soncino in December stated this to be the intention, and Ayala in the following July, after the expedition had sailed, complained that its intended course would bring the English into trespass upon the Spanish discoveries in the region covered by Columbus.

An alternative suggested reason for going to Greenland was that it would enable Cabot to avoid facing the westerly winds that blow across the North Atlantic in British latitudes. Some remarks on the weather conditions, as they were experienced in the sixteenth century, have already been given.[1] In 1497, with an outward passage of thirty-five days, John Cabot could not have been much dissatisfied with them; and on his then knowledge he had no great incentive to seek an indirect course. Neither in fact did his more experienced successors, the Newfoundland fishermen of the

[1] See above, pp. 62-3; and also Document 34.

following age. There is no evidence that it was their general practice to sail by any but the direct course. By making the weather factor the main reason, as some have done, for sending Cabot to Greenland in 1498 it is possible to reconcile such a course with an eventual objective in his original New Found Land, and to avoid the North West Passage complication. But the whole is nothing but a building-up of suppositions unsupported by evidence.

Towards those suppositions one sixteenth-century writing can be adduced, but only, on close examination, to be found devoid of relevance. In 1541 the Spaniard Alonso de Santa Cruz completed a manuscript *Islario General de todas las Islas del Mundo.*[1] For its north-western parts he drew information from a book published at Strasbourg in 1532 by Jacobus Ziegler, a German, who gave some particulars about the Cabots and a north-western voyage. Ziegler in his turn had copied from the *Decades* of Peter Martyr, the Italian historian who worked in Spain and produced the first section of his book at Alcalá in 1516. Peter Martyr apparently knew nothing about John Cabot, for he never mentioned him, but gave a description of the north-western voyage of Sebastian Cabot, whom he knew personally. By some careless blunder Ziegler, in paraphrasing Martyr, altered the explorer's Christian name to Antoninus, and ascribed the voyage to 'Antoninus Cabotus'. Years later Santa Cruz used Ziegler as his authority and miscopied Antoninus as Antonio, thus making the captain's name Antonio Gaboto. So Antonio Gaboto, at third hand, now stood for Peter Martyr's Sebastian Cabot. But Santa Cruz knew Sebastian Cabot's correct name. Santa Cruz failed to realize that his 'Antonio' was really Sebastian, and assumed instead that Antonio must be the father of Sebastian, of whom he had heard something. Thus Santa Cruz wrote that Greenland was called the land of the Labrador 'because a *llabrador* of the islands of the Azores gave notice and information about it to the King of England, when he sent in search of it Antonio Gaboto, the English pilot and

[1] Document 39.

father of Sebastian Gaboto'. Here then apparently João Fernandes the *llabrador* is contemporary in England with John Cabot. But in reality there was no connection with John Cabot but only an alleged contemporaneity with Sebastian, whose voyage 'in search of it' was at a later date; for, as we have seen, Antonio Cabot was Ziegler's Antoninus, who was the Sebastian of Peter Martyr, the original authority. Santa Cruz, unknown to himself, was writing only of Sebastian, whom by his following of Ziegler's mistake he doubled into two persons, father and son. His statement is therefore no evidence that John Cabot ever met the *llabrador*. This passage constitutes a tortuous muddle, so tortuous that it is not easy to unravel in a lucid manner. If the explanation is hard to follow, the present writer makes his apology.[1]

It is now possible to go forward with the veritable story of the voyage of 1498. Not much of it is proven fact, and a good deal of what must be said consists of possibilities, which need to be considered, even if discounted. First, a comparatively recent piece of information requires mention: that John Cabot himself did not survive the voyage. Polydore Vergil was an Italian priest who came to England in 1502 in the service of another Italian who obtained the see of Hereford. Thenceforward Vergil lived mainly in England, although he died in 1555 at a great age at his birthplace of Urbino in Italy.[2] He wrote his History of England, *Anglica Historia*, in 1512–13. A manuscript of it is now in the Vatican Library. It was printed at Basle on three occasions, in 1534, 1546 and 1555. The printed versions contain no mention of the Cabots or their voyages. In 1937 Mr (now Professor) Denys Hay examined the manuscript and found that it had a passage on

[1] Ziegler's words are as follows: 'Petrus Martyr Mediolanensis in hispanicis navigationibus scribit, Antoninum quendam Cabotum solventem a Britannia, navigasse continue versus septentrionem, quod incideret in crustas glatiales mense Julio, inde ergo conversum remigasse continue secundum litus sese incurvans austrum versus, donec veniret ad situm contra Hispaniam supra Cuba insulam Canibalum' (Jacobus Ziegler, *Schondia etc.* (Argentorati, 1532), f. xcii b). This is a geographical work in which the matter on Sebastian Cabot is merely incidental.

[2] Denys Hay, 'The Anglica Historia of Polydore Vergil', *Camden Series*, vol. LXXIV (Royal Historical Society, 1950), pp. ix–xi.

Cabot,[1] which stated, among other particulars, that he set sail for the west and was believed to have been lost with his ship, since after that sailing he was nowhere seen again. This is the sense of the Latin words, but they should be considered in the original: 'Deinde in occidentem versus vela fecit, qui ad postremum creditur nullibi alias invenisse terras, quam in imo Oceani fundo, in quod una cum navi, descendisse putatur raptus ab ipso Oceano, quoniam post eam navigationem, nusquam amplius comparuit.' The statement means to convey that Cabot's ship was 'missing', in the technical sense in which the word is now used, and that no circumstances of her fate were known. It affords no information, perhaps because there was none, of the part of the voyage in which she was lost, whether on the passage out, on the American coast, or on the way home. There is an indication that, before writing in 1512, Polydore Vergil had not had full information of the occurrence, for Professor Hay found that in the manuscript a blank space had been left for the explorer's name, and that it had been supplied subsequently. So soon was the memory of John Cabot fading out in the England which he had served. By 1534 the matter was considered no longer important enough to be worth printing.

In spite of the fact that Vergil was not in England as early as 1498, we may regard the above as good evidence that Cabot lost his life in some unknown disaster in the course of his second expedition. It was formerly thought possible that he was alive and in England in 1499, because his pension of £20 was paid 'in one tally' at some date in the financial year Michaelmas 1498 to Michaelmas 1499.[2] The payment was evidently made to his representative, most likely his wife. It shows that in or after September 1498, and probably well on into the following year, John Cabot was not known to be dead; and this accords with the 'missing' statement of Polydore Vergil. The death was no doubt presumed in due course. Nothing further is known about the pension, but the records which would deal with it are incomplete after September 1499. An exactly parallel testimony, conveying

[1] Document 33.　　　　　[2] Document 29.

no more than that of the pension, is afforded by Philip Grene's Rental of properties in Bristol for the year Michaelmas to Michaelmas 1498–9.[1] It shows that Cabot's house in St Nycoles Street was rented from Grene at £2 per annum. It does not show at what date in the year, or by whose hand, the payment was made.

The fleet of five ships sailed from Bristol in May. In July Ayala wrote that news had been received from Ireland to the effect that a gale had struck them and that one ship had been damaged and had returned to an Irish port. 'The Genoese', he added (meaning Cabot), had continued his voyage. In Ayala's letter as we have it these are two separate statements with no conjunctive words between them, and it has always been assumed that the ship which took refuge was not the one in which Cabot was sailing. But Polydore Vergil has something which causes us to reconsider Ayala. Polydore says: 'As a result of the rumour about the unknown lands, King Henry at the request of one John Cabot, a Venetian by birth and a most skilful mariner, ordered to be prepared one ship, complete with crew and weapons; this he handed over to the same John to go and search for those unknown islands. John set out in this same year and sailed first to Ireland. Then he set sail towards the west.'[2] Polydore, then, asserts that it was Cabot's ship that put into the Irish port, and that in her Cabot subsequently continued the voyage westwards. It is not what Ayala implies. His implication arises from the lack of any connecting word or phrase between his two sentences. We must consider the fact that Ayala's Cabot statement was part of a long dispatch on several important matters, which was sent in cipher from London. In Spain it was deciphered on receipt, with the inexactness characteristic of so much authorship and secretarial work at the time. G. A. Bergenroth saw this and made a revised decipherment for his *Spanish Calendar* of 1862. But we have no

[1] Document 30.
[2] Polydore Vergil's Latin is given in Document 33. The phraseology of part of the above quotation shows that its source was common to that of the London chronicles already quoted; but Vergil proceeds to tell more than the chronicles do.

text of what Ayala originally wrote or dictated to his secretary in London. We have only the ciphered version that the secretary made of it; and secretarial persons were sometimes careless, as has already been noted. Thus it is possible that Ayala did not mean to imply that it was a ship other than Cabot's that returned damaged to port. It is also highly probable that he did not care whether he implied it or not, for he was not writing scientific history and the matter was a minor detail in the communication he was making. On the whole then it would appear that we should accept Polydore Vergil. His testimony is that Cabot entered an Irish port and thence sailed alone for the west; and that was the last ever heard of him.[1] Polydore says nothing of the other ships, although he must have read of them in the archetype document which he used in common with the London chroniclers.

After this evidence of the ship returning to Ireland there is no direct information of the proceedings of any part of the expedition. The chronicles that mention its start merely say that no news had been received by mid-September, the end of the London mayoral year. It was a fault of the chronicle form that if the writer of the record had known of any tidings coming in subsequently he could not have fitted them in at the point where he dropped the subject. He would have needed to reopen it in another mayoral year. Perhaps no further tidings ever did come, perhaps the ships returned to Bristol, certainly they brought no rich cargoes of spices. The chroniclers were writing only of outstanding London events. If there was a straggling back to Bristol with a report of commercial failure, a London writer may not have thought it

---

[1] I record this without an absolute belief that it is true. Polydore was evidently summarizing some evidence unknown to us, and he may have done it clumsily. However, that is his statement, and I believe it to be a sound principle to accept what evidence we have unless it is contradicted by fact, circumstance or strong probability, although with the expressed reservation that the evidence is not so perfect as it might be. In this case the only contradiction is that the new evidence is contrary to what had been assumed to be the truth on no good evidence at all, the implication of Ayala's not well attested arrangement of his words. In sum, Ayala's implication, as we have it, is less convincing than Polydore Vergil's statement.

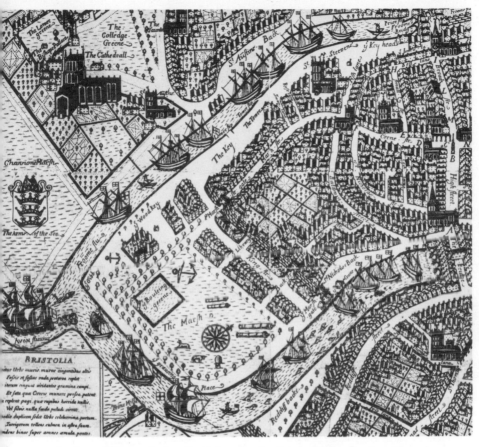

III. The Port of Bristol: detail of the plan by James Millerd, 1671. Showing the quays and mercantile area in the west part of the city, at the junction of the Avon and Frome rivers. The Custom House stood on the Marsh; and the plan marks the streets, mentioned in Philip Grene's Rental of 1498–9 (Document 30), where John Cabot and the Bristol merchants had their houses

worth while to make a new reference to the subject. 'The Venetian' had been the strong character who excited London enthusiasm. He did not come back, but no news of his death came; he slowly faded out. The silence of the chronicles proves neither that the whole expedition was lost nor that part of it returned.

There are indirect indications, cumulatively very strong, that some of the explorers did return, with extensive discoveries to report. Before considering them there is one point of probability to notice. It is that not all the five ships are likely to have been lost on the voyage. In the history of Atlantic exploration for the ensuing century, beginning with the Corte Reals of Portugal in 1500 and going forward to Gilbert and Frobisher and Davis and the Virginian pioneers of Ralegh's time, there is no instance of a multi-ship expedition having been entirely wiped out by an unknown disaster; and we are entitled to say that the odds were heavily against it in 1498.

On the course of the voyage there is another possibility. We have been inclined to assume that, leaving one ship in Ireland, the other four sailed across the Atlantic in company and explored together on the other side. But again the history of the Atlantic does not justify such an assumption. Gales and fog may have separated the ships, and there could have been no rendezvous accurately attainable without great loss of time. We have to allow for separate explorations and separate, not synchronous, returns. Long absences were possible if Ayala was right in saying that the fleet was victualled for a year.

Now for the indirect indications. One of them is an apparent change in English thought about the transatlantic objective. In the winter of 1497-8 London was fired with the promise of reaching the empire of the Grand Khan and the riches of Cipango, and everyone believed that on the other side of the ocean lay the coast of Asia. Not only did Pasqualigo and Soncino witness this, but Ayala grew angry at the intrusion upon his sovereigns' rights to the same Asia, and the archetype English document on which the chroniclers drew spoke of 'the island replenished with rich commodities', which can only have been Cipango. But after 1498 all this disappears. Thenceforward there were more English voyages to the end of Henry VII's reign, and scanty records exist of them. But there is no more talk of Asia as lying on the other side of the ocean. It is always 'the New Land' or 'the New Found Land', with no suggestion of a direct spice trade. The great geographical concept that inspired Toscanelli and Columbus and Cabot died out of English thought, upon which it had so recently impinged. What killed it? By inference—of proof we have none—it may have been the voyage of 1498. And the inference hangs on an if. If the voyagers explored the coast westwards and southwards as they meant to do, we know what they found: primeval tracts and Indian tribes, no great state or government, no cities, seaports, ships or trade, no spices and silks for barter—in a word, no Asia. Did any of them come back to tell this? The change in English outlook suggests that they did. It is certain that by 1509 the English had the concept of America, for in that year Sebastian Cabot tried to make his way round America to reach Asia. It is probable that they had it from 1498–9. If they then made the voyage they intended, they must have had it. Of John Cabot's personal defeat we cannot tell. Perhaps he was spared it, drowned on the outward voyage. But if he made the long coasting that never revealed China and Japan his last days were bitter.

Pietro Pasqualigo, a resident of Lisbon and brother of Lorenzo Pasqualigo of London, wrote in October 1501 of the homecoming of a ship of Gaspar Corte Real's expedition of that year.[1] He said that the crew had got from the Indians a piece of a broken gilt sword which seemed to have been made in Italy, and a pair of silver ear-rings which appeared to be of Venetian manufacture. This made the writer think that the coast must be continental, since he had heard of no previous ships going there, the implication probably being that the articles had travelled right across Asia by the land routes from Europe. The expedition of 1501 visited Labrador, Newfoundland and perhaps a part of Nova

[1] Document 38.

Scotia, but there is no indication of the locality at which the sword and ear-rings were found. Here we have a probable clue to the appearance of at least one of Cabot's fleet of 1498, since the *Matthew*'s company in 1497 had had no contact with the natives. It would be a certain clue but for the pre-Cabotian visits of Bristol men to Newfoundland or its neighbourhood. The incident conveys no proof of the presence of Cabot himself at the place indicated, wherever it may have been. In an expedition that must have comprised between one and two hundred men it is not to be supposed that he was the only one armed with an Italian sword: the blades of Milan were articles of trade esteemed throughout Europe; and the fragment only 'seems to have been made' in Italy. As for the Venetian ear-rings, sailors acquired such things in many ports, and commonly wore them. However, the story is an indication that part of the expedition of 1498 reached the neighbourhood explored in 1497. If the Indians gained the things in a fight, it might mark the end of Cabot and his crew. But the supposition is very speculative. It was more probably by barter.

The North American part of the La Cosa map offers some possible but uncertain evidence. The section of the flagged English coast which has no place-names, but only the off-shore inscription *Mar descubierto por inglese*, may or may not be a reporting from 1498. We have no means of telling. Farther west and down to the frame of the vignette in the latitude of Cuba, the coast may be imaginary, but it has features with a plausible appearance of having been derived from real information, particularly one delineation that might stand for the eastern end of Long Island Sound. Certainly La Cosa meant to convey that there was a continental coast there. It is beyond his line of English flags, and he did not therefore ascribe its discovery to the English; but there was no one else who could have discovered it. South of this again there is another stretch of continent bordered by an archipelago, evidently the Bahamas, reaching down to Cuba. It is easier to believe this, now that we realize that La Cosa's North America is not drawn to a uniform scale and proportion with exact latitudes;

for on the interpretation suggested by his drawing the whole coastline between New Jersey and Florida is simply omitted, and those two regions are contiguous. It points to the suggestion that La Cosa had information from two or more ships making separate explorations. But all this map-interpretation is hopelessly uncertain, and from it one may argue almost anything that comes into one's mind. The historian wants written statements. For the North American part of the voyage of 1498 there are none.

Farther south, in the Caribbean, the La Cosa map has a feature worth examining. In 1498 Columbus had touched the main continent of South America in the neighbourhood of Trinidad. In 1499 Alonso de Ojeda, with Juan de La Cosa and Amerigo Vespucci in his company, sailed westwards along this coast, the Spanish Main of later days, until he reached Cabo de la Vela in Venezuela. From that point he turned north for the Antilles and arrived in Hispaniola. He then went to the Bahamas for slaves and finally returned to Spain, where in the second half of 1500 La Cosa made his map. On examining La Cosa's map of America as a whole, one is struck with the fact that no part of its coastline, North or South, is more accurately drawn than the tract from Trinidad westwards along the Main and the northern side of the Isthmus of Panama, terminating at the edge of the vignette.[1] For the eastern portion of this well-drawn coast such accuracy is not surprising, since the cartographer had himself sailed along it. But the terminus of his coasting was at Cabo de la Vela. At that point La Cosa plants his westernmost Spanish flag, and there also he ends his nomenclature of coastal features. But beyond Cabo de la Vela, and right on past the Gulf of Darien to the edge of the vignette, the outline is also remarkably good, its only fault being that it does not make the Gulf of Darien extend deeply enough to the southward. La Cosa himself had not been on this coast, and there is no record of any Spanish expedition that was there in time to afford him information. On this mysteriously appearing coast there are no flags and no names. We are left to consider whether La Cosa

[1] See Fig. 3.

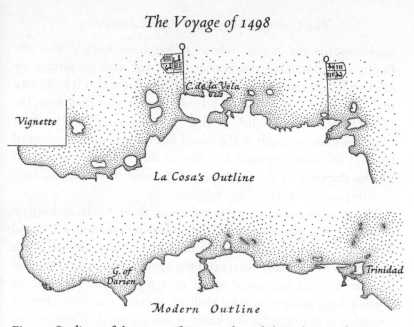

Fig. 3. Outlines of the coast of Venezuela and the Isthmus of Panama,
as drawn by La Cosa (1500), and in the modern chart

drew it entirely by conjecture or whether he had information
unknown to us. In the map itself there is no answer to this question. Like much other map evidence, this piece of map-work
records a fact without saying how it was arrived at.

So far we have been dealing in vague possibilities. We now
come to some better authority for the belief that at least one ship
of the English expedition penetrated southwards through the
Spanish islands into the Caribbean. This passage is the only part of
the voyage which is based upon historical evidence—of a sort.
On 8 June 1501 Ojeda received a licence from the Spanish
sovereigns to make another South American voyage.[1] The grant
prescribed the coasts he might visit, an extension westwards of
what he had already discovered, and laid down conditions, among
them the following: 'that you go and follow that coast which you
have discovered, which runs east and west, as it appears, because it

[1] Document 40.

goes towards the region where it has been learned that the English were making discoveries; and that you go setting up marks with the arms of their Majesties...in order that it be known that you have discovered that land, so that you may stop the exploration of the English in that direction . . . likewise their Majesties make you gift in the island of Española of six leagues of land . . . for what you shall discover on the coast of the mainland for the stopping of the English, and the said six leagues of land shall be yours for ever.'

The Spanish government, as we know from Ayala, had notice of the tropical intentions of Cabot when he sailed in 1498, and now in 1501 there had been time for them to learn where Cabot's expedition had actually been; and the Spanish authorities believed that the English had sailed south to a region that lay west of Ojeda's 1499 discovery. The Gulf of Mexico was then entirely unexplored. It might (as we know it does) provide a continuous coast linking North and South America. It might (as some hoped right on to 1517–18) be an open sea or a strait completely separating the two Americas and leading the European voyager on to the coastline of Southern Asia. The contemporary makers of world maps did not know the answer, and La Cosa prudently covered the unknown region with his vignette containing St Christopher's picture. The framers of the Ojeda patent believed that the English had advanced southwards into the area of the vignette, or even farther, and that it was important that the Spaniards should lay claim to whatever coasts existed there, since the future trade with Asia might depend upon it. The belief is clear enough in the wording of the patent. The questions that arise are: how correct was the information, and whence did it come?

That Spain had obtained information, true or false, of an English advance southwards is obvious, but the extent of the advance is open to question. It may have been, on a literal reading of the patent, right down into the western Caribbean; or it may have been that the information was muddled and the English had not gone nearly so far. We must remember that the Spanish authorities—more precisely, Bishop Fonseca's rudimentary ministry for colonial affairs—had no authoritative maps to work upon, and that the reports they received were deficient in figures of latitude. On English activities the information may have amounted to no more than that someone said that the ships had sailed a vaguely estimated number of leagues on an inaccurately located and oriented coast. The situation also was changing rapidly. Each year brought new reports that must have been debated with much disagreement in the Spanish colonial department: at the very time that Ojeda's instructions were being issued in 1501, another Spaniard, Rodrigo de Bastidas, was actually performing the exploration west of Cabo de la Vela, although he did not get back to Hispaniola with his report until 1502. These circumstances warn us not to be too confident that the Ojeda patent is strict evidence of an English arrival in the Caribbean. On the other hand, that conclusion cannot be ruled out. It is supported by a sober and responsible Spanish historian, Fernández de Navarrete.[1] Writing in 1829, before the discovery of the La Cosa map, he said: 'It is certain that Ojeda in his first voyage [1499] encountered certain Englishmen in the vicinity of Coquibaçoa.'[2] Two commentators consulted by the present writer consider that Navarrete may have been making an unwarranted jump in advance of the evidence, a guess based on the mention of Coquibaçoa in Ojeda's privileges. But the historian's statement is unqualified: *Lo cierto es*, he wrote, 'it is certain'. He can have seen a document that has since disappeared. Such losses of documents have occurred. In England at the very same date we have the loss of one of the Household Books that Craven Ord worked on.

So we must leave this question tantalizingly uncertain. One thing may be added, that the Spanish information need not have been obtained through England. If Navarrete is right, it could

---

[1] M. Fernández de Navarette, *Colección de los viages y descubrimientos*, vol. III (Madrid, 1829), p. 41.

[2] Coquibaçoa is marked on some early maps (not on La Cosa's) a little to the east of Cabo de la Vela.

have been gathered from the Englishmen encountered at Coqui-baçoa, and these men may never have reached home. The ship concerned may even have been John Cabot's missing flagship. Possibilities: nothing more.

There is another hint, even more nebulous. In 1499–1500 the three Columbus brothers were all in Hispaniola and were intensely unpopular among the Spanish settlers and adventurers. It was to this situation that Francisco de Bobadilla put an end when he arrived from Spain in 1500 and immediately sent the three brothers home under close arrest. Las Casas, the friend of Christopher Columbus, gives a long account of the spiteful calumnies that were invented and circulated about them. Some of the accusations of their ill-doings were true, and accounted for the full powers that the Spanish government gave to Bobadilla. But among the slanders was the following: 'Also, they accused him of refusing to give licence to gather gold, in order to conceal the riches of that island and of the Indies, so as to take them for himself with the support of some other Christian King.'[1] It was not true, for Columbus was never disloyal to his sovereigns. But his brother Bartholomew had once been in treaty with Henry VII, and if there had been an English ship in the Caribbean in 1499 the charge would have gained plausibility. Ferdinand and Isabella showed that they did not believe in it, but there may have been a suspicion in Fonseca's circle. John Day, if his proceedings were known to them, may have looked like an intermediary between Columbus and Henry VII. Bobadilla's action in chaining Columbus was very drastic, and he was not reproved for it.

In sum we have no positive knowledge of the discoveries made by the second Cabot expedition, although the evidence of the Ojeda licence is that some southward advance was made. The ships were equipped for trade and provisioned for a year. The leaders expected to make a longer voyage than that of the *Matthew* in 1497. No news had come home by September. Cabot's ship

---

[1] Bartolomé de las Casas, *Historia de las Indias*, in *Documentos inéditos para la historia de España*, tom. LXIII (Madrid, 1875), pp. 493–4.

was lost at some unknown point. The others may have kept together on the American coast, or they may have become separated, to come back at different dates with different stories; and it is not improbable that some continued the voyage into 1499. The lack of a focal point in the return of the expedition, and its failure as a commercial venture, account for its passing-over by the chroniclers. People waited for the return of Cabot, and he did not come. As the months passed they gave him up for lost.

The year 1498 was critical in the long story of the expansion of Europe, although general historians have failed to notice it. In that year the simple, almost unicellular, governments of Spain, Portugal and England were concerned with questions of global strategy as far-reaching as those that have rumbled through the great staffs of the modern states of our time. The three powers were simultaneously seeking tropical Asia, and there were three questions awaiting answer. Was Columbus right in his contention that in his Indies he was already there? Would Cabot with his coasting approach be the first to reach China? Would Vasco da Gama sailing south open the way to India? The facts of geography foiled England and Spain and gave the prize to Portugal, thereby directing on the course we know the history of European domination in southern Asia.

At this stage we leave John Cabot, and may essay some estimate of him. In his Venetian period he was a merchant of enterprise sufficient to take him to Mecca and to think of new ways of working the Far Eastern trade. He had read Marco Polo and mastered the information on China and Japan which enabled him to expose the falsity of the Spanish claim to have reached Asia. The mastery of Marco Polo may not seem remarkable to us who are the heirs of five centuries of commentators and who bring to the subject a vast amount of background knowledge; but in Cabot's time it was the mark of an original and penetrating mind. He had studied also cartography and could express his ideas not only by maps but on a globe, a considerable professional achievement. The Venetian documents on his property transactions about

1482 show that he was not altogether a poor man at that time, although possibly not a rich one. We do not know how he was living at Valencia ten years later (if he was Cabot Montecalunya), but he had evidently the status from which to urge a public project that secured King Ferdinand's approval. In the same way we do not know how he lived at Bristol and supported his family there.

That he was an able advocate and spoke with authority is clear from his acceptance by Henry VII and the grant of the letters patent. Soncino testifies to his eloquence and conviction, and both Soncino and Pasqualigo suggest a certain magnificence and magnetism which fired the ignorant public no less than it drew support from the wary circle round the King. We may discern that John Cabot was a veritable leader of men, deprived of rounded historical greatness by premature death and lack of record. There he was unfortunate, for his son Sebastian did not play the part of Las Casas and Ferdinand Columbus, without whose devotion Christopher Columbus would not today be the great figure that he is. Sebastian did nothing for his father's reputation. The other sons, Ludovico and Sancio, are unknown men, their names appearing only on the patent of 1496. We would gladly know more of Mattea, the wife who kept house for her husband and sons in foreign Bristol; but she also is little but a name.

John Cabot's position in the enterprise may be seen more clearly since the publication of the John Day letter. The Bristol men had already found their Brasil and knew the way to it. There is no hint that they based any plan of Asiatic trade on their discovery, which was of so small promise that London, for all we can tell, had not heard of it. Cabot, seeking aid in Lisbon and Seville, where there were Bristol men to talk with, learned of it and decided that England must be his base. That would appear to have been his entry into the affair, although we lack the dates to prove it. There was land in the west, well clear of the Spanish activities. This land could be a stage on the way to Cipango. He came in therefore not only as a navigator but as a geographer and a specialist in the spice trade and, it is clear, as the commander in full control. He would extend a fishing voyage into a new trade-route that would divert the richest of all trades to an English port. It was sound enough had the world-map been true as he and Columbus viewed it. But the unsuspected presence of America defeated them both.

VIII

BRISTOL AND THE NEW FOUND LAND

IN SEPTEMBER 1499 the Household Book reveals that a Portuguese embassy came to England. The King bestowed £60 on 'the ambassador of Portugal', £50 on 'the doctor of Portugal', and £5 on a minor member of the party.[1] This liberality to foreign ambassadors was not unusual but customary. Puebla and Soncino both received money gifts, and Ayala was made Archdeacon of London and a canon of St Paul's in 1502.[2] We have no information on the business of the Portuguese envoy in 1499. It may have been on some purely European matter. But it can have been to give notice to Henry VII that the King of Portugal claimed all lands across the Atlantic that were not within the rights of Spain, for this was a Portuguese policy actively operated during the next three or four years. It is to be noted that in July 1499 one ship of Vasco da Gama's squadron had arrived in the Tagus with news that he had reached India and was on his way home. Gama himself came in on September 9. In October the King of Portugal issued a new patent for Atlantic discovery. As will be shown, there is a possibility that all the above events were inter-connected.

We have already had occasion to mention João Fernandes the Azorean *llabrador*.[3] His property was in the island of Terceira, and in 1892 Ernesto do Canto, a historian of the islands, published a document concerning a lawsuit in 1506 for trespass on lands in Terceira. In the lawsuit one Pedro de Barcelos claimed that the

---

[1] Document 26.

[2] *Letters and Papers, Richard III and Henry VII*, vol. II, p. 378. These were sinecures, as was his later appointment by his own sovereigns to be Bishop of the Canary Islands. Governments found the payment of their debts by this disguised taxation of the Church very convenient.

[3] See above, p. 98.

trespass on his land had taken place while he was away for three years with João Fernandes, exploring with the licence of the King. The defendant, as other evidence showed, took possession of some land in January 1495, and Barcelos was shown to have been back in Terceira in April. All this fitted neatly together to prove that João Fernandes had been engaged on exploration for the three years 1492–5 and must have been known as an explorer at the time of John Cabot's voyages. One thing was lacking from the documentary evidence, the licence granted to Fernandes by King John II, who died in 1495. Admiral S. E. Morison probed the whole story for his book *Portuguese Voyages to America in the Fifteenth Century* (1940), and his elucidation is summarized here. He showed that although the royal licences and similar documents are well preserved, copied into large manuscript registers now in the Torre do Tombo of Lisbon, no licence can be found from King John II to Fernandes or Barcelos; and that, owing to the general completeness of the series, this furnishes a strong inference that such a licence was never issued. There is, however, a patent from King Manoel, who succeeded John II in 1495. It permitted João Fernandes of Terceira to discover 'certain islands in our sphere of influence', and promised him their captaincy with the usual privileges. It made no reference to any previous discoveries by Fernandes, which is significant, for it was the common form of such grants to allude to previous discoveries if there had been any. This patent was dated 28 October 1499. Admiral Morison's research went farther still. He found that the land occupied in 1495 by the defendant in the lawsuit of 1506 was not the same land as that about which Barcelos complained, but an estate three or four miles distant from it; from which it followed that the complaint did not relate to 1495 and that the three years at sea with Fernandes need not have been the years 1492–5, but could have been 1499–1502, when we know by other evidence that Fernandes was engaged in oceanic exploration. It would be more natural also for Barcelos to take legal action four years after the trespass than to wait eleven years before doing so.

The effect of Admiral Morison's investigation is to knock out the supposed evidence that João Fernandes was at sea as an explorer in 1492–5, and to show that there is no evidence of any such activity before the grant of his indubitable patent at the end of October 1499. In practice that means that Fernandes made no voyage of discovery before 1500, for he would hardly have started at the close of the year.

The Bristol customs records show that a man named Fernandes and another named Gonsalves, in whom we shall be interested, were trading in and out of Bristol as early as 1486. In September in that year, among the merchants' names in a Portuguese ship from Madeira, are to be found 'ffornandus' and 'Gunsalus' (without indication of the Christian names).[1] Taken separately, these names can provide only a very flimsy identification with the João Fernandes and João Gonsalves whom we shall find in Bristol in 1501; but the fact that they are found in association at both dates somewhat strengthens the likelihood. Again in January 1493 we find 'Johannes ffornandus' exporting goods from Bristol to Lisbon.[2] There is no other customs ledger until 1503. On the whole it appears probable that the Fernandes and Gonsalves of 1501 were known in Bristol several years earlier. But it is not an essential link in the story of the Bristol enterprises.

On 12 May 1500 King Manoel issued a comprehensive grant for discovery to Gaspar Corte Real, a nobleman of the Portuguese court, who owned property in Terceira. He was empowered to make voyages for the discovery of mainland as well as islands, and to be governor of such lands, with judicial and administrative rights and financial privileges.[3] The locality is not indicated, but appears from the subsequent proceedings of the grantee. The grant was issued in time for Corte Real to make an expedition in 1500. He sailed first to the east coast of Greenland and, being

[1] P.R.O., E 122, 20/5 (Ledger, 1–2 Hen. VII).
[2] P.R.O., E 122, 20/9 (Ledger, 8–9 Hen. VII).
[3] The text of the patent, with translation, is given by H. P. Biggar, *The Precursors of Jacques Cartier*, 1497–1534 (Ottawa, 1911), pp. 32–7.

stopped by ice, rounded Cape Farewell and tried the west coast, after which he returned to Lisbon. In view of the knowledge of Greenland, dim and vague as it may have been, that undoubtedly existed in the fifteenth century, it is not probable that Gaspar Corte Real went there with any hope of founding a rich patrimony on its shores. His purpose must have been other than that. João Fernandes was similarly interested in Greenland, as we shall see by evidence to be produced in its place. His patent was not superseded by that granted to Corte Real: he was entitled to anything he could independently discover. We do not know what he did in 1500. He may have made a voyage of his own to the Greenland coast, he may have sailed with Corte Real, he may not have gone to sea at all. It is possible that he had not sufficient money or influence to equip an expedition when a more powerful man was making a call on the available resources. Shipping and investment capital must have been short in Lisbon that year when Cabral was setting out with the great second expedition to India. Whatever he may have done João Fernandes saw his prospects in Portugal blighted by the Corte Real enterprise, and before the end of the year he came to Bristol, he and two other Azoreans, and took service under the King of England.

Why this Portuguese interest in Greenland? It had an economic motive, for no one at that time made explorations solely in the interest of geographical science. The land itself supplied no such motive and could not have been expected to. Can any motive be suggested other than that of trade with Asia? It is a question that the commentator must face. The facts were that Cabot in 1498 had not got through to Asia by his south-western course from his New Found Land, that Columbus was bogged down in Hispaniola amid the crimes and dissensions of his colonists, and that Vasco da Gama had come home with one-third of his men from a two-year voyage that had brought him only to Calicut, an entrepôt for the trade in spices, but very far short of their producing area. A long hard voyage by Gama's route, no voyage at all by Cabot's route, an evident decline in the Spanish drive behind

Columbus: was there no easier solution? Fernandes and Corte Real thought so, a northern passage through the polar region, which the globe showed to offer by far the shortest line to China and Japan. These Portuguese captains were willing to try it; and although King Manoel wisely put his main effort into the certainty of the Cape route, he let them have their chance. So far as the present writer can see, this explanation alone accounts for the Greenland push. A corollary must be that it was known in 1499 that the Englishmen's New Found Land was not the coast of Asia.

It was incumbent on Portugal to follow a generally northern rather than a markedly north-western direction because she was bound by the Treaty of Tordesillas and its meridian of demarcation. A meridian was not exactly determinable, but some approximation had to be observed.

To return to João Fernandes. He and others received a patent from Henry VII in March 1501, and this implies that he was in England well before the end of 1500. He may have arrived in the middle of the year, soon after learning the intentions with which Gaspar Corte Real set out. From various pieces of evidence we learn that Fernandes advocated the advantages of a voyage to Greenland, and it has been commonly assumed that he had himself made one. The evidence does not go so far as that. The Wolfenbüttel map of c. 1530 has an inscription saying that the Land of the Labrador (Greenland) was discovered by the English from Bristol, 'and because he who gave the information [el aviso] of it was a labrador of the Azores they gave it that name'. This was a Spanish map, and Alonso de Santa Cruz had evidently seen a copy of it, for he said: 'It was called the land of the Labrador because a labrador of the islands of the Azores gave notice and information about it to the King of England.'[1] Fernandes introduced the Greenland project to England, but is nowhere said to have already been there himself. The above two testimonies give the story in its complete form and have therefore been mentioned first, but they are late and by themselves might be suspect. But there is good

---

[1] Document 39.

map-evidence that Greenland was named the Land of the Labrador from about 1503 onwards.[1] The King-Hamy map of 1503 or a little later gives the name as 'Terra Laboratoris'. The map known as Kunstmann II, now dated as post-1506, entitles Greenland 'Terra de Lavorador'. The Oliveriana map, assigned to 1508–10, calls the southern point of Greenland 'Cavo Laboradore', and an imaginary adjacent island 'Insula de Labardor'. The Kunstmann IV map, of about 1519, has on Greenland the name 'Do Lavrador'. Greenland therefore owed its name of Labrador to the man who came from the Azores in 1500, and is almost certain to have been João Fernandes. The name continued to be applied to Greenland until about 1570, when it began to be shifted to its present location on the mainland of America. The shift is noticeable in the *Discourse* of Sir Humphrey Gilbert, written in 1566, and published ten years later. Meanwhile our present Labrador was included in the general designation of the New Found Land.

In the spring of 1501, while Fernandes was in England obtaining recognition from Henry VII, Gaspar Corte Real sailed on a new voyage from Lisbon. He went again to the west coast of Greenland, but ice stopped his progress and he crossed Davis Strait to America. Here he appears to have visited in turn part of the true or modern Labrador, the east and south coasts of Newfoundland, and perhaps part of Nova Scotia; and it was somewhere on these coasts that he picked up the sword and ear-rings which we have considered above as evidence that the English had already been there. He had three ships on this expedition. He sent two home in September, and they safely reached Lisbon. He continued the exploration with the third and was never seen again, lost like John Cabot with all his company. In May 1502 his brother Miguel sailed with three ships, but did not go to Greenland. His prime object was to find his lost brother, who might have been wrecked on the American coast. Miguel Corte Real dispersed his ships to search the Newfoundland and adjacent coasts, with a rendezvous fixed for August 20. Two of the ships met at the place and date,

[1] See also below, pp. 310–12; and Pls. IX, XIV.

but not the commander's. Miguel Corte Real, like Gaspar, was missing and was never again heard of. Another expedition went out in 1503 to look for them both, but had no success. After this, Portugal gave up the idea of the northern passage, but she did begin the exploitation of the Newfoundland fishery. By 1506 the importation of Newfoundland cod to Portugal was sufficient to warrant the imposition of a new tax. At some time, probably rather later, the Bretons and French came in, and it has been commonly supposed that Cape Breton is so named from the former. But Ganong pointed out that in writings of the period the English were sometimes referred to as Britons, and he was inclined to think that Cape Breton was a relic of John Cabot.[1]

It must be clearly stated that the foregoing explanation of the Portuguese interest in Greenland and the coast of the true Labrador is tentative and based on circumstantial evidence, which, however strong, does not comprise any document explicitly stating that Portugal was looking for a northern passage to Asia.[2] If it is thought a likely explanation, it carries the undoubted implication that the Portuguese leaders believed North America to be a continent separate from Asia.

The Cantino map is an illustration of Portuguese ideas and policies.[3] It includes the information gained by the Gaspar Corte Real expedition of 1501, whose ground covered may have exceeded that of the expeditions of 1502 and 1503. In October or November 1502 an Italian named Alberto Cantino obtained from a Portuguese cartographer a map of the world to the order of Ercole d'Este, Duke of Ferrara. The cartographer put into it the latest Portuguese findings about the North Atlantic. In doing so he ignored Cabot and the English as if they had never been, and used the opportunity for a piece of propaganda for Portuguese claims. He brought Labrador, Newfoundland and perhaps a part of Nova Scotia together as one land and entitled it *Terra del Rey de Portu-*

[1] See also below, p. 168.
[2] But on a late map (Gemma Frisius, 1537) there is an explicit statement. See below, p. 167.   [3] See Pl. IV.

guall, and he placed this land comfortably on the near or Portuguese side of the line of demarcation. But he had to admit that the whole of the West Indian islands were in the Spanish sphere, and this involved placing the larger part of the North American coastline (from Florida northwards) far to the west of the line of demarcation. Consequently there is a very wide oceanic gap between Terra del Rey de Portuguall and the rest of North America. So far as the map is concerned, it was possible to sail north-west in Spanish waters through this gap. But it may be that the cartographer knew that there was no great gap between Nova Scotia and the rest of North America—La Cosa at any rate had filled it a year before—and that the only way into the North West lay between Terra del Rey de Portuguall and Greenland, or, in modern nomenclature, up Davis Strait.[1] Having made the western side of the Davis Strait opening a Portuguese annexation, our cartographer provided for the eastern side by giving a surprisingly accurate outline of Greenland, on which is inscribed, the title *A ponta d*   , of which Asia may well be the missing word; for on an adjacent scroll it is stated:

This land was discovered by licence of the most excellent Prince D. Manuel King of Portugal, and they who discovered it went not ashore, but viewed it and saw nothing but very thick mountains, whence according to the opinion of cosmographers it is believed to be the peninsula of Asia.[2]

There are two Portuguese flags planted on Greenland, and two on Labrador-Newfoundland. The whole delineation is a neat and able piece of political map-making designed to show Portuguese ownership of the two gateposts of the entry of the northern passage to tropical Asia.

The identification of Greenland with a point of Asia was a conception that had already had, and was destined to have, a long life.

[1] A Portuguese cartographer cannot have failed to hear of the Cabot expeditions by means of the Portuguese ships and traders in Bristol and the English in Lisbon.
[2] Translation from Morison, *op. cit.* p. 52.

But it took two forms, of which the earlier dated back at least to the middle of the fifteenth century. In this form Greenland projected *westwards* from Northern Asia, and by consequence there was no way east of Greenland to reach tropical Asia; the voyager attempting it would find himself in a great enclosed gulf and could never pass round Siberia towards the warmer regions.[1] The fact that Corte Real in 1500 tried first the east coast of Greenland indicates that this interpretation was not implicitly believed by him. In the other form, long current in the sixteenth century, Greenland was an *eastward* projection of North East Asia, curving in a great horn round the northern edge of 'the New Found Land' and separated from it by the waterway which men sought as the North West Passage. But the proceedings of Gaspar Corte Real show that he was prepared to try either way, and that it was the local ice on the east coast of Greenland rather than any geographical conception that halted his first northern probe. It is an interesting question, how far the explorers based their plans on what the cartographers told them, and how far the cartographers relied on the findings of the explorers. Some at least of the map-conceptions surrounding Greenland were the fruit of medieval speculations of a somewhat schematic and fanciful nature, such as those which seem by surviving allusions to have been embodied in the lost *Inventio Fortunata.*

Such was the state of Portuguese activities when a new Bristol undertaking was launched by the grant of letters patent from Henry VII on 19 March 1501. As explained in dealing with the Cabot grant, this implies a considerable period of prior negotiation and formalities, and carries the initiation of the project back into 1500. It should be noted that hope of the return of John Cabot must then have been abandoned, and that his son Sebastian was not more than nineteen or twenty years old; but that nevertheless the Cabot patent was uncancelled and able to be kept in operation by the heirs of the dead man and their deputies.

[1] I owe this to information on fifteenth-century maps kindly given me by Mr R. A. Skelton. See also below, p. 309.

The patent of 1501[1] was granted to João Fernandes, Francisco Fernandes and João Gonsalves, described as squires of the Azores, and Richard Warde, Thomas Asshehurst and John Thomas, merchants of Bristol. As with the Cabot patent, we are not justified in assuming that anything not stated was intended.

The patent is long and detailed. It gives permission to sail in all seas, southern and northern, eastern, western and Arctic, in order to discover or recover in any part of the world heathen lands 'which before this time were and at present are unknown to all Christians'. The grantees may annex and subdue such lands, the sovereignty being reserved to the King. All the King's subjects have a general licence to dwell and trade in the lands so found, under the governance of the grantees, who may make and enforce suitable laws. For the first ten years unprivileged subjects shall go to the new lands only with the permission of the grantees, and thereafter, with permission from the King and the grantees jointly. The grantees may import any goods in any ships into any ports of England. For the first four years they may import goods in one ship free of all customs, subsidies and other dues, but they must pay at the usual rates on their other ships. During the first ten years the grantees may levy on unprivileged subjects a toll of one-twentieth of the goods brought home, provided that they act as factors for such subjects in the new lands. Any foreigners who intrude into the new lands may be expelled by force, even though they are of a nation in amity with England. The grantees may appoint resident officers and deputies in the new lands, and may exercise therein and in the adjacent seas the office of Admiral, with jurisdiction as in England. They are to hold the conquered territories in perpetuity by fidelity alone, without fee or tribute, the King's dignity and sovereignty always reserved. The three Azoreans and their children are accepted as the King's naturalized subjects for all purposes except the payment of customs and subsidies, for which they shall continue as foreigners.

There are two copies of the document, the draft in the warrant

[1] Documents 42 and 43.

under the Privy Seal which authorized the Lord Chancellor to seal the patent, and a final version inscribed upon the patent roll after the Great Seal had been affixed. The first, but not the second, contains an additional clause to the effect that no foreigner, by virtue of any grant formerly made or in future to be made, shall expel the present grantees from their title to the new territories. This clause in the Privy Seal is struck through, and it makes no appearance in the completed patent.

The scope of this grant should be recognized. It enabled its possessors to sail the seas anywhere including (a new designation) the Arctic, but in conquest or occupation of lands it limited them to regions hitherto unknown to Christians. This prevented any overlapping with the Cabot patent. What Cabot had discovered was in 1501 obviously known to Christians, and trespass in it by the 1501 syndicate was not allowed. Equally, Cabot's patent applied only to lands discovered by himself and his successors in his rights, and those successors could not claim anything newly discovered by the 1501 grantees. Hence there was no necessity for the restrictive clause against the Cabots, which was omitted from the completed patent of 1501. The Cabot patent, it must again be emphasized, did not expire on the death of John Cabot. It was inherited by his sons and continued to be a valid instrument. Of two of the sons we know nothing, but Sebastian was living in 1501 and continued to live for more than half a century afterwards. In 1550 he obtained a re-issue of the Cabot patent, a true copy of the original of 1496, from the Chancery of Edward VI. The grant of 1501 had the effect of placing in the field of discovery two separate and possibly competing groups of operators. This had been essentially the policy of the Portuguese kings in grants to their subjects —each to draw benefit from what he himself discovered, and no limit to the number at work. Henry VII was following the Portuguese model. Later in the Tudor period, with the patent granted to the Muscovy Company in 1555, the Crown did something different, conferring a great regional monopoly of all new discovery north of the British latitudes, with no competitors allowed. Probably old Sebastian Cabot, then in England, obtained his copy of the Cabot grant in order to make some claim for compensation. The movement for a grant for all northern discovery was in agitation for some years before 1555, and Sebastian himself was a counsellor and consultant on it.[1]

The bearing of the 1501 grant on Portuguese operations appears to be as follows. It was known in March 1501 that the Portuguese had been on the Greenland coast in 1500: João Fernandes certainly knew that. So, even if we suppose that its previous knowledge by Christians was ignored, it was not a coast that the Bristol men were licensed to occupy. They cannot have wished to do so. The Greenland seas were more in their interest than the lands, and the seas were open to them. The Corte Real discoveries in the voyage of 1501 had not taken place when Henry VII issued the patent. Its grantees were therefore free to exploit anything on the American side of Davis Strait which lay north of the region discovered by John Cabot.

What status in the matter the pre-Cabot Bristol discoverers had is unknown. They were not incorporated, and their interests were not protected by any patent. As individuals some of them may well have been among the merchant backers of John Cabot and have been represented by his patent.

The Household Book[2] contains the following entry under the date 7 January 1502: 'Item to men of bristoll that founde thisle, Cs.' That is the only administrative reference to the proceedings at sea in 1501, but it is sufficient to prove that a voyage of exploration was made. The word 'isle' was common form in these records

---

[1] In June 1550 Sebastian Cabot, having obtained his certified copy of the 1496 patent, was granted £200 'by way of the King's reward'. These are two isolated facts, for the reason for the award was not stated (Taylor, *A Brief Summe of Geography*, p. iv). The surrender of the Cabot patent would have been necessary to clear the way for the new general grant in contemplation, and the £200 was probably Cabot's compensation. The general northern patent was not completed until 1555, but it was nearly so in 1553, when the death of Edward VI took place before the Great Seal had been affixed. The new grant was probably in contemplation from the time of Sebastian Cabot's return to England in 1548.

[2] Document 26.

for a new discovery, and need not be construed literally. On 24 September 1502 there are two entries, 'to a mariner that brought haukes, X s.' and 'to an other that brought an Egle, vi s. viii; d'. These may have nothing to do with our subject; but a week later, on September 30, there is something indubitably relevant: 'to the merchauntes of bristoll that have bene in the newe founde launde, xx li.' There are thus two voyages proved, in 1501 and 1502. Nor is this all, for on September 26 the King bestowed pensions of £10 each upon Francisco Fernandes and João Gonsalves 'in consideracion of the true service they have doon unto us, to oure singler pleasure, as Capitaignes into the newe founde lande'.[1]

The Fabyan Chronicle, as rendered by Hakluyt and Stow, contains a short statement relating to one of the voyages of 1501 and 1502.[2] The Hakluyt version says that in the seventeenth year of the King's reign, 22 August 1501–21 August 1502, three savage men taken in the new found island were brought to the King. They were clothed in beasts' skins, ate raw flesh, and their speech was unintelligible. Two years afterwards two of them were still to be seen about the Palace of Westminster, and the chronicler, who saw them, said that by their appearance he was unable to distinguish them from Englishmen. Stow's version gives the date as '1502, ann. reg. 18', which would be after 21 August 1502. The scanty details seem to indicate that the men were Eskimos rather than Indians.

That is all the documentary evidence we have about the two voyages made under the patent of 1501. We have to consider their location and motive. The patent itself is evidence that they were not made to the coasts discovered by John Cabot and his associates. One of the directing men was João Fernandes, whom we know to have been interested in the Greenland seas, the *llabrador* whom the maps from 1502–3 onwards commemorate by naming Greenland Terra de Labrador. The earliest map evidence is near enough in date to be reckoned as applying to the events of 1501 and 1502. A later map, by Diogo Ribeiro in 1529, writes the

[1] Document 46.   [2] Document 31.

tradition of Tierra de Labrador as the land 'which the English of Bristol discovered and in which they found nothing profitable'.

Taken altogether the evidence points strongly to two voyages towards the north-west, and to contact with the coast of Greenland, named Labrador. There is no suggestion of contact with the coast of our modern Labrador, but it is not ruled out. The map information is apparently from Portuguese sources, but English information may be embodied. The Portuguese may have lost interest in Greenland after 1500, but they were asserting their right to Newfoundland and modern Labrador; and this can be a reason for their suppression of any Bristol work on those coasts, as we know that Cantino's draughtsman suppressed John Cabot's work.

There must have been a certain Anglo-Portuguese animosity. The Portuguese government could only resent the secession of three of its captains to English employment, and the English could only resent the Portuguese annexation of Newfoundland (for that is what 'Terra del Rey de Portuguall' amounted to) in contempt of the fact that the English had been there first. It is possible that the Portuguese embassy of 1499 came to make the claim to Newfoundland by virtue of the papal donation. In 1501–2 we have what look like more communications from Portugal. Household Book entries show payments as follows: 8 January 1501, 'to Edward of Portingale in Rewarde, iiij li.'; 20 June 1501, 'to an herrald of portingale in Rewarde, vi li. viij s. iiij d.'; 1 January 1502, 'to Edward le portingale in Rewarde, xxvj s. viij d.'; 18 February 1502, 'to Edward portingalle in Rewarde, iiij li.'[1] Edward the Portugal was evidently a man below ambassadorial value, but may have been a trusted emissary.

The English voyages of 1501–2 can have been made to Newfoundland and the modern Labrador as well as to Greenland. That they accomplished something very promising is evident. Henry VII declared his 'singular pleasure' with what had been done, and his rewards to Gonsalves, Francisco Fernandes and the unnamed Bristol men were liberal. There was no reward to João Fernandes,

[1] Document 26.

with whom, and with Warde and Thomas, the King was evidently displeased, according to the tenor of a later document. Now, what important work could have been done up there between Greenland and Labrador, in the waters of Davis Strait? First, we must remember that before 1501 it was not known to be a strait, for no one had been far enough to prove the fact since the Norsemen of long ago. La Cosa in 1500 knew of no Davis Strait. It looks as though the thing that pleased the King was the discovery of open water to the north-west, with promise of a North West Passage round the New Found Land to Asia. This, as our present knowledge stands, is but a conjecture; and the reason for advancing it is that it fits such facts as are known, while no other explanation appears adequate to do so. An economic motive is essential to any explanation. The spice trade had been the motive since John Cabot had come on the scene. His second expedition, whatever may have happened in it, had shown that he was working in the wrong direction. The patentees of 1501 were making a new beginning in a new direction. The conjecture that they subscribed their money to discover the North West Passage to Asia appears reasonable, and also that in 1501–2 they thought that they had achieved their aim.[1] They were indeed only on its threshold, but they were not alone in premature optimism. We shall find their contemporary Sebastian Cabot in the same mind a few years later; and far on in the sixteenth century Martin Frobisher and John Davis each asserting from a like basis that the Passage was found.

The patent contemplated the foundation of colonies, or at least of some permanent possessions. England at that time had no surplus population, as a century later she was thought to have, and therefore had neither the human material nor the incentive to found true settlement colonies. Under Henry VII the purpose was to make factories for the collection and forwarding of trade goods, and the human material is suggested by the promise of 'all the malefactors' to Cabot in 1498. It may be objected that a post in

[1] Map evidence may have a bearing on this. See R. A. Skelton's 'Cartography of the Voyages'; below, pp. 310–12.

Newfoundland or Labrador would have been nothing like half-way to China, but that was not the belief of the time. Men thought that, having rounded the New Found Land, there would not be much farther to go. As late as 1519 John Rastell could write: 'But these Newe landes by all cosmographye from the Cane of Catous lande can not lye lytell paste a thousande myle'[1]—or half the distance from England to Newfoundland. With the Portuguese claiming 'Terra del Rey' there was an immediate motive for the English to stake their claim there; and their patent had a significant clause empowering them to remove by force any foreign intruders, even though they belonged to a nation in amity with England. Whether any post was established in Newfoundland or modern Labrador in 1501–2 cannot be said. The voyage of 1501 evidently had a very late return, since it was not noticed in the Household Book until January 1502. This may suggest considerable business on the coast. Again Gonsalves and Francisco Fernandes are not named in that entry, but only, and with great commendation, in September 1502, which may suggest that they did not come home at all in the winter of 1501–2. But these are faint indications on which nothing positive can be based.

Meanwhile the holders of the Cabot patent, not perhaps the young sons of John Cabot but the merchants who stand as his deputies, were possibly at work. Their reserved area was the coast discovered in 1497 and whatever may have been further reported by the expedition of 1498, together with any extension they could make in their turn. We do not directly know their names, but it is a fair supposition that among them were Robert Thorne and Hugh Elyot. At some time these two made a south-pointing voyage down the American coast. It may have been pre-Cabotian, it may have been with John Cabot in 1497, or more likely in 1498, and it may have been after that date. The younger Thorne records the fact, but not the year. But it was not a voyage in association with the syndicate of 1501–2, which was debarred from Cabot's coast.

[1] *A New Interlude*, by John Rastell (brother-in-law of Sir Thomas More), London, *c.* 1519.

There are some recorded facts which show that Robert Thorne and Hugh Elyot were business allies, and also that they could have made an Atlantic voyage together in 1502.

On 7 January 1502 Robert and William Thorne and Hugh Elyot, having recently bought in Normandy a ship of 120 tons, renamed by them the *Gabriel* of Bristol, were granted a remission of £20 from the duties payable on her cargo on her next arrival from Bordeaux, where she was then lading.[1] It is possible that she arrived in Bristol before the authority from the Exchequer permitting the remission, in which case the Bristol customs would have exacted the full duties. On 4 May 1502 a certain Thomas Thorne was paid £20 by the Bristol customers on presenting a tally from the Exchequer.[2] There is no proof that the one piece of business had any connection with the other, but the surnames and the amount are coincident. A possible explanation is that Robert and William Thorne and Hugh Elyot were all absent from Bristol in May, leaving Thomas Thorne as their agent to collect the £20. In that case the two Thornes and Elyot could have been engaged on some long expedition in 1502. But in default of the discovery of some other evidence this remains only a remote possibility. It is unfortunate that the Bristol customs book for this year, giving the movements of ships and merchants, is missing. The possibility, however, reminds us that the Cabot patent and that of 1501 were both living instruments, and that American operations may have been in progress under both.

The next development is the issue by the King of a new patent, dated 9 December 1502.[3] It was granted to João Gonsalves, Francisco Fernandes, Thomas Asshehurst and Hugh Elyot, and to their heirs and deputies. There is good reason to believe, as has been already noted, that the named principals were not the only investors, and that others were in it as sub-partners. The patent permitted the grantees to sail all the seas and 'to find, recover, discover and search out' (*ad inveniendum, recuperandum, disco-periendum et investigandum*) any heathen lands in any part of the

[1] Document 44.   [2] Document 45.   [3] Document 47.

Bristol and the New Found Land

world, and to annex in the King's name any such places by them found. There is a highly significant omission of a phrase contained in the previous patents, about the lands concerned being hitherto unknown to Christians. Instead of this there is a prohibition against entering lands *first discovered* by the King of Portugal or other friendly princes and *now in their possession*.

The purpose of this provision is evidently to clear up the relation in which the English pioneers stood to the Portuguese. Both had been operating in the same general direction, the north-west, in 1501–2; and there may well have been Anglo-Portuguese recriminations, or even some conflict on the spot. Henry VII adopts the doctrine of effective occupation: if you find the Portuguese in occupation of any territory which they have discovered, respect it; but if it is merely territory which they claim to have discovered, but which they have not occupied, then it is open to you. So early does the doctrine of effective occupation make its appearance on the colonial scene.

The existence of three patents was likely to produce some complication in the mutual relations of the English pioneers. The grant of 1502 rules as follows. The patent of 1501 is not cancelled, but the rights under it of João Fernandes, Richard Warde and John Thomas are expressly limited: these three are not now to resort to lands found, recovered or discovered by the new patentees without licence from them. In other words they are reduced to the status of ordinary unprivileged subjects. As regards the Cabot patent, there is no word of prohibition to its holders. So far as it goes, they are evidently free to continue their operations in lands discovered by them and previously unknown to Christians. But they do so in a subordinate position, for the grantees of 1502 have an overriding power to 'recover' the Cabot discoveries which are not now excepted by an 'unknown to Christians' proviso. It seems that without any formal cancellation the King has dictated a fusion of interests under the grant of 1502. In that grant there is the new name of Hugh Elyot. It may be that he was one of the Cabot operators and that his presence in the 1502 list signalizes a substantial amalgamation. The operators of 1502, among whom we shall find Hugh Elyot taking a leading part, were in control in the next following years. A document of 1506 shows that they were then known as the Company Adventurers to the New Found Land.[1]

Household Book entries[2] show that a voyage was made in 1503. On September 15 there was a payment of 6s. 8d. to the servant of Sir Walter Herbert for bringing to the King 'a brasil bow and two red arrows'. This, while worth noting, is of no demonstrable relevance unless the allusion was to the Island of Brasil. But on November 17, twenty shillings were paid 'to one that brought hawks from the Newfounded Island'. There had certainly been a voyage that season, but its destination is not indicated. White falcons, it is true, were found in Greenland, but 'hawks' might mean any kind. In 1504 a new voyage was in preparation, and on April 8 'a priest that goeth to the new Island' received forty shillings. This suggests a permanent settlement, since it was not usual for priests to sail on a mercantile voyage simply to minister to the crew. For 1505 we have a more detailed statement. On August 25 there are two entries: 'to Portingals that brought popinjays and cats of the mountain with other stuff to the King's Grace, £5', and 'to Clays going to Richmond with wild cats and popinjays of the Newfound Island, for his costs, 13s. 4d.' The popinjays or parrots did not come from the cold North West, and they are evidence that this voyage had been southwards down the coastline discovered by John Cabot. Finally there is a cryptic entry on 20 February 1506: 'to Griffeth Rede's servant for bringing upe a [   ][3] don at Penbroke by portyngales'. No certain interpretation of the contracted word has occurred to the present writer or those whom he has consulted. As a far-fetched guess it might be 'portolan', much mangled by a clerk unfamiliar with it.[4] The Portuguese at Pembroke may have nothing to do with the

---

[1] Document 49.   [2] Document 26.
[3] The contracted word, here omitted, is shown in the photograph of the MS, reproduced facing this page.
[4] The *OED* shows that the word portolan first came into English use in the nineteenth century. If the 'Portyngales' used it the clerk would have been puzzled to spell it.

Va. Endorsement of John Day's letter to the Lord Grand Admiral (1497)
Vb. Entry in the Household Books of King Henry VII, 20 February 1506

Bristol venturers, but a ship bound for Bristol could have been driven in there by bad weather. To the end of the reign the Household Books have nothing more.

Two questions arise from the above evidence: to what localities were the voyages made, and were any settlements founded? At the outset the emphasis was on the North West, and João Fernandes undoubtedly directed the effort to Greenland and Davis Strait, where the objective can only have been the passage to Asia. We can be fairly sure of what followed on that, for it followed in every known project of the North West Passage until modern times. After a certain initial progress dependent on the fortitude of the men and the luck of the season, the ships were stopped ultimately by ice. For, as we now know, there is no North West Passage open to such expeditions as the sixteenth century could send out. So we have the early hopes of 1501–2, followed by the reconstruction of the syndicate after the withdrawal of three of its members. In spite of that the stronger patent of 1502 shows that the King and the leaders were in winning mood. They thought that they really had something worth developing. They were prepared to resist exclusive Portuguese claims in Labrador-Newfoundland, and to continue visits to John Cabot's coast, which had openings that may have appeared to be those of through channels. In spite of its exacting legal language the patent of 1502 is worth close attention, replete as it is with regulations for colonies, monopoly rights, privileges for the promoters and their seamen, and strong measures for expelling intruders. This was a plan for exploiting a bigger trade than the north-western region itself could promise. It can only have been a trade in the commodities of Asia, reached through a passage that was to be an English monopoly. The plan was the outcome of the discovery that John Cabot's coast of 1497 was not the coast of Asia.[1]

[1] I have been careful in this book not to make any unqualified assertions for which direct evidence is lacking. Such direct evidence is lacking for the belief that after 1498 the English knew that the western continent was not Asia. But the presumptive evidence is so powerful that I think we must accept it, and date the discovery of America in its true light from 1498.

But, however bright the hope, the discovery needed financing. The cash resources of merchants were small, and it was not possible for them to pay for a series of expeditions without some current income. This may help to explain the authority given in the 1502 patent to intrude on the Cabot interests, which included the fishery. Several cargoes of stockfish each year could have paid the cost of small vessels probing northwards into the ice. So also might some barter trade with the natives of the warmer southward coastline: the popinjays suggest that it was going on. But after a few years most of these hopes would fade, leaving nothing substantial but the fishery. The fishery was so widely extended that it was not possible to monopolize it, and it became an international industry; and the Company Adventurers to the New Found Land died out, although we do not know precisely when.

On colonial settlements the indications are that one or more were founded. Two purposes appear likely, as half-way bases for the North West Passage, and as bases for the fishery. The indications are as follows. First, the obvious intention to make settlements, expressed at length in the patents. Next, the pensions to Gonsalves and Francisco Fernandes, described as 'Capitaignes into the new founde lande'. The word captain as then used applied rather to service on land than at sea, for which meaning master or pilot would be more appropriate. The King's ships indeed had captains, but they were military commanders for battle, and the King's armed ship was thought of in the same category as the King's castle on the shore. It looks, as we have noticed, as though Gonsalves and Fernandes may have been overseas during the winter of 1501–2. The priest in 1504 also suggests that a settlement existed. The most likely place for a colony was on the shores of Newfoundland or Nova Scotia. There stockfish could have been dried, and there could have been export of mast-timber and the furs of creatures conveniently described as wild cats. In these years we know that the Portuguese were working the fishery, and the creation of settlements by either party would have served to stake its claim to the coast. But all these things are indications and not solid evidence. We cannot positively say that any English colony existed.

For the year Michaelmas 1503 to Michaelmas 1504 there survives an account book of the Bristol customs.[1] It is a document on our subject, but its length renders it impracticable to print it in full, although its entries relating to the *Matthew* are given in Document 20. First it should be said that the book yields no evidence of the importation of goods from America. This is what might be expected, since the patent of 1502 allowed the Company to import the ladings of two ships duty free, and fish if caught by Englishmen was not in any case dutiable. The customs book of course contains no notice of any shipping not containing dutiable cargo. For the ordinary commerce of the port the book gives the names of the ships and of the merchants lading them. An analysis of the entries reveals that certain merchants were not doing business, and thus presumably were absent from Bristol, between the following dates: Hugh Elyot, having been mentioned four time in the winter of 1503-4, does not appear from 22 February to 16 August 1504; William Thorne is out of the record from January 16 to August 28; William Clerk, a Londoner who traded at Bristol and belonged to the Company,[2] was doing business at Bristol until February 9, and thereafter not again until August 12; Thomas Asshehurst appears but once in the book, on August 12, not having been mentioned in the previous winter. Thus four merchants, Elyot, William Thorne, Clerk and Asshehurst all resume work in August in ordinary European business, three of them not having been mentioned since the previous February, and one not since the beginning of the record in September 1503. It is a possible inference that Elyot, William Thorne and Clerk together made a voyage to the New Found Land between the end of February and the beginning of August, and that Asshehurst came home with them, having been absent overseas all the winter.

Ship movements are not so conclusive, since a ship might be out of the record for various reasons, repairs, chartering to another

[1] P.R.O., E 122, 199/1.   [2] Document 49.

port, and so forth. But, for what they are worth, some ship entries may be given. The *Frances* of Bristol entered from Ireland on 2 January 1504 and is no more mentioned until August 9, when she sailed for Portugal. The *Gabriel*, which belonged to Elyot and the Thornes, entered from Spain on January 16 and appears no more in the book. Two other vessels, the *Austen* and the *Mary Bonaventure*, are first mentioned on August 16 and August 29 respectively. They may have been newly built in 1504, or they may have been extant but away from Bristol throughout the winter and early summer of 1503–4. The entries as a whole are consistent with but do not prove the use of these four ships in the American trade.

Robert Thorne was not away on a long voyage in 1504, since the entries name him about once a month throughout that summer, engaged in short-distance trade. Similarly the *Matthew* is fully accounted for, and did not cross the Atlantic that year.

There is no customs book for 1504–5 or for any other year to the end of the King's reign. But the Household Book shows the Portuguese returning from the New Found Land in August 1505 and a doubtful entry about them in the following February; and that is the last datable expedition of the Company.

In 1506, however, we have a lawsuit in the Court of Chancery between William Clerk and Hugh Elyot. Clerk was the plaintiff, and part of his suit concerns the voyage of the ship *Michael* from Bristol to San Lucar in September 1505. This is irrelevant to our purpose, but in another bill of complaint of 1506,[1] probably October, Clerk goes into some detail about the Company's affairs, saying that he has paid sums of money on Elyot's behalf and has supplied stores and victuals for the ships. The Company is twice mentioned: 'Item, payd for the same hewghe to the Company adventurers into the new founde ilondes, xx li.'; and 'Item, for the costes that the same hewghe causyd the said William to have in the viage for the Company Aventurers preparyd into the new fownd londes, iiij li. xv s.' The date of this voyage does not appear.

---

[1] Document 49.

Last of all there is a complaint in the Chancery by Francisco Fernandes against the oppressive behaviour of Hugh Elyot.[1] The bill is not dated, but its form places it in or after 1504. By its matter it probably belongs to 1506 or later. Fernandes states that Hugh Elyot has been suing him in the Constable Court of Bristol for an alleged debt of £100, which Fernandes says that he does not owe, but that on the contrary Elyot owes him £160. In spite of this Elyot is maliciously keeping Fernandes in prison at Bristol, and accordingly the Lord Chancellor is prayed to intervene and see justice done.

Together these two cases show dissension in the Company and may indicate its break-up. Up to the present no further traces of it have been found in the records. But the negative proves nothing in a matter like this, which depends at best on the merest documentary scraps. It is quite possible that the operations went on longer.

The period 1502–10 is fairly rich in surviving maps bearing on the region discussed in this chapter. They are dealt with at length by Mr R. A. Skelton in the concluding section of this book, but some suggestions on the historical bearings of a few of them may be included here. The earliest are of Portuguese origin or derivation and record Portuguese achievements. The Cantino map of 1502 has already been mentioned. Similar in origin and general conception is the Caveri map of slightly later date. The anonymous planisphere in the Biblioteca Oliveriana at Pesaro is of possible date 1508–10.[2] It presents Greenland and Labrador-Newfoundland as in the Cantino and Caveri maps, and a large mainland, which may be meant for Asia, a long way west of Labrador-Newfoundland. Its island of Cuba is of the same hooked shape as in La Cosa.

The Portuguese map now agreed to be wrongly ascribed to Salvat de Pilestrina (Kunstman III),[3] probably drawn *post*–1506, is

---

[1] Document 50. [2] See Plate IX.
[3] See Plate XIII. The Kunstmann maps are a group found preserved in Bavaria and excellently reproduced in colours by Friedrich Kunstmann, *Atlas zur Entdeckungsgeschichte Amerikas*, Munich, 1859.

not a world-map but a chart of the Atlantic. Its Greenland and Labrador-Newfoundland, the latter with a number of place-names and the general title Terra de Cortte Reall, are perhaps the best expression of Gaspar Corte Real's discoveries, since a surprisingly accurate scale of latitudes is given. More than this, the coast of modern Labrador is extended north-westwards to 62°–63° by the map's own scale. The extension (north of 56°) bears no place-names, but appears to be copied from an actual survey. There is no evidence that the Corte Reals went as far north as this, and Mr Skelton suggests that there may have been an unrecorded Portuguese voyage before September 1502.

The present writer thought also of an unrecorded English voyage by the holders of the Cabot patent in 1499, or more probably in 1500. He looked for some scrap of evidence upon it in the English documents of those dates, but found nothing. But the Record Office rolls are filled chiefly with entries on matters obviously irrelevant to the present enquiry, and anything to our purpose must be as a pinhead of gold in a desert of dross. These rolls are searched by students working on historical subjects quite other than ours, and there is still a hope that something on the voyages may be turned up inadvertently by someone not intentionally searching for material of its type. Such has been the process of some important discoveries of evidence already incorporated in the history of the voyages.

The map of Pedro Reinel (Kunstmann I)[1] has been diversely dated by good authorities. Dr Armando Cortesão assigns it to c. 1504. Others have given somewhat later dates. It makes Davis Strait about the right breadth at its southern end but becoming very narrow. Its Labrador-Newfoundland is a continuous coast with plentiful Portuguese names, and it shows unmistakably our present Cabot Strait between Newfoundland and Cape Breton, with a more vaguely known part of Nova Scotia, perhaps from English information, beyond. But upon Nova Scotia, west of Cabot Strait, there is a Portuguese flag. Kunstmann II is an anony-

[1] See Plate XII.

mous Italian map of probable date *c.* 1506 or later. It shows a small part of Greenland, named Terra de Lavorador, and is thus excellent evidence of the bestowal of that name close to the time at which João Fernandes was active. There are seven Portuguese names on the Greenland coast and adjacent islands, but there are none on Labrador-Newfoundland except the general title Terra de Corte Reall. There is no delineation of any other part of the North American coast. It would appear that this map embodies information available soon after the return of the two ships of Gaspar Corte Real's expedition of 1501. The Greenland names might result from his voyage of 1500.

The group of Portuguese maps dating from 1502 or a little later, none of them earlier, was evidently inspired by the voyage of 1501 at the end of which Gaspar Corte Real lost his life. The other Corte Real voyages, of 1502 and 1503, have not left evident cartographical traces and may not have contributed much to discovery.

In the later years of this decade there were some maps of Italian and German origin which used information from all sources and expressed conclusions on the large question of the identity or non-identity of North America and Asia. A printed world map was designed by Giovanni Matteo Contarini and engraved at Florence in 1506.[1] The British Museum has the only known copy and has reproduced it in facsimile. The South American continent is shown so far as it had been revealed by Columbus, Ojeda, Pinzon and Cabral as late as 1500 but not thereafter, and it is an isolated land-mass far remote from the continent in the north. The Spanish Antilles are drawn in too high a latitude, and with no continent but a broad expanse of ocean to the west of them; and in this ocean, west and south of Cuba, lies the island of Cipango. Far away west of that stretches the mainland of Eastern Asia, with names drawn from Marco Polo. The north-eastern corner of this Asia is immensely extended towards Europe, to serve as the land discovered by John Cabot and the Corte Reals. It is more roughly drawn than in the Portuguese maps, but an inscription attributes

[1] See Plate VIII.

the discovery to the Portuguese. On the whole this map is of a design smacking more of the 1490's than of 1506: La Cosa in 1500 is more advanced on the North American question. Omitting South America, the design would serve very well to illustrate the ideas of John Cabot in 1497; and his map, which so exasperated Ayala, was most likely of this general type. This Italian cartographer was convinced, in the year of Columbus's death, that the transatlantic continent was Asia; and no one accepting his interpretation could have embarked on the search for a north-west passage to Cathay.

The same general conception, with the proportions modified, appears in a world map drawn by the Dutchman Johan Ruysch and printed in the edition of Ptolemy produced at Rome in 1508. The Newfoundland region is better drawn, and there is a gulf representing Cabot Strait, but it is all continuous continent with Marco Polo's Asia. Although there is not much sign of it, one would expect to see an English influence in Ruysch's map, for his editor Marcus Beneventanus stated that Ruysch had sailed from southern England and had reached the shore of Asia in the latitude of 53° N. This is somewhat puzzling because the map-information appears to be mainly of Portuguese origin, although one name, Baia de Rockas, looks English, and the name given to the Newfoundland coast, Terra Nova, is distinctively English. Ruysch reveals nothing of John Cabot's 1497 nomenclature, and evidently had not sailed with him. Equally he does not show the penetration of Davis Strait recorded in some of the Portuguese maps. Near the Greenland coasts are three inscriptions of traditional stories which he could have acquired without sailing there. Ruysch's voyage was probably with some fishing expedition, and difficulty of language may have prevented him from learning much from the ship's company. Formerly, when not much attention was paid to the post-Cabotian Bristol voyages, Ruysch was thought to have been engaged with John Cabot, and much effort was spent on reading his map as Cabot evidence. It does in fact represent the continental conception held by Cabot in 1497-8. Its drawing of

Newfoundland indicates later experience, unless, improbably, we have here the pre-Cabotian Isle of Brasil found by the men of Bristol *en otros tiempos*.

The Inset Map of Martin Waldseemüller, 1507,[1] is the earliest to show, without the least doubt of its interpretation, Eastern Asia and the whole of America as two distinct continents, separated by a broad ocean in which is sited Cipango. North America reaches only to about 50° N, with a possibility of making the North West Passage in open water round it. It extends southwards to a fairly well shaped Florida and a Gulf of Mexico shaped long before there is any record of Europeans in those waters. A long isthmus connects this northern continent to South America. The northern edge of North America and the whole of the western coasts of both Americas and the isthmus are in straight lines indicating that they are as yet unexplored. Here we have an academic geographer of Western Germany expressing the dominant truth of the connection of the two Americas and their separation from Asia by an ocean not yet named the Pacific, ten years after the return of John Cabot from his first voyage. If Waldseemüller could obtain by 1507 the information which he welded into this conception, it seems evident that the exploring captains of Western Europe must have had it some time earlier. The Inset Map goes far to support the inferences derived earlier in this chapter from the Portuguese voyages and the patents issued by Henry VII.

Some general conclusions can be stated about the Bristol voyages of 1501–5. North-western discovery was the originating motive, introduced, so far as the evidence goes, by João Fernandes with his hope of the utility of the Greenland coast. On this conception the coast of our modern Labrador was part of a new continent, not Asia; and between it and Greenland lay the strait that would bring the explorers round to the economically useful lands and seas of Asia which had not yet been reached. The idea that the Englishmen's New Found Land was a new continent barring the direct way to Asia probably sprang from the failure of

[1] See Plate VI.

the second Cabot expedition of 1498. The 'north-western' interpretation of the voyages of 1501–2 depends on this interpretation of the voyage of 1498. In other words, it is not a strictly proved proposition.

Yet there is no other proposition which will account for the north-western push by the English and the Portuguese, which resulted (as the maps show) in considerable discovery on either side of the approach to Davis Strait. The cold barren lands and ice-strewn waters of the North West had no conceivable economic attraction of their own; and an economic attraction was indispensable to the financing of discovery. The distant lure of Cipango and Cathay was the magnetic pull to draw men through the sub-Arctic waste. Yet we should do wrong to these men if we held the economic to be the only incentive. They imperilled their lives, and some lost them—Cabot, the two Corte Reals and many others—for achievement, the motive which has characterized the best Europeans throughout Europe's history.

The north-western push by the Bristol syndicates died out in the ice-fields. So also did that by the Portuguese. Later history shows that unless success came quickly lack of money closed the effort. There remained the fishery. Its exploiters, English, Portuguese, French and Spanish, pursued it in the sixteenth century in mutual competition and without serious hostilities. There was fish for all, and the assertion of a monopoly would have required armed forces such as no kingdom was prepared to find.

What in detail took place in these Bristol voyages we do not know. Lack of record precludes a narrative. We have only administrative fragments, the patents expressing great intentions, and the maps which speak with the uncertain voice of delphic oracles. Chronicles ought to supply the narrative, but we have none from Bristol, and those of London are interested only in London events, such as Eskimos at Westminster, and have no space for Bristol ventures. But there was an undertaking of discovery, trade and colonization, and its history is lost because we cannot penetrate the mists and read it.

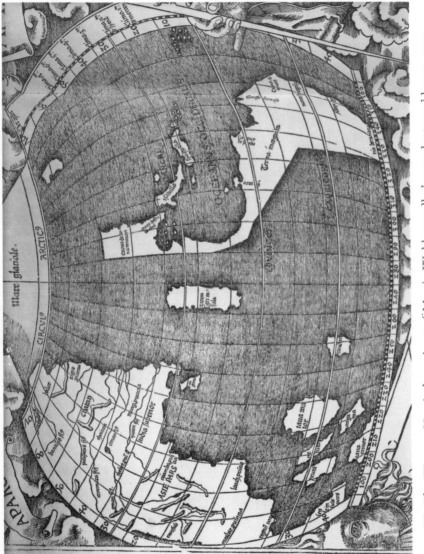

VI. The Western Hemisphere: inset of Martin Waldseemuller's woodcut world map, 1507

IX

THE NORTH WESTERN VOYAGE OF SEBASTIAN CABOT

IF WE accept the years 1480–3 as covering the date of his birth, Sebastian Cabot was twenty years old, more or less, when the operations of the Bristol syndicates began in 1501. His father's patent was inherited by himself and his brothers. John Cabot's discoveries were expressly reserved to them by the terms of the 1501 patent, which allowed the new combination to work only in lands unknown to Christians. The grantees of the 1502 patent were allowed to work on the Cabot discoveries, but the owners of the Cabot patent were not debarred from working there as well, and there is some indication of an amalgamation of the interests in the Company of 1502. But in all this there is no hint of any part being played by Sebastian Cabot. Apart from the somewhat misleading statement on the Paris Map of 1544, bracketing Sebastian with John as discoverers of the New Found Land, there is no sure mention in history of Sebastian Cabot from his inclusion with his family in the patent of 1496 to his appearance as principal in a new grant made by Henry VII in April 1505.[1] The new grant was that of an annual pension of £10 charged upon the customs of the port of Bristol, 'in consideracion of the diligent service and attendaunce that our well beloved Sebastian Caboot Venycian hath doon unto us in and about the same'. The reason for the award is service in Bristol, not service into the New Found Land as in the previous cases of Fernandes and Gonsalves. If Sebastian had sailed as a commander we may be fairly sure that it would have been mentioned.

It appears therefore that Sebastian Cabot had not served in the recent voyages from Bristol, except perhaps in some apprentice

[1] Document 51.

capacity, but had nevertheless been so employed as to give the King cause for satisfaction. How he had been employed can only be guessed, perhaps in cartography and the study of navigation. The Spanish government was to recruit him in 1512 and afterwards to promote him, partly for his knowledge of these subjects. But so far as it concerns his position at Bristol the suggestion is a mere possibility.

About Sebastian Cabot's own voyage in English service there are as yet no administrative documents known. Those who do not believe that the voyage took place in 1508-9 may find this lack of record significant. But in these matters lack of record proves nothing, although search for record illustrates what we already know, that the records are extremely defective. The evidence is therefore of a nature quite different from that concerning the Anglo-Azorean voyages of 1501-5. It consists mainly of extracts from historical and geographical writers over a period of more than half a century after the voyage was made. Their testimonies are either ill-informed or much curtailed, and their standards of accuracy and chronology were low. Out of them, by sifting and criticism, it is possible to extract a date and the bare outline of a narrative. The plan here adopted will be to consider and evaluate each writing in turn and to note its salient points, leaving the reader to make his own judgment with the aid of the full texts as presented among the Documents, and then to try to arrive at the truth through a synthesis of the facts held to be established. In this process there may be unconscious persuasion on the author's part, but the cards are on the table, and the sceptic is invited to be vigilant.

In the autumn of 1512 Sebastian Cabot was in Spain with the English army commanded by the Marquis of Dorset and intended to act in alliance with King Ferdinand in an invasion of France. Sebastian was in communication with the Spanish government, and was transferred to the Spanish service with the consent of his immediate commander Lord Willoughby. The most obvious reason for his voluntary transfer is that he could get no further backing in England, whose new king had not the outlook of Henry VII. Thenceforward for thirty-six years his residence was chiefly in Spain, although in the earlier part of that time he made one or two visits to England, and in 1526–30 he was absent in command of a Spanish expedition to the River Plate. In 1518 Charles V appointed him Pilot Major of Spain, and before that date he had been consulted about voyages of discovery.

The first of the writers to deal with his English voyage is Peter Martyr of Anghiera, an Italian historian of the discoveries who lived in Spain.[1] His *De Orbe Novo Decades* was written in Latin, and the Third Decade (of eight) was published at Alcalá in 1516. In the Third Decade, in the course of a disquisition on ocean currents and the possibility of a strait between North and South America, opening through the then unknown waters west of Cuba, he cites Sebastian Cabot as a witness to what he has to say and gives a short account of the voyage which Sebastian has made to the north-western seas and the North American coast. He implies that his information comes solely from Sebastian himself, who is a personal friend of his and sometimes stays at his house. The story is that Sebastian Cabot equipped at his own cost two ships with three hundred men and steered first for the north, where in July he found great icebergs, although the ice had melted off the land. The ice compelled him to turn and make for the west, where he followed the coast southwards almost to the latitude of Gibraltar, and was almost in the longitude of Cuba before he returned to England. In the course of this coasting he passed and himself named the Baccalaos, the region of the great fishery. He said that the inhabitants there were clothed in skins and not devoid of intelligence, and that there were great numbers of bears which caught and ate the fish. Martyr further states that at the time of writing (1515) Sebastian Cabot was expecting shipping to be provided for him to discover 'this secret of Nature hitherto hidden', which the tenor of the whole passage shows to mean the supposed intercontinental strait through the Gulf of Mexico to the

[1] Document 52.

Pacific. Sebastian expected to sail in March 1516. Martyr adds that some of the Spaniards denied that Cabot was the first finder of the Baccalaos and did not allow that he went so far westwards as he claimed.

On the above we may note that no date is given for the voyage, nor purpose in making for the north, and that no highest north latitude is mentioned. Spaniards who knew some such facts as were supplied in John Day's letter—and Juan de Fonseca, Bishop of Burgos and virtual secretary for colonial affairs, was undoubtedly one of them—may well have known that Sebastian Cabot was not the first finder of the Newfoundland fishery; and it was in their interest to deny that an English expedition had been farther south on the United States coastline, since they had themselves a design for making a colony there. In October 1511 the Castilian government gave instructions to a captain named Juan de Agramonte to explore and colonize the New Land south-west of the fishing region.[1] No expedition resulted, although it is perhaps significant of this interest that Cabot was invited into the Spanish service a year later. Cabot never sailed on the other proposed expedition through the Gulf of Mexico because King Ferdinand died early in 1516, and there was a period of confusion before the new king, his grandson Charles, arrived from the Netherlands to take charge. In the interim the Spaniards of Cuba made their own investigations of the Gulf of Mexico and reported that there was no strait. Peter Martyr was a reliable historian, generally careful of his facts. When we read his statement on Sebastian Cabot in its full context we see that it is merely illustrative of the chief subject in Martyr's mind, the coastwise current and the inter-continental strait. He is thus under no obligation to go into full detail about Cabot's voyage. Cabot on his side felt no necessity to state his purpose in going north, for the discoverer of a north-west passage for England would not have been popular in Spain. In the documents of 1511 the Spanish authorities recognized the Portuguese interest, and they knew the Portuguese claim that

[1] Biggar, *Precursors*, Documents XXXII, XXXIII.

148

Newfoundland-Labrador was in the Portuguese sphere by the Treaty of Tordesillas. Spain was hoping for an all-Spanish route to Eastern Asia through the unexplored Gulf of Mexico, and Sebastian was ready to conduct the search. It was obviously impolitic for him to talk of the North West Passage.[1] With the conquest of Mexico and afterwards of Peru, bringing a Pacific coast and a treasure route along it, the revelation of a north-western access from Europe would have become ever more damaging to Spanish interests. Sebastian Cabot had to keep silent for a generation about a discovery which, as will be shown, he really believed that he had made. He was silent, however, only to Spaniards. There were others to whom he talked under pledge of secrecy, as will appear.

In his Seventh Decade, in a passage written in 1524, although not published until 1530, Peter Martyr supplied the omission of the date of Sebastian Cabot's voyage.[2] He there made mention of 'the Baccalaos discovered by Cabot from England in the sixteenth year backwards from this [*anno abhinc sexto decimo*]'. This by subtraction from 1524 yields the date 1508 or 1508–9.

Peter Martyr's original account of the voyage appeared again after his death, and in an amplified form, in a general history of the West Indies published at Venice in 1534.[3] Broadly the matter is the same, but there are some additions, which may have been made by Martyr himself or by another hand. He introduces Cabot's voyage after the former reference to the coastal currents, and after a new one, to the belief of some that America is joined by the north to Europe: 'but this last opinion conflicts with the voyage made by . . . Sebastian Cabot'. The writer mentions the two ships but not the 300 men. He gives Cabot's direction as 'between the west and the north', and says that he reached 55° N before being turned back by floating ice. Although the voyage was towards the North West there is no suggestion of Asia as the ultimate destination, and in fact no reason for the expedition is supplied.

---

[1] It may have been worse than impolitic. See below, p. 151.
[2] Document 54.   [3] Document 53.

In 1520-1 Sebastian Cabot, although Pilot-Major of Spain, was in London negotiating with Wolsey and Henry VIII on the command of an English expedition across the Atlantic. It appears that this was done openly, with the knowledge of Charles V, who was then in friendly alliance with the English king. Charles, however, was absent from Spain from May 1520 to July 1522, attending to important business in the Netherlands and Germany; and he was therefore out of touch with his colonial advisers. The English expedition did not take place. Its ostensible destination had been the New Found Land of English discovery, which would not have been very offensive to Spanish interests, since the fishermen of all the Western nations were already using its waters. But there are various indications, amounting to proof, that the real objective was a push through the North West Passage to Eastern Asia;[1] and this to Charles V would have been treachery on the part of his Pilot-Major. In those years (1519-22) Magellan with a Spanish expedition was away on the discovery of the South West Passage through the straits at the end of South America, which did lead the Spaniards to the Spice Islands. The surviving ship of Magellan's expedition came home in September 1522, when it became known that Magellan had entered and crossed the Pacific. Sebastian Cabot was then in the perilous position of having instigated or connived at a rival English project, and he was in deadly fear lest his secret should leak out. He himself had been imprudent. While in London he had talked to Venetians and had spoken of admitting Venice to a share in the English expedition, and these Venetians had reported

[1] No one can read carefully the extracts from the records of the Drapers' Company given in Document 71, without realizing that the 'Newefound Ilond' mentioned as the objective is not the Newfoundland to which the West-Country fishermen were regularly resorting. If a voyage to the fishery had been in question it would have been absurd to say that no English sailors knew the way there, and that the ships for that voyage must be victualled for a whole year; and there would have been no point in objecting that Sebastian Cabot had never been there when so many others obviously had. This 'Newefound Ilond' was not the well known fishery region, but something much more distant, and Sebastian had not been called from Spain to lead a fishing expedition. The destination must have been on the farther side of America, and the island was very likely Cipango, about which John Cabot had spoken in times past, as the London objectors mentioned.

the matter to the Council of Ten. Then, in the autumn of 1522, when the English plan had been abandoned and Charles V was back in Spain, Cabot was dismayed to be approached at Valladolid by the Venetian ambassador with a letter from the Ten desiring to be apprised of all the details. He read the letter and became pale and confused, and said to the ambassador: 'I most earnestly beseech you to keep the thing secret, as it would cost me my life.' He then admitted a conversation with a Venetian agent in London: 'I said I had the means of rendering Venice a partner in this navigation, and of showing her a passage whereby she would obtain great profit, which is the truth, for I have discovered it.'

All this would not have been necessary for the ostensible voyage to the New Found Land alone, and it is abundantly clear that Sebastian Cabot was claiming to have discovered the North West Passage.[1]

The rest of the intrigue is not relevant to our present purpose. Sebastian Cabot was thoroughly scared, and edged his way out of the demand to explain himself in Venice. He realized that the North West Passage by the English was more than ever a matter of treason in Spain, now that the Spaniards were the discoverers and monopolists of the South West Passage.[2] But the whole affair is evidence on his former discovery—as he believed it to be—of the North West Passage. It is the earliest statement that he had discovered it, and it is from his own lips, at a time when he took a great risk in making it. If he had led the English expedition through to Asia he would have had a great future in English service. If he had led it and failed, he would have had no future in England, and certainly none in Spain. He must have believed in it.

[1] For the London project as well as Cabot's intrigue with Venice, see Documents 70 and 71. The difficulty in London was financial, the merchants being unwilling to subscribe, and Cabot appears to have thought that Venice might supply the necessary capital.

[2] The Spanish authorities, however, knowing the difficulty of Magellan's Strait, did decide to search for a more direct opening to the Pacific through warmer waters. In 1523 the Emperor commissioned Estevão Gomes to look for an opening through the coastline of what is now the United States. Gomes sailed in 1524, but had no chance of success (Biggar, *Precursors*, Documents, XLIV–L).

Several years later, in 1536, a report on Sebastian Cabot was made to the Venetian Senate.[1] It stated that he had had two ships from Henry VII, and with 300 men had sailed into the frozen sea. He had turned back without accomplishing what he had intended, with a resolve to resume the project at a better season. When he reached England he found that Henry VII was dead and that his son would not support the enterprise. This yields a clear date for the voyage: it began before and ended after 21 April 1509, when Henry VII died.

Giovanni Battista Ramusio, a Venetian historian, made a large three-volume collection of voyages. The first volume, published in 1550, contained a piece on Sebastian Cabot, produced in somewhat unusual circumstances.[2] Ramusio said that some months before writing it he had been one of a house-party which had discussed such matters. One of those present was 'a Mantuan gentleman' whose name he withheld 'out of respect'. The Mantuan said that several years previously he had had an interview with Sebastian Cabot at Seville. Sebastian declared that his father had died at the time when news was brought of Columbus's discovery of the Indies, a thing much talked of at the court of Henry VII. He, Sebastian, had thereupon proposed to the King that he should lead an expedition to find a shorter route to the Indies by the north-west. This was in 1496. Sebastian sailed with two caravels provided by the King, with the expressed intention of reaching Cathay. But he found the land running to the north and then to the east, and at 56° N he had to turn back down the American coast, going southwards and looking for a passage that should lead to the Indies. In this way he went as far as Florida and thence returned to England. There he found civil wars and disturbances and no further thought of discovery. On account of this he went to Spain, where the King and Queen Isabella received him well and sent him to explore the coast of Brazil, where he discovered the River Plate. After that he made many other voyages until old age compelled him to rest at his post at Seville.

[1] Document 55.   [2] Document 56.

Sebastian no doubt was not very precise in his talk with this gentleman, who obviously knew little about the history of discovery. But it is the Mantuan who must bear the blame for the major inaccuracies of this wild story: for he was a man totally devoid of the chronological sense. He made Henry's difficulties with the Scots and the Cornish rebels in 1497 the reason why Cabot went to Spain in 1512. There Cabot was kindly received by Queen Isabella, who had died in 1504, and she and her husband, who died in 1516, despatched him on the voyage to the River Plate, which began in 1526. So much for the Mantuan as a witness to the discourse of Cabot, who certainly did not say these things. But what are we to think of Ramusio, a professional historian? He swallowed the yarn whole, keeping it in memory until he wrote it down some months later, and printed it without the slightest qualm on the chronological impossibilities. Out of the whole story there is only one thing we can believe, that Sebastian sailed at some time in search of the North West Passage; and we should hardly believe that unless we otherwise knew it to be true. The evidential value of the Mantuan's story is small. Ramusio called it 'a great and admirable discourse'.

In his third volume, published in 1556, Ramusio told something more about Sebastian Cabot.[1] Many years ago, he said, Cabot had written to him that he had sailed beyond the land of New France, and had gone a long way west and a quarter north until on June 11 he had reached the latitude of $67\frac{1}{2}$ degrees. There he found the sea open and believed that he could have gone on to Cathay, but the ill-will of the master and crew compelled him to turn back.

It must be remarked that Ramusio's 'many years ago' must mean 'not many years ago', for it is hardly credible that he had had this letter when he printed the Mantuan's story.[2] For the account he received from Sebastian Cabot was detailed and sensible. Ramusio gives us only a brief summary of a letter which we would gladly

---

[1] Document 57.

[2] Cabot was certainly corresponding with someone in Venice, probably Ramusio, in 1551, on the matter of his mother's property (Almagià, p. 26).

have entire, for it contained the only known account of the voyage written by Cabot himself. Can we suppose, for example, that he would have specified June 11 without giving the year? Ramusio does not give it, perhaps because it was not the 1496 which he had adopted so uncritically from the Mantuan. In 1548 Cabot had come permanently to England and was free, as he had not been in Spain, to write of the North West. He was no doubt in possession of Ramusio's first volume and indignant at the nonsense it attributed to him. His letter to Ramusio may have been his correction of it. Ramusio, at any rate, decided not to print the letter. The new facts that the abridgment does tell us are that Sebastian sailed beyond the land of New France, the name given since Cartier's voyages to eastern Canada, that his course was west and a quarter north (from a locality unspecified), and that he claimed to have reached $67\frac{1}{2}°$ N, that is, to have crossed the Arctic Circle. Ramusio lets his readers down. He should have apologized for printing the Mantuan's nonsense and published Sebastian's letter in full.

In 1552 the Spanish writer Francisco Lopez de Gomara published a history of the Indies at Saragossa.[1] In it he said that Sebastian Cabot was the first to bring news of the Bacallaos or fishery, and that he promised Henry VII to go by the north to Cathay and find a quicker route to the spices than that of the Portuguese. He took 300 men and went by way of Iceland to the cape of Labrador until he reached 58 degrees, 'although he himself says much more'. In July he found so much ice that he turned westwards, refreshed himself at the Baccalaos, and sailed down the coast to 38 degrees, whence he returned to England.

Most of Gomara's statement is copied from Peter Martyr's Third Decade, but he is more specific in giving the course by way of Iceland to the point of Labrador, which means Greenland's Cape Farewell, within a degree of the latitude he mentions. Gomara is also clear that the objective was a passage to Asia, which Martyr had not stated. Gomara's work, printed three or four years after Cabot had left Spain, may reflect something of what

[1] Document 58.

the explorer was saying in England. There was time also for Gomara to have corresponded with Ramusio after the latter had received Cabot's letter, which may account for 'he himself says much more'. If Gomara had seen the Mantuan's story, he would as a Spaniard have detected its anachronisms.

André Thevet was a Frenchman who lived to become Geographer Royal of France. Whatever may have been his geographical talents, his historical mind was as uncritical and unchronological as that of the Mantuan Gentleman. In his book on the French in America, published at Paris in 1558, he discussed the Baccalaos and made a few statements on Sebastian Cabot.[1] He said that Cabot had been sent by Henry VII to seek a northern passage to Cathay, and that also he proposed to settle Englishmen in 'Peru and America'. But in fact he put 300 men on shore 'in the direction of Irlande [Iceland?] towards the north', where they nearly all died from the cold, although it was in July.

On this it may be observed that no such country as Peru was known or heard of in the opening decade of the century. What was in Thevet's muddled mind was that in 1552 the Duke of Northumberland was meditating an expedition to ascend the Amazon and plunder Peru, and that after Northumberland's death Cabot reported this to the Emperor in 1554. The 300 men come from Peter Martyr. Their deaths from cold are possibly a reflection of the fate of Sir Hugh Willoughby in 1553-4, when he and two ship's companies, not nearly 300 strong, were frozen to death on the coast of Lapland: Sebastian Cabot was the governor of the company which sent them out. Thevet tells us nothing not otherwise known, and mixes up events half-a-century apart.

The only Portuguese collection of voyages to mention Sebastian Cabot is that of Antonio Galvão, published at Lisbon in 1563.[2] He says that in 1496 Sebastian Cabot, influenced by the news of Columbus's discovery and by the fact that the globe showed that the islands of Asia were 'in the same latitude as and much nearer to his country [England] than to Portugal or Castile', obtained two

[1] Document 59.   [2] Document 60.

ships and 300 men from Henry VII. He sailed westwards to land in 45 degrees, and then went on by that land to 60 degrees, where they found great cold and many icebergs. This caused him to turn back and coast the same land southwards, examining every bay, river and creek, to see if it passed to 'the other side'; and so went on to the latitude of 38 degrees or, as others say, to the cape of Florida in 25 degrees, before returning to England.

This story is a composite, a muddle like Thevet's, but considerably more valuable because it consists of two and perhaps three components which in themselves give valid information. Galvão confused them because he had not heard of John Cabot and attributed everything to one voyage by Sebastian which, as the two ships and 300 men indicate, was based on Peter Martyr. The date 1496 is that of John Cabot's patent, and the westward passage to land in 45 degrees, i.e. Nova Scotia, is an echo of John Cabot's first voyage. Then, immediately linked to it, is Sebastian Cabot's veritable voyage to the northern ice, with its return down the American coastline searching for a westward opening. This search Galvão, in common with Martyr and Gomara, declares to have ended at about 38 degrees, the latitude of Gibraltar. Then, surprisingly, Galvão adds that some say he reached 'the Cape of Florida which is in twenty-five degrees'. This is the only attribution of so low a latitude to Sebastian Cabot[1]; and that is why Galvão's account is described above as having possibly three components. For the latitude of the Cape of Florida may conceivably be derived from the lost second voyage of John Cabot in 1498.

The last of our continental historians is very much later in date.[2] In 1579 Urbain Chauveton, in a work on the New World printed at Geneva, said briefly that in 1507 Sebastian Cabot sailed in search of Cathay by the north and reached 67 degrees before being compelled by ice and cold to give up. The statement is obviously compiled from previous works, but the date 1507 is peculiar to

---

[1] The Mantuan (above, p. 152) spoke of Florida, but not the Cape of Florida. In 1550 the name Florida covered the whole coastline south of New England.

[2] Document 61.

Chauveton. It may be derived from Peter Martyr's 1524 statement of 'sixteen years ago', with an error in arithmetic.

The remaining testimonies to Sebastian Cabot's discovery are by Englishmen, or in one instance by a Frenchman writing in England. They belong to the period after Cabot's return in 1548. He came at the invitation of some members of Edward VI's council who wished for his advice on the opening of new trades. The most important outcome was the formation of the joint-stock company afterwards known as the Muscovy Company, of which Cabot was appointed governor. Its purpose was to open a northern passage to Asia. In this it failed, but it did open a new trade with Russia by the White Sea. Its charter of 1555 gave it the monopoly of all exploration and new trade north of British latitudes. This included the north-west, and in the reign of Elizabeth I the search for the North West Passage became prominent. It gave rise to some important allusions to the work of Sebastian Cabot. He himself died in 1557.

In 1555 Richard Eden published an English translation of Peter Martyr's first three Decades. In some prefatory remarks he spoke of Sebastian Cabot 'yet living', as the discoverer of the Baccalaos. But he added that Cabot touched only in the north corner and most barbarous part, from which he was repulsed by ice in July.[1] Although Eden was a friend of Cabot in the last phase of his life, it might appear that the personal acquaintance had not begun when the above was written, or we should have a better account.

Jean Ribault, a French Huguenot captain, published *The Whole and true discovery of Terra Florida* in English in 1563.[2] No French version of the book has been found. Its only relevance to the north-western discovery is that it gives the date of Sebastian Cabot's voyage as 1498.[3]

Sir Humphrey Gilbert makes some brief remarks of more importance in his *Discourse* on the North West Passage, published in 1576, but written ten years earlier.[4] He says: 'Sebastian Cabot

---

[1] Document 62.   [2] Document 63.
[3] See below, p. 160.   [4] Document 64.

by his personal experience and travel hath set foorth and described this passage in his Charts, which are yet to be seene in the Queens Majesties privie Gallerie at Whitehall'. Gilbert goes on to speak of the latitude of 67½ degrees reached on June 11, and of the certainty of reaching Cathay on that voyage but for the mutiny of the crew. He says that Cabot's course was on the north side of Terra de Labrador; and the whole tenor of the *Discourse* shows that Gilbert uses the name Labrador in our modern sense and not as meaning Greenland. The Cabot charts seen by Gilbert have disappeared. It is evident that they were not identical with the Paris Map of 1544, which does not show any possibility of the North West Passage. Cabot, if he sanctioned the use of his name on that map, had to keep silent on the Passage. Later, when in England, he could tell a different story. One of the charts seen by Gilbert at Whitehall may well have been the engraved issue 'cut by Clement Adams' in 1549, of which no copy is now known. This map appears to have been a revised version of the now well-known map of 1544, for Hakluyt reproduces from it the Eighth Legend about the Cabot discovery of North America in 1497. The 1549 Adams version evidently showed a North West Passage, and to effect this was probably the reason why it was re-engraved.[1]

The most detailed testimony to Sebastian Cabot's statements in his last English period occurs in *The History of Travayle in the West and East Indies*, published by Richard Willes in 1577. The relevant extracts are given in Document 65, and should be closely read. Their effect is that the maps and globe of Gemma Frisius substantially set forth Sebastian's discovery, and that a map drawn by Sebastian himself was in 1577 extant in the Earl of Bedford's library. This map showed that the entrance of the North West Passage lay between 61 and 64 degrees of north latitude, and that the strait continued westward through about 10 degrees of longitude, and then turned southerly and broadened out until it merged in the Pacific under the tropic of Cancer.

This is the only detailed account we have of the discovery which

[1] Hakluyt, *Principall Navigations* (1589), p. 511.

Cabot claimed to have made, and it is so circumstantial that a map could plausibly be drawn from the figures given by Willes. The relevant surviving work of Gemma Frisius, a famous Flemish geographer of the generation before Mercator and Ortelius, was a globe formerly preserved in Germany, but now reported to have been destroyed in the last war. Another copy, however, has been found in Italy and is now in Vienna. This will be referred to in the synthesis of evidence on the voyage.

George Beste, one of Frobisher's officers, wrote an account of the Frobisher voyages in 1578.[1] In it he said that Sebastian Cabot sailed in 1508, 'pretending' to discover the passage to Cathay. 'Pretending', as the word was then used, carried no implication of deceit. It was equivalent to our 'intending'.

Lastly, in 1582 Richard Hakluyt in his *Divers Voyages* wrote that all Sebastian Cabot's maps and discourses were then in the custody of William Worthington, an associate of Cabot in his last years, and would shortly be edited and printed.[2] Hakluyt probably meant to do this himself, but never did. The reason is unknown, but the effect is that all this valuable material has been lost. Not a trace of it is known to exist today.

In attempting to reconstruct Sebastian Cabot's voyage from this varied collection of evidence, some of it inaccurate and none of it giving a full story, the first point to consider is the date of the expedition. Three authorities give the date as 1508 or 1508–9. They are Peter Martyr in his Seventh Decade, the report made to the Venetian Senate, and George Beste. Chauveton, who may be only an inaccurate copyist of Martyr, says 1507. Then we have the Mantuan and Galvão, who both say 1496; and Ribault, 1498.

Of all these the earliest in time is Peter Martyr, who wrote in 1524 with the advantage of personal conference with Sebastian Cabot; and his statement is quite clear, 'in the sixteenth year backwards from the present'. The Venetian report of 1536 is probably the most authoritative, for an official document of this sort was

[1] Document 66.　　　　[2] Document 67.

expected to be accurate. It reads like a piece of independently acquired knowledge and not entirely a copy of Martyr's statement, and it may have come from Cabot himself: the voyage began before and ended after the death of Henry VII on 21 April 1509. An unqualified statement from such a source may be thought fairly conclusive. George Beste corroborates, but he wrote twenty years after Cabot's death, and we do not know the source of his information. It may have been Peter Martyr's Seventh Decade, in which case Beste has no independent value; or it may have been derived from Sebastian Cabot's papers then under examination by Richard Willes. The Elizabethans dealing with this matter were a small group and personally in touch with one another.

The Mantuan Gentleman says that the voyage took place in 1496, actually the year of issue of the Cabot patent. Possibly Sebastian Cabot mentioned that date in talking to him, and the Mantuan's confused mind applied it to the voyage. But 1496 is an impossible date for Sebastian to have led an expedition, and we know that John Cabot was then in charge. Galvão also gives 1496, and his opening sentence has a faint suggestion of the Mantuan's account. But wherever Galvão may have had the date, it is obviously inadmissible. This leaves Jean Ribault with his assertion of 1498. When we read Ribault's very brief notice we see that it has nothing about Sebastian Cabot's push into the icy North West or even about the Baccalaos. It is concerned with the coast between Cape Breton and the Cape of Florida. Sebastian, as we shall see, covered at least part of this coast after leaving the north-west. But Ribault's words may be an allusion to the second voyage of John Cabot, for the region they cover is exactly that which he meant to explore in 1498. If Ribault's date is right, it is certainly the second John Cabot voyage that he intends, and not the Arctic voyage of Sebastian Cabot. Why then should he give the latter's name? Simply because it was what they all did from Peter Martyr onwards. The map of 1544 did name John Cabot, but not one of the sixteenth-century writers previous to Hakluyt in 1582 ever did so. For them John Cabot was an unknown name, and Sebastian stood for the sum of English discovery. Jean Ribault took the name without question. He was not a critical historian or an Englishman, but a French man of action who died fighting the Spaniards in Florida two years after he wrote his book.

A fair review of the evidence of the date of Sebastian Cabot's voyage leaves no doubt that it was 1508-9. It may here be remarked that in any evidence of date coming from an English source the year 1508 means the year ending by our modern calendar on 24 March 1509. The Venetian report pins us to the date of the King's death, 21 April 1509. It may mean that Sebastian sailed in the spring shortly before that date and returned at any time after it; and if the start was in March, George Beste's '1508' would not be in contradiction. It may alternatively mean that Sebastian sailed in the season of 1508, made a long voyage, and did not come back until after 21 April 1509. This is rather what Peter Martyr implies. But Martyr probably got his date from Sebastian, who may have used the English calendar. Strict chronology, as we have seen, or any chronology at all, was not a matter of great concern to these sixteenth-century historians. The outcome is that Sebastian Cabot's voyage either began in the spring of 1508 and lasted a full year, or began in the early spring of 1509 and ended at any time thereafter.

Histories of that century were full of the deeds of persons and did not deal much with backgrounds, and the writers we have quoted knew nothing of the Bristol background of Sebastian Cabot. Yet he had one. He and his brothers were the inheritors of the Cabot patent. It was uncancelled, and they were free to act upon it. The Company Adventurers of 1502 was also free to trespass upon its area of operations. There may have been a fusion of interests between the Cabot patentees and the Company. Sebastian Cabot in 1505, at the age of about twenty-three, had been doing some work at Bristol which earned the King's reward. We lose sight of the Company after 1506, but that is no proof that it ceased to operate. There is therefore a possibility that all this Bristol interest was behind Sebastian Cabot two years later. His voyage can have been an effort of the Company Adventurers. It is not impossible that he had been to sea himself; in fact it is probable, or he would hardly have been qualified for command. We know that the Bristol men had been to Greenland, and that probably they and certainly the Corte Reals had been on the Newfoundland-Labrador coast. The maps show a certain penetration of Davis Strait well before 1508, although they do not distinguish between English and Portuguese discovery. The position was that both English and Portuguese had looked for the North West Passage. It appears that both parties had given it up, although we cannot be certain. The time was opportune for a new leader to revive the search. It is a testimonial to Sebastian Cabot's reputation that Bristol and the King provided the money to equip him, for we may be certain that he did not find it all himself. Henry VII and the Thornes, Asshehursts and Elyots were old hands at the game, and they saw something in Sebastian Cabot.

One circumstance, however, may remind us that the above remarks on the Bristol support given to Cabot are speculative. It is that not one of our authorities mentions the port from which he sailed. It is natural to suppose Bristol, but the venture may have been independent of Bristol, and he could have sailed from the Thames and made his way up the east coast to the point of Greenland and thence into Davis Strait. Frobisher went this way in 1576.

The cost of the expedition was borne, according to Peter Martyr, by Sebastian Cabot himself; but most of the others say that the cost was at the King's expense. From what we know of other expeditions neither statement is likely to be strictly true. In no other venture, not even in the well-attested equipment of 1498, do we find that the whole cost was borne by any single person, not even the King. The merchants between them found most of the ships, and if the King provided one the merchants paid for the lading. It is most probable that the voyage of 1508-9 was a combined royal and mercantile undertaking.

Peter Martyr's original testimony in 1516 that 300 men went on the expedition is puzzling. The number seems impossibly large, and yet Martyr was a man of great knowledge of oceanic voyages, and his words carry weight. The figure was repeated in the Venetian Senate statement, and by Gomara, Thevet and Galvão, possibly all on the authority of Peter Martyr. A little arithmetic shakes faith in it. For fighting service in the English Channel in the early Tudor period the King's great ships were manned on a scale of 1 man to $1\frac{1}{3}$ tons; and they were seldom long at sea and were able frequently to renew victuals and water. On this scale 300 men would have required 400 tons of shipping. Sebastian Cabot went with two ships on a long voyage without much certainty of renewing supplies, and for him such a scale is unlikely. We can hardly believe that he took 300 men, for at the lowest these two ships would have been of 200 tons each and their crews would have been starving before they reached the North West. Ships of that size were above the ordinary for merchantmen—we have seen the Thornes and Elyot receiving a bounty for acquiring a vessel of 120 tons. Experienced explorers, as the English now were, did not favour large ships, whose deep draught and lack of handiness were dangerous on unknown coasts. It is most improbable that Cabot's two ships together comprised anything like 400 tons, and virtually impossible that he took 300 men. Peter Martyr's figure must be a slip of some sort, uncritically accepted by his successors. There is one possibility to be considered, that some of the men were not seamen, but reinforcements for a colony, to be landed as soon as possible. But there is no evidence to that effect, except perhaps Thevet's, if one can call it evidence, and even so the discrepancy between tonnage and men would seem to be too great.

The contrast between evidence arising in Sebastian's Spanish period and that dating from his last English period is on the whole well marked. When he went to Spain in 1512, and for long afterwards, the discovery of the North West Passage by a line anywhere east of the New Found Land was contrary to Spanish interests. Spain herself was bound not to intrude in waters delimited to the Portuguese by the Treaty of Tordesillas. Both Spain and Portugal appear to have been honestly prepared to observe that treaty, although the difficulty of fixing a meridian allowed room for some divergences of opinion. We should remember that, during the whole period in which Portugal remained an independent power, Spain never sent one ship round the Cape of Good Hope into the Indian Ocean. Magellan's *Victoria* came home that way, but it was of necessity, not choice. In North America Portugal claimed the Newfoundland–Labrador coast as within her reserved longitudes, as may be seen from the Cantino map. Spain admitted that claim in her instructions to Juan de Agramonte in 1511 to open up 'cierta Tierra Nova' within the Spanish rights and to respect the King of Portugal's sphere 'within the limits marked out between ourselves and him'. Agramonte was directed to the United States coastline, and so also was Estevão Gomes in 1523–4.[1] A western passage was legitimate for Spain, but not a north-west passage past the Baccalaos and Labrador. England of course was not bound by Tordesillas, and the North West Passage was exactly what Sebastian Cabot had been trying to find when he joined the Spanish service in 1512. Probably King Ferdinand knew it, and one of his reasons for employing Cabot may have been to disarm a dangerous man by taking him into his pay. Cabot, as Martyr tells us, was intended to look for a Spanish western passage through the Gulf of Mexico.

All this explains why Sebastian Cabot did not publicly claim to have discovered the North West Passage, and why he was in such mortal fear of the revelation of his intrigue with England and Venice in 1520–2. The only published evidence for the Cathay destination in 1509, emanating from Cabot in his Spanish period, was that of the Mantuan Gentleman, gathered some years before it came into print in 1550. There he did, according to the Mantuan, avow that he sailed into the north-west seeking a road to Cathay, but he also added that land barred his way and he did not find the passage. It was a partial indiscretion in a private conversation without witnesses, and not a very damaging one.

[1] Biggar, *Precursors*, Documents XXXII, XXXIII, XLIII–L.

Sebastian Cabot's North Western Voyage

After 1548 Sebastian Cabot was in England and could say what he pleased. He produced charts and discourses to prove that he had been far into the north-west, round the northern corner of America, and had found a passage trending southwards into the Pacific, and could have gone on to Cathay but for the mutiny of his company. We ask, first, whether he had had these charts in his possession ever since 1509, a dangerous possession in Spain; and second, whether he was romancing, telling a fictitious tale in order to gain credit in England and justify the large pension allotted to him as an expert in northern discovery. On the first, we do not know: the charts and documents existed at his death and were examined by Elizabethan students. They have vanished now.

The other question, whether he told the truth, is the crux of our enquiry. The details are provided by Richard Willes, who is our research agent in the Cabot documents. Willes says that the strait opened between 61 and 64 degrees latitude, continued at the same breadth for about 10 degrees of longitude westwards, then turned southerly and broadened out to merge into the South Sea under the tropic of Cancer. On the modern map we find that Hudson Strait opens in 60½ degrees, its northern shore covers about 13 degrees of longitude in a direction about two points north of west, and it then turns southward into Hudson Bay, opening out into a large sea which Cabot could pardonably claim to be the Pacific. He underestimated the length of Hudson Strait, and he got its direction a little wrong; or perhaps Willes may have contributed to these errors. The length was by dead reckoning, never strictly accurate. The direction was by a compass almost useless so near the magnetic pole,[1] and by observations of the pole star, which may have been difficult to see at midsummer in the neighbourhood of the Arctic Circle. But out of this we have the fact that can scarcely be denied, that he passed through Hudson Strait and entered Hudson Bay. To argue that he invented those two geographical realities is to ask too much from coincidence. The further state-

---

[1] See E. G. R. Taylor, 'Hudson's Strait and the Oblique Meridian', *Imago Mundi*, vol. III (1939), pp. 48–52.

ment, that his new sea was the Pacific with free passage to the tropics, was an assumption that was certainly not a wild one. Henry Hudson a century later also made it, and died in the belief that he had opened the North West Passage. He knew nothing of his predecessor Cabot in those waters, and neither did anyone else who had not availed himself of Richard Willes.

The parallel between Cabot and Hudson is close. Both got through to the Bay, found it full of floating ice, and believed it to be the Pacific. Both thought that they were on the way to China and were stopped by mutiny. Cabot was turned back by his mutineers. Hudson was murdered by his.

Cabot's highest claimed latitude was $67\frac{1}{2}$ degrees. In the conditions it can only have been an approximation. He may have recorded it at his turning-point from the Strait to the Bay, especially if he followed the northern shore of the Strait. The latitude here would actually be about 64 degrees; but in view of the difficulties the error is not great.

The cartographer Gemma Frisius had information of Sebastian Cabot's discovery, but evidently not from Cabot himself. The Gemma Frisius globe, formerly preserved at Zerbst in Germany, was made in or before 1537, in the period in which Sebastian in Spain was keeping silence on his north-western proceedings. But inevitably others besides Cabot knew of the discovery, the crews and the interested merchants and, we can hardly doubt, Cardinal Wolsey and his staff, who promoted the project of 1521 to open an important national trade by way of the North West. Some of these people could have talked of the matter and exhibited maps, and the probability that they did so is strong. It is also probable that, the information being a valuable economic property, there was an attempt to keep it unpublished, as we can see by reading the transactions of 1521 between the King and the cardinal on the one hand and the City companies on the other. In them the orthodox New Found Land of the fishery was ostensibly made to bear a burden of negotiation and large-scale planning that was out of proportion to its value and was, in the present writer's opinion, a cover for something else.[1] Here, however, we must not fall into the error of attributing the leakage of Sebastian Cabot's secret necessarily to the affair of 1521. It could very well have occurred quite soon after the event of 1509, when the Portuguese were interested in the North West and would have appreciated the importance of Cabot's story. At any rate, it was apparently through the Portuguese that Gemma Frisius learned of the discovery and to them ambiguously attributed the credit for it. But even so, he did it with a second thought in favour of the English. It would be most interesting to know what was truly in his mind as he worked on his globe; what he had seen and heard, who were his informants, and why he was not wholly certain of his main statement.

The globe[2] shows a strait opening westwards a little south of the Arctic Circle, narrow at first, then broadening while turning in an arc south-westwards until it becomes a wide sea merging in the Pacific. All the south-westward extension is, even on Sebastian Cabot's own claims, conjectural, for he said only that he had gone part way through the passage. The general idea of the strait is consonant with Willes's description of Cabot's chart.

But Gemma Frisius does not mention Sebastian Cabot. His entitlement of the strait is: *Fretum arcticum sive trium fratrum per quod lusitani ad orientem & ad Indos & moluccas navigare conati sunt.* The three brothers of the inscription have been presumed to be the three Corte Real brothers, although only two of them explored in the North West, the eldest, Vasqueanes, having been restrained by the King of Portugal from doing so. To assert that in the above inscription Gemma Frisius declared that the Portuguese had discovered the strait is to go beyond the words. Gemma may imply it, and perhaps means it, but what he says is not that the Portuguese discovered the strait but that they attempted to use it. In Eastern Asia Gemma marks a cape as *Promontorium Corterealis* and gives a somewhat confused legend saying that Gaspar Corte Real *ultimum orientem lustraret.* This undoubtedly implies that

---

[1] See above, p. 150, n. 1.   [2] See Pl. VII.

Gaspar went right through the North West Passage and is obviously fanciful. Gaspar's voyage of 1501 covers the greatest recorded extent of Portuguese discovery, and its written record does not say that he went so far as the entrance of Hudson Strait. On the other hand, Portuguese maps of the pre-1508 period do indicate the opening of the strait. This points to an unrecorded expedition. We do not know of any from Portugal, but we do know of two from England in 1501 and 1502, of which no details are known except that Henry VII expressed his great pleasure with the result; and it may be on this unrecorded success that Sebastian Cabot founded his own push into the strait in 1509. This, however, is conjectural, and unrecorded expeditions are a dangerous base of argument.

Returning to the strait of Gemma Frisius, we find an attribution of credit to others than the Portuguese: on the land close along the coast on the southern shore, and well to the west of the narrow entrance, is inscribed *Terra per britannos inventa*. Some have seen in this a confusion of the strait with the course of the St Lawrence, first ascended by the Breton Jacques Cartier in 1535 and reported by him in the summer of 1536. It is hardly a tenable suggestion, for the waterway is evidently not intended for anything so narrow as the St Lawrence, and its mouth is above sixty degrees north and is not behind but well to the north of the island of Newfoundland, marked *Terra Corterealis*. The whole delineation bears no evidence that Gemma Frisius had heard of Cartier's second voyage. The globe may have been drawn and even engraved in 1536. Its assumed date of publication in 1537 rests on the fact that a companion celestial globe is so dated.[1] The *britannos* of the inscription are therefore more likely to be Sebastian Cabot's English than Cartier's Bretons. This was strongly held by W. F. Ganong, whose careful description and re-drawing of the outlines and inscriptions are very informative and suggestive.[2] If this was so the Gemma Frisius globe is a rather stronger testimony to an

---

[1] See below, p. 320, n. 2.
[2] Ganong, 'Crucial Maps', v, 157–62.

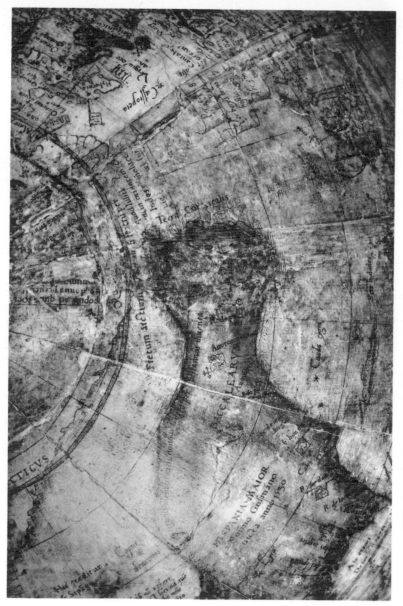

VII. Detail of terrestrial globe by Gemma Frisius, engraved c. 1537. Showing the Strait of the Three Brothers, leading to the Pacific

English than to a Portuguese discovery of Hudson Strait and Bay. A point of mere possibility, not of probability, is that the three brethren of the title could have been the three Cabots. We do not know anything of Lodovico and Sancio in 1509, and they might have accompanied Sebastian. If the name had been derived from the Corte Reals, who were probably never in the strait, it would more fittingly have been the Strait of the Two Brothers.

One other inscription needs accounting for, appearing at large on the land forming the northern shore of the strait: *Quii populi ad quos Iohannes Scolvus danus pervenit circa annum 1476.* This is not relevant to our subject, since it refers to a very hazily attested Danish expedition which, if it took place at all, reached Greenland, not Hudson Strait.[1]

The foregoing analysis, it may reasonably be suggested, shows that, according to Gemma Frisius, while the Portuguese knew of the entrance of Hudson Strait, the English may have penetrated it and entered the Bay. The English interpretation of Gemma's inscriptions is backed by the evidence of Sebastian Cabot as rendered by Richard Willes. The Portuguese claim to the discovery has no other backing. But Sebastian Cabot is a witness whose reputation is under a cloud, because he never, save in the Eighth Legend of the Paris Map, made any refutation of the false impression that he alone had led the original English voyages of discovery. If he had told the true facts of 1497 to Peter Martyr the true record would then have been established, and later historians would have been saved from great error. So we have to be careful in assessing Sebastian's story that he discovered what we know as Hudson Strait and Bay. He told this story after his return to England in 1548, when he had ample opportunity of seeing the published work of Gemma Frisius. An obvious suggestion is that he may simply have lifted his strait from Gemma Frisius. But that opens a new question. Who discovered the strait of Gemma Frisius if it was not Sebastian Cabot? The pre–1509 map evidence leads only to the entrance of Hudson Strait. Gemma Frisius takes

[1] See above, p. 12.

his *Britanni* well within it and shows it opening into a sea. There is no Portuguese candidate for this achievement. Again, Sebastian claimed long before 1537 that he had discovered a strait of great value for trade with Asia. His claim lies in the records of 1521–2, in the English discussions with Sebastian of a rich island which John Cabot had spoken of, but which had never yet been reached; and in Sebastian's own statement to the Venetian in Valladolid, that he had discovered the important strait. All this was pre-Gemma, and may have formed part of Gemma's information.

The conclusion of the present writer is that Sebastian Cabot did discover Hudson Strait and part of Hudson Bay in 1509 or 1508–9.

Sebastian Cabot was not primarily a geographer seeking scientific fame but an explorer for an economic prize, the short way to Asia. When he was forced back from the North West he looked for another solution. He turned southward to the fishery, and thence down the United States coastline. Other English expeditions had been there before him. But the seaboard was of great extent, and there were several promising openings. The Spaniards had hopes of this coast with Gomes's expedition in 1524, and there were others, so that not until the end of the century did the possibility fade of a passage through temperate North America. Cabot looked for a channel leading westward through the land, and failed to find one. At about the latitude of Gibraltar he turned for Europe. He reached England some time after April 1509 to find Henry VII dead and the new government uninterested in discovery. It is not certain whether he accomplished all this in a single season or whether he wintered somewhere on the American coast.

The first period of English discovery ended at the death of Henry VII, and it is fairly evident that he himself was its patron. He was not perhaps its inspirer, for the initiative came from Bristol; but he was sympathetic and was prepared to make oceanic discovery an element in his foreign policy. His direct expenditure of money upon it was small, but by taking the risk of antagonizing Spain and Portugal in a diplomatic situation that was always difficult and sometimes threatened his throne, he made a noticeable contribution to the cause. The reason is clear: the prize was an English trade with Asia; and Henry was an economist of the mercantile school which linked foreign trade with national greatness. He was his own chief minister, and we cannot discern any councillor who may have acted as his deputy in handling the oceanic business. At his death the interest was checked, and his son did not revive it for several years.

Of Sebastian Cabot as a person up to the time he left England for Spain we have no information. There is nothing on record about him save that he gained the King's favour in 1505 and led the expedition of 1509. What sort of commander he then was we cannot tell. When he took service with Ferdinand he was about thirty. In his Spanish period his portrait is that of a man respected for his attainments, but not loved; although Peter Martyr speaks of him with an approach to cordiality. The great men thought well of him, but the lesser men did not. Charles V, Henry VIII, Wolsey, were impressed with his qualities. Most of his subordinates in the River Plate exploration disliked him. So also, we may conclude, did the younger Robert Thorne, who invested money in the expedition, but markedly refrained from mentioning its commander's name in the well-known letter to Dr Lee. If he had had any enthusiasm for Sebastian Cabot, Thorne would have shown it in that letter. Sebastian in his Spanish period was a man with a secret to guard, occasionally unbending but commonly holding himself in, with the great matter of the North West Passage in the background of his mind. In his old age, in his last ten years in England, he was a different man, liked, trusted, looked up to. Northumberland and his associates paid him well, made him governor of their new trading monopoly, and gave him a free hand with the planning of the voyage. Richard Eden visited him when his health began to fail and his mind to wander. To Stephen Borough the sea captain he was 'the good old gentleman Master Cabota', who went down to Gravesend to wish God-speed to an exploring expedition, made great cheer at the inn for the ship's company, and 'entered into the dance himself amongst the rest of the young and lusty company'. That was little more than a year before the old man's death, and it is the liveliest picture we have of him in the whole of his life.

No portrait exists of John Cabot, and no scrap of his handwriting. There was formerly a painting of Sebastian Cabot, seen by Purchas at Whitehall in the reign of James I, and rediscovered in a private house in 1792. An engraving was made of it, and has been reproduced in several books. Richard Biddle bought the original picture, which was lost when his house in Pennsylvania was burnt in 1845. It is not certain that this portrait was painted during the lifetime of the subject: it may have been commissioned by the Muscovy Company some time after his death, when his reputation in England continued to advance; for the inscription upon it does not appear to be contemporary.

The story of the early efforts in discovery has been progressively built up in the past hundred years, but even now it has not gained a place in the canon of our national history. A bare sentence or two is as much as it receives in general histories. This is no doubt because the obscure and controversial nature of many of the topics makes considerable reading necessary to their understanding. But the subject cannot fairly be shirked, since the first navigators between England and North America were the beginners of the United States and the British Commonwealth.

DOCUMENTS

DOCUMENTS

BRISTOL AND THE ATLANTIC IN THE FIFTEENTH CENTURY

1

BRISTOL TRADE WITH ICELAND IN THE FIFTEENTH CENTURY

From the Bristol Customs Records in the Public Record Office. These are examples of a larger number of entries relating to Bristol trade with Iceland. There is no possibility of confusion with Ireland, which is always named Hibernia. The customs records are incomplete for Edward IV and fragmentary for Henry VII.

(i) *E. 122/161, 31. Undated ledger, temp. Hen. VI*
The bark called the John the Evangelist in which Germanus Lynch is master came from Iseland the xijth day of June and has in it
 for Thomas Rowley, denizen, iiij lastes and a half of salt fish, value xlv pounds, subsidy xlv shillings
 for the same, v lasts giltfissh, value xxv pounds, subsidy xxv shillings
 for the same, j last and ij hundredweight titeling, value lx shillings, subsidy iij shillings
[The *Ive* of Bristol arrived from Iceland on the same day.]

(ii) *E. 122/19, 1. Ledger, 1 Ed. IV*
[1461] The ship called the John of Fowey in which Hugh Davy is master came from Norbarn on this day [August 20] and has in it
for John Jay, denizen, vij last stokffish, value xxxv pounds, subsidy xxxv shillings;
 for the same, ij last tetelyng, value v pounds, subsidy v shillings;
[Several more merchants imported fish in this ship, and two other vessels arrived from Norbarn on the same day.]¹

---

¹ Norbarn was in Norway, but the entry is given for its mention of John Jay.

(iii) *E. 122/19, 7, Ledger, 10 Ed. IV*

[1471] The ship called the Antony of Bristol in which John Deanfitz is master came from Islond on this day [September 10] and has in it
    for John Forster, denizen, xxxv last lyng, value lxx pounds, subsidy lxx shillings
    for the same, xv last stokfysshe, value lxxv pounds, subsidy lxxv shillings
    for John Gregorie, denizen, j last salt fish, value x pounds, subsidy x shillings

(iv) *E. 122/19, 11. Ledger, 15 Ed. IV*

[1476] The bark called the Mary Byrde in which William Orner is master sailed for Iseland the xxvijth day of April and has in it [a general cargo laded by John Godeman].

(v) *E. 122/19, 13. Controlment, 17–18 Ed. IV*

[1478] The ship called the Antony of Bristol in which John Brislie is master sailed for Iselond on this day (March 6) and has in it [general cargo for John Forster].

[1479] The bark called the Ive of Bristol in which John Geough is master sailed for Iselond the xvijth day of February and has in it [general cargo for John Forster].

(vi) *E. 122/19, 14. Ledger, 19–20 Ed. IV*

[1481] The bark called the Leonard of Bristol in which John Gogh is master sailed for Iseland on this day [February 12] and has in it [general cargo for Dionisius Bracy].

[1481] The bark called the Christopher of Bristol in which Thomas Sutton is master sailed for Iseland on this day [February 14] and has in it [general cargo for John Shipward].

(vii) *E. 122/20, 5. Ledger, 1–2 Hen. VII*

[1486] The ship called the Trinity of London in which Thomas Sutton is master came from Islonde on this day [September 18] and has in it [fish and brimstone].

176

(viii) *E. 122/20, 9. Ledger, 8–9 Hen. VII*

[1493] The bark called the Michael, Robert Gege master, sailed for Island on this day [May 8].

[1493] The bark called the Barbara, John Pembroke master, came from Island the xvth day of September.

2

THE SPHERE AND THE WESTWARD PASSAGE TO ASIA

Cardinal Pierre d'Ailly, *Imago Mundi* (written *c.* 1410; printed *c.* 1480).

The Eighth Chapter. Of the extent of the Earth that is habitable.

For the investigation of the extent of the habitation of the earth it must be understood that habitation is considered in two ways. In one way in respect of climate, or how much is habitable by reason of the sun's heat and how much is not, and of this we have spoken generally above. In another way it may be considered in respect of water, or to what extent it is hindered by water; and of this we are now to consider. Concerning which matter the opinions of the wise are varied. For Ptolemy in his book of the disposition of the sphere holds that about a sixth part of the earth is habitable with respect to water, and all the remainder is covered by water. And also in the second book of the Almagest it states that habitation is known in only a quarter of the earth, or that in which we live, whose length is from the east to the west and is half that of the equator, and its breadth is from the equator to the pole and is a fourth of the great circle. But Aristotle in the end of his book of the sky and the earth has it that more than a quarter may be inhabited. And Averroes confirms this. And Aristotle says that the sea is little between the farthest bound of Spain from the east and the nearest of India from the west. And he does not speak of the nearer Spain that is now commonly called Spain, but of the farther Spain that is now named Africa, of which certain authors speak, such as Pliny, Orosius and Isidore. Moreover Seneca in the fifth book of the things of nature says that this sea is navigable in a few days if the wind be favourable. And Pliny teaches in the second book on natural things that it is navigated from the Arabian Gulf to the Herculean Gades in no very great time. Whence, from these and many other reasonings, on which I shall touch more fully when I speak of the ocean, some conclude that manifestly the sea is not so great that it can cover three-quarters of the earth. The authority of Esdras in his fourth book supports this, who says that six parts of the earth are inhabited and the seventh is covered with the waters; the authority of which book the saints held in reverence and confirmed the sacred truths by it. And therefore it seems that although the extent of habitation known to Ptolemy and those who follow him may be confined within a fourth part, more nevertheless is habitable. And Aristotle could have known more about this by the aid of Alexander, and Seneca by that of Nero, who were both accustomed to investigate the uncertain things of this world, as Pliny states of Alexander in his eighth book, and Solinus also, and Seneca tells of Nero in his book of natural things. Whence it seems that more trust is to be placed in them than in Ptolemy and also in Albategnus, who states that even less is habitable, namely the twelfth part only; but proof is lacking for that to be advanced. But for brevity I pass on, and also because the unfolding of this matter will better appear in what follows. From the foregoing therefore, and from what is to be said below, it appears that the habitable earth is not round like a disc as Aristotle says, but is as the fourth part of the surface of a sphere, of which fourth the two outermost parts are to some extent cut off, namely those which are not inhabited by reason of too great heat or cold. And this cannot be shown as conveniently in a plane as in a spherical diagram.[1]

[1] A globe. Terrestrial globes were evidently known to d'Ailly, although none of his time has survived.

3

FIFTEENTH-CENTURY INDICATIONS OF UNKNOWN
LANDS IN THE ATLANTIC

Bartolomé de las Casas, *Historia de las Indias*, lib. I, cap. xiii (first printed
1552).

Christopher Columbus says then, amongst other things that he
wrote in his notebooks, that speaking with mariners, various persons who were accustomed to navigate the western seas, especially
to the islands of the Azores and Madeira, amongst others a pilot of
the King of Portugal, named Martin Vicente, told him that, finding himself on one occasion 450 leagues to the west of Cape St
Vincent, he saw and took into his ship from the sea a piece of
wood artificially worked, and, as he judged, not by means of an
iron tool, from which circumstance, and because there had been
west winds for many days, he imagined that this timber came
from some island or islands lying to the westward. Also another
man named Pero Correa, a brother-in-law of the same Christopher Columbus, married to his wife's sister, informed him that
in the island of Puerto Sancto he had seen another piece of wood
which had come with the same winds and was fashioned in the
same shape, and that he had also seen very large canes which could
contain in their cavities three measures of water or wine; and
Christopher Columbus says that he heard the King of Portugal
say this, speaking with him on those matters, and that the King
ordered the canes to be shown to him [Columbus]. And he held
for certain [said Columbus] that the said canes were from some
islands or island which was not very distant, or were brought from
the Indies by the force of the wind and the sea, since in all our
parts of Europe there are none, or at least he did not know that
there were any like them. It confirmed him in that belief, that
Ptolemy, in Book I, cap. 27 of his *Cosmographia*, says that such
canes were to be found in India.

Again it was made known to Columbus by some inhabitants of
the Azores that when the wind blew strong from the west and

north-west the sea brought certain pine-trunks and deposited them on the coasts of those islands, especially in the islands of Graciosa and Fayal, there being no part of those islands which grew pines. Others told him that in the isle of Flores, which is one of the Azores, the sea had brought up the bodies of two dead men who seemed very broad in the face and of an appearance different from that of Christians. Another time, they say that in the Cabo de la Verga, which is in . . . , and in that neighbourhood, they saw hollowed trunks or canoes with a movable covering, which by chance, passing from one island or place to another, the force of the winds and the sea brought thither, and those whom they carried, not being able to turn back, perished, and the canoes, since they never sink, came to land in time at the Azores.

In the same manner a certain Antonio Leme, dwelling in the island of Madeira, told him that having sailed once with his caravel far to the westward, he had seen three islands to which he came close, which may have been true or not; at least they say that there were many reports among the people, especially in the islands of Gomera and Hierro, and many in the Azores affirmed and swore, that every year certain islands were seen towards the west. To that Columbus said that they might be the islands of which Pliny declares in Book II, cap. 97 of his *Natural History*, that towards the north the sea washes away certain woods from the land, which have such great roots that it carries them like rafts upon the water which from a distance resemble islands. Seneca supports that, who says in Book III of *Naturalia* that there is a kind of stones so porous and light that in India they form as it were islands which go floating on the water, and of the same sort must be those which they call St Brandan's in whose history they say that he read that there were many islands seen on the sea about the isles of Cape Verde and the Azores, which were always burning and must be like those above mentioned: there is a notice of the same in the book named Inventio fortunata.

Moreover, Columbus says that in the year 1484 he saw in Portugal that an inhabitant of the island of Madeira came to seek from the King a caravel to go to discover a certain land that he swore he saw every year and always in the same manner, in which he agreed with the people of the Azores. Whence it followed that, in the charts made in times past, there were depicted certain islands in that sea and vicinity, especially the island called Antilla, and they placed it little more than 200 leagues west of the Canaries and the Azores. This was the judgment of the Portuguese, and to this day they do not forsake the opinion that it may be the island of the Seven Cities, the fame and desire of which has reached us also, and has caused many to act foolishly in quest of it and to expend much money with no profit and with great loss, as, if God pleases will appear in the course of this history. This island of the Seven Cities, say the Portuguese, according to report, was peopled by them at the time when Spain was conquered in the reign of the King Don Rodrigo; and they say that to escape that persecution seven bishops and many people embarked, and with their ships came to land at the said island, where each of them made his settlement, and lest the people should think of turning back they set fire to the ships. And it is said that in the time of the Infante Don Enrique of Portugal there ran there a storm-driven ship which had sailed from Oporto and did not stop until it came there, and when they landed those of the island took them to the church to see if they were Christians and used the Roman ceremonies, and seeing that they were, they asked them to stay there until their lord should come, who was some distance away, but the sailors, fearing lest they should set fire to the ship and detain them there, suspecting that they did not desire to be known by anyone, returned to Portugal very gladly, hoping to receive a reward from the Infante; whom, they say, he ill-treated and ordered them to go back, but the master and the others dared not do so, for which reason, once out of that kingdom they never again re-turned there: they say also that the sailors gathered certain earth or sand for their cook-room, and found that great part of it was gold.

Some have started from Portugal to seek that land which, by common use, is called Antilla, amongst whom sailed one named

Diego Detiene, whose pilot, Pedro de Velasco, an inhabitant of Palos, assured the same Christopher Columbus, in the monastery of Sancta María de la Rábida, that they had set out from the island of Fayal, and went 150 leagues with the *viento lebechio*, which is the north-west wind, and on putting about they discovered the island of Flores, guiding themselves by the numbers of birds they saw flying thither, for they recognized them as land birds and not seabirds, and so they judged that they must go to some land to sleep. Afterwards, they say, they went so far to the north-east that they reached Cape Clear, which is in Ireland towards the east, where they observed the west winds to blow very strongly and the sea was very smooth, from which they believed that it must be because of the land that must be there which gave shelter in the western direction; which they did not follow up by going to discover it, for it was in August, and they feared the onset of winter. This, it is said, was forty years before Columbus discovered our Indies. In agreement with this is what a decrepit sailor told the said Columbus, in the port of Santa Maria, that in a voyage that he had made to Ireland he had seen a land that others believed to exist there, and they imagined it was Tartary which projected that way by the east, which I believe truly was that which we now call the Bacallaos, which they could not approach on account of the terrible winds.

Again, a sailor named Pedro de Velasco, a Galician, told Columbus in Murcia that, going on an Irish voyage they were sailing and running so much to the north-west that they saw land to the west of Ireland, and those who were in that voyage believed it must be what a certain Hernan Dolinos sought to discover, as shall presently be told. A Portuguese pilot named Vicente Diaz, an inhabitant of Tavira, making from Guinea for the island of Terceira in the Azores, having passed the locality of the island of Madeira, and running westwards, saw or seemed to see an island which he was certain was veritable land; and he, coming to the said island of Terceira, told the secret to a very rich Genoese merchant, a friend of his, whose name was Lucas de

Cazana, whom he persuaded earnestly to fit him out for that discovery, with all things that were necessary; who, after having obtained licence from the King of Portugal to do so, sent security for his brother Francisco de Cazana, living in Seville, to equip a vessel with all speed and deliver it to the said pilot Vicente Diaz; but the said Francisco de Cazana frustrated the design and would not accomplish it. The pilot returned to Terceira, and then the said Lucas de Cazana equipped him, and the pilot set out three or four times to seek the said land to a distance of a hundred leagues and more; and now he could find nothing, so that the pilot and his backer lost hope of ever finding it. And in his notebooks Columbus relates all this, which the same brother Francisco de Cazana told him, and he added further that he had seen two sons of the captain who discovered the said island of Terceira, who were named Miguel and Gaspar Corte Real, go at different times to seek that land, and that they perished in the quest one after the other without anything being heard of them.

4

PORTUGUESE PROJECTS FOR FINDING THE
SEVEN CITIES AND OTHER ATLANTIC ISLANDS

Lisbon, Archivo nacional da Torre do Tombo. Original Portuguese printed by Bernardino José de Senna Freitas, *Memoria historica sobre o intentado descobrimento nos annos 1649–1770* (Lisbon, 1845), App., Documents B, E, G; also in *Alguns documentos da Torre do Tombo* (Lisbon, 1891), pp. 32, 37, 58.

[1462] Dom Affomsso,[1] etc., to all who shall see this charter we make known that the Infante Dom Fernando my very esteemed and beloved brother has informed us that one Guomcallo Fernamdez, an inhabitant of Tavira, coming from the fisheries of the Rio de Ouro in the direction north-west of the Canary Islands and the island of Madeira, had sight of an island, and because the weather was contrary he could not land on it, which [island] my

[1] King Afonso V, 1438–81.

said brother sent to discover by certain signs that they gave him of it, and they did not find it; and that inasmuch as he now wishes to send again to seek it, [and] asks us that by favour we shall give it thus and in the form in which we have given him the other seven isles that Diego Affomso, his esquire, found near Cape Verde: and that we, having seen his petition begging [us] to make him grace and grant, we hold it for good, and we bestow the said island that he has found, or that may at any time be found by his ships or by any others whatsoever in the said region. And we desire that he shall have and hold it from us fully, with all dues and rights and power of justice, thus and in the manner that he now has and holds the said seven isles of which we have made him grant. And meanwhile we order all our magistrates, judges and officers of justice, and persons to whom the knowledge of these presents pertains and to whom this our charter may be shown, that they accomplish it and observe it and cause it to be accomplished and observed as if in there is contained and has been contained [what is] in the other charter of grant that we have made to him of the seven isles, without there being placed on it hindrance or doubt, for thus and not otherwise he holds our grant. Given at Lisbon the twenty-ninth of October in the year of Our Lord Jesus Christ 1462.

[1475] Dom Affomso, etc. to all who shall see this my charter I make known that I have made a grant by a charter of mine to Fernam Tellez, governor and chief majordomo of the Princess my very beloved and esteemed daughter, of any islands to be discovered by him, and by his ships or men that he sends for this purpose, or that go to seek them for him, provided that they (the islands) be not in the seas of Guinea. According to what at greater length is contained in the said charter it does not make clear [whether they be?] uninhabited islands and those which the said Fernam Tellez by himself or others may cause to be peopled. And it might happen that, in thus sending out to seek them, his ships or people might find the Seven Cities or some other inhabited islands which at the present time have not been navigated to or discovered or traded with by my subjects, and it might be said that the grant I have thus made must not extend to them on account of their being thus inhabited. I declare by this my [present] charter that my intention and purpose then at the time I thus gave them was that the said charter comprises islands both inhabited and uninhabited, and that it is my pleasure that he shall have in them all the lordship and jurisdiction and power over the inhabitants and for them the same privileges and liberties, that I gave by the said charter for the inhabitants of the other islands. And in case he should wish to forbid that any persons of my kingdoms and lordships, and of any others whatsoever, should enter or go to them without his licence or authority, and [only] by contract that they may make with him, as I granted to the Infante Dom Amrique[1] my uncle, whom God have in his keeping, and now have granted to the prince my most beloved and esteemed son, I decree, desire, order and forbid all my said people and subjects, and all others of whatsoever nations they may be, that without licence, authority and orders of the said Fernam Tellez they shall not go to nor enter any inhabited islands whatsoever that may be discovered by the said Fernam Tellez or his ships or people, in the same manner that I have forbidden it in Guinea. And this on condition that the said islands shall not be in the seas adjoining Guinea which I have already given to my said son, and shall not hitherto have been traded with or visited by my subjects of these my realms of Castile and Portugal. And I desire and command all my officers of justice that, against those who shall do the contrary and shall trespass against this my charter of prohibition and command, they shall fully execute and cause to be executed all the penalties set forth and imposed on those who without licence of my said uncle should have gone to Guinea or who now should go without the licence of my said son; because thus it pleases me that it shall be done and accomplished by the said Fernam Tellez, who has the desire to send to seek and discover them and to take care that if they should be found great advantage may come to my realms.

[1] Henry the Navigator, d. 1460.

And also, because the said Fernam Tellez has done for me in the said realms so many and signal services, I am pleased to do him this and much greater favours, and it is my pleasure and desire that all this shall thus be observed and accomplished from now and for all time. And in witness of the same I order him to be given this charter signed and sealed with the seal. Given in the Chamber the tenth of November at the date of 75 years.

[1486] Dom Joham,[1] etc., to all who shall see this our charter we make known that we have seen a deed of contract and gift made between Fernam Dulmo and Joham Afomso do Estreito, an inhabitant of the island of Madeira, the tenor of which is word for word as follows: In the name of God amen, know you who shall see this deed of contract that in the year of Our Lord Jesus Christ 1486, on the 12th of July in the city of Lisbon, there appeared in the Notarial Bureau Fernam Dulmo, gentleman of our lord the King's household and Captain of the island of Terceira, who now goes as captain to discover the Island of the Seven Cities by order of our lord the King; and there appeared also Joham Afomso do Estreito, an inhabitant of the region of Funchal in the island of Madeira, and thereupon the said Fernam Dulmo presented to me the notary a document of the following tenor: Dom Joham, by the grace of God King of Portugal and of the Algarve on this side of the sea, and on the other in Africa Lord of Guinea, we make known that Fernam Dulmo, gentleman and Captain in the island of Terceira for the Duke Manuel my very esteemed and beloved cousin, came now to us and told us how he wished to discover a large island or islands or mainland by the coast, which is supposed to be the Island of the Seven Cities, and all this at his own cost and expense, and that he prayed us that we should make him a grant and royal donation of the said island or islands or mainland that he, or another by his orders, may thus discover or find; and so we grant him the right of all justice, with power of death and of all other penalties of the said island, etc. [continues with details of grant].

1 King John II, 1481–95

5

BRISTOL TRADE WITH MADEIRA

From the Bristol Customs Records in the Public Record Office.

(i) *E. 122/19, 14. Ledger, 19–20 Ed. IV*

[1480] The bark called the Mawdeleyn of Kimperley [Quimperlé] in which Johannes de Chayston is master sailed for Madeira the xviijth of May and has in it [cargo for English merchants].

(ii) *E. 122/20, 5. Ledger, 1–2 Hen. VII*

[1486] The bark called the Mare Petat in which Lusianus is master came from Madeira the xixth of September and has in it [sugar and bowstaves for various Portuguese merchants, including 'Gunsalus' and 'ffornandus', their Christian names not given].

6

THE VOYAGE OF 1480

Statement from the *Itinerarium* of William Worcestre, a manuscript preserved at Corpus Christi College, Cambridge (MS 210). The MS was first edited by James Nasmith, Cambridge, 1778. Mr John Harvey, F.S.A., F.R.S.L., who is now (1960) working on this MS, has generously extended to the present writer the use of his transcript of the relevant passage in the MS, accompanied by, in his own words, 'a rough literal translation'.

[p. 195] Johēs Jay sēds maritus Johāne sororis mee obijt die. 15. mes maij a° x̄p̄ī

.   .   .   .

1480 die. 15. jullij Navis   et Johīs Jay junioris ponderis. 80. dolior/ jncepeɍ/t̄ viagū apd. portum Bristollie de Kyngrode vsqz ad insulam de Brasylle in occidētli pte hibernie sulcando maria per   et   Thloyde est magist^r navis. scientificus marinarius tocius Anglie. et nova veneɍ/t̄ Bristollie die lue. 18. die septēbris qd. dicta navis velaueɍ/t̄ maria p̄ c^{r}ca. 9. mēses nec jnveneɍ/t̄

jnsulam sed p̄ tempestas maris reuersi sūt vsqz. portum   in
hibernia p₀ reposic̄ōē navis & marinarior/.

John Jay the second, husband of my sister Joan,[1] died on 15 May
in the year of Christ

. . . .

1480 on the 15 day of July the ship   and of John Jay junior,
of 80 tons burden, began a voyage at the port of Bristol from
King Road to the Island of Brasylle on the west part of Ireland,
ploughing the seas for   and   Thloyde is the ship's
master, the [most] knowledgeable seaman of the whole of England; and news came to Bristol on Monday 18 September[2] that
the said ship had sailed the seas for about nine months but had not
found the island; but had been turned back by storms at sea to the
harbour of   in Ireland to refit the ship and [refresh] the
crew.

7

THE VOYAGE OF 1481

(i)

From an Inquisition at Bristol, 3 September 1481. Bristol Customs
Records in the Public Record Office: E. 122/19, 16. Document discovered by Professor W. E. C. Harrison and included in his unpublished thesis (1931) in the University of London; translation
published by him in *The Mariner's Mirror*, vol. XVI (1930), pp. 198–9.
Original Latin text printed by D. B. Quinn, *The Mariner's Mirror*, vol.
XXI (1935), p. 283. Here re-translated.

Thomas Croft of Bristol, armiger, customer of the said lord the
King in the port of his town of Bristol aforesaid on the sixth day
of July in the aforesaid year [1481] of the aforesaid King at Bristol
aforesaid was owner of an eighth part of a ship or balinger called
the *Trynite* and of an eighth part of a certain ship or balinger called
the *George*, and in each of the said ships or balingers the said

---

[1] Mr Harvey notes: 'Johannes Jay secundus maritus, etc.' may mean John Jay
the younger, but could mean John Jay the second husband, etc.
[2] Correct for 1480.

Thomas Croft on the said sixth day of July in the aforesaid year at Bristol aforesaid laded, shipped and placed forty bushels of salt of the value of twenty shillings for the repair, equipment and maintenance of the aforesaid ship or balinger, and not with the intention of trading but of examining and finding [*causa scrutando & inveniendo*] a certain island called the Isle of Brasil.

(ii)

From a Pardon issued to Thomas Croft, 20 January 1483. M.R., L.T.R., E. 368/255, Recorda, Hilary Term, 22 Edward IV, m. 10. The document was discovered by Professor Quinn and printed by him, *loc. cit.*

It is found amonges other thinges that Thomas Croft of Bristoll squier oon of our custumers in our said porte of Bristowe aforesaid was possessed of the viij th part of a shipp or Balinger called the *Trinite* & of the viijth part of an other shipp or Balinger callyd the *george* & in to every of the said shipps or Balingers the said Thomas Croft the same vj day of July the foresaid xxj yere of our reigne at Bristowe afore said shipped and put xl buschels of salt to the value of xx s. for the reparacion and sustentacion of the said shippes or Balingers and not by cause of marchandise but to thentent to serch & fynde a certain Isle called the Isle of Brasile as in the said Inquisicion more playnly yt dothe appere.

THE CABOTS TO 1495

8

JOHN CABOT'S NATURALIZATION AT VENICE

Venice, Archivio di Stato: (i) Senato Terra, Reg. VII, fol. 109v; (ii) Privilegi, Reg. II, fol. 53. Italian texts printed by H. P. Biggar, *The Precursors of Jacques Cartier* (Ottawa, 1911), pp. 1–6, with English translation.

(i) *The Grant: 29 March 1476*

That a privilege of citizenship, both internal and external, be made out for John Cabot on account of fifteen years' residence, as usual. Ayes, 149. Noes, 0. Neutrals, 0.

(ii) *Terms of the privilege*

That since whoever has resided in Venice continuously for fifteen years or more, and during that period has fulfilled the duties and borne the charges of our government, is to be henceforward a citizen and one of our Venetians, and is to enjoy for ever and everywhere the rights, liberties and immunities exercised and enjoyed by the other Venetians our citizens: wherefore as the prudent man [name inserted] has notified us by proper and clear proofs which have been carefully verified by the magistrates of our municipality, that he has inhabited Venice continuously for fifteen years, conducting himself towards us and our duchy faithfully and worthily, with wholehearted devotion, and submitting regularly to the duties and charges of our government, things worthy of reward, we have received and do receive the said person, the proper formality having been observed, as a Venetian and our citizen within and without, and have created and do create him a Venetian and our citizen within and without, and desire him to be and act and be held and treated as a Venetian and our citizen in Venice and without, everywhere, in such a manner that the said person may for the rest freely enjoy and make use of all the liberties, rights and immunities that the other Venetians, our citizens, have and enjoy within and without, it being understood that he cannot himself trade or carry on trade through others by sea or in the German warehouse or with Germans, unless he has given security for this to our government within the year. In witness and more complete evidence whereof we have caused the present privilege to be drawn up, and our leaden seal to be affixed thereto. Given in our Ducal Palace on . . . in the year of our Lord's incarnation. . . .

9

STATEMENT THAT JOHN CABOT
WAS OF ENGLISH ORIGIN

From MS notes in the Boston Public Library. Printed by C. R. Beazley, *John and Sebastian Cabot* (London, 1898), pp. 293–4.

In the copy in the above library of *Ragguagli sulla vita et sulle opere di Marin Sanuto*, by Rawdon Brown (Venice, 1837), its author, who had made deep research in the Venetian archives, has inserted these manuscript notes. The documents to which he refers have not otherwise come to light.

'Mr Rawdon Brown will gladly show Mrs R. E. Apthorp what he considers documentary evidence of John Cabot's English origin, and of his never having come to Venice (where he married a Venetian woman, who bore him Sebastian and his other sons) until the year 1461. Casa della Vida, Thursday, 2 p.m.'

[on another page] 'I printed this in the year 1837; but in 1855–6 it became manifest, through documents discovered in the Venice Archives, that John Cabot really owed his birth to England.'

10

NAMES RESEMBLING CABOT AT BRISTOL, 1483–6:
JOHN CORBET, JOHN DE SAVOT, JOHN CHAVET

From the Bristol Customs Records in the Public Record Office.

(i) *E. 122/20, 1. Ledger, 1 Rich. III*

[19 August 1483] The bark called the Seint Spryte of Fontarabia, in which Johannes de Savot is master, sailed for Spain the xixth day of August.

(ii) *E. 122/20, 5. Ledger, 1–2 Hen. VII*

[15 October 1485] The bark called the Michael of Bristol, in which Johannes Corbet is master, sailed for Welba [Huelva] the xvth day of October [with cargo of cloth for various merchants, including Robert Thorne and John Jay].

[17 March 1486] The bark called the Michael of Bristol, in which Johannes Corbet is master, came from Welba on this day [with cargo of wine and oil for numerous merchants, including Robert Thorne].

[18 April 1486] The bark called the Michael of Bristol, in which Johannes Corbet is master, sailed for Andalusia the xviijth day of April [with cloth for various merchants, including John Jay].

[18 June 1486] The bark called the Mary of Saint Sebastian, in which Johannes Chavet is master, came from Spain on this day [with cargo, partly of iron, evidently from North Spain, for John Jay and others].

[18 September 1486] The bark called the Michael of Bristol in which Johannes Corbet is master, came from Lisbon, the xviijth day of September [with cargo for numerous merchants including Richard Warde, John Jay, and Robert Thorne].

11

RECORDS OF JOHN CABOT AT VENICE, 1482–4

Venice, Archivio di Stato. Extracted and first published by Rodolfo Gallo in *Atti della Accademia Nazionale dei Lincei*, Cl. Sc. Mor., Stor., Fil., ser. VIII, vol. III (1948), pp. 209–18. Of Signor Gallo's fifteen documents, the first deals with Cabot's naturalization, as recorded in our Document 8. Nos. ii–v are concerned with the property before Cabot's name is mentioned, and provide no evidence about him. Nos. vi–xv are translated below, in chronological order. For the translations, here printed by kind permission of Signor Gallo, the editor is indebted to Professor D. B. Quinn and Mr J. P. Maguire. The passages evidential on

John Cabot and his family are here given. The formal clauses and numerous signatures of officials, together with the registration numbers of the original manuscripts, are omitted but are printed in full in the volume noted above.

(ix) *27 September* [1482]

I, Joannes Grifonus, son of Messer Dominicus, as guardian of Marieta, daughter of the late Pasqualis Bragandinus, my kinsman, for whom I and also my successors give a legal undertaking of sale of the same things, that in the name of God and Christ I do give, sell and make over to you Joannes Caboto, son of the late Egidius, merchant, and your successors all that property, which is certain houses of sergeants, partly habitable and partly ruined, with all etc., situated within the boundaries of S. Jacobus de Luprio, for the price of 500 ducats, according to the form of the written contract in the name of the said Marieta.

(x) *27 September 1482. In Iachomo de Lorio*

Messer Giofani Grifon, son of the late Messer Domenego, guardian of Donna Marieta, daughter of the late Messer Pasqual Bragadin, as such gives a legal undertaking of sale to Messer Zuane Chaboto of further houses of sergeants with all their possessions and appurtenances, situated within the boundary of San Iachomo de Lorio, for 500 ducats, according to the terms of the contract of sale drawn up on behalf of the said Donna Marieta.

(xi) *17 December 1483. In San Iachomo de Lorio*

Messer Zuan Gaboto has had registered with the Court of the Proprio a piece of property within the boundary of San Iachomo de Lorio which he bought from Messer Zuan Grifon, the guardian of Marieta, daughter of the late Messer Pasqual Bragadin, for 500 ducats, according to the agreements drawn up at the Mcsetaria.

(vii) *13 January* [1484]

I, Johannes Caboto, son of Messer [blank], with my successors, make manifest in the name of God and of Christ, that I do give, sell, make over and give bond to you, Mathye, my beloved wife, and to your successors, for security of your dowry, which was and is in sum 75 gold ducats together, all that certain property which is a house of sergeants, with all its possessions and appurtenances, situated within the boundaries of S. Nicolas, and a small piece of meadow land in the district of Clugia and three saltworks in the same. With condition that in the event of any restitution of the 75 ducats by me or by my heirs you are to restore the said things.

(viii) *13 January 1484. In San Nicolo*

Messer Zuan Chabotto gives and makes over to Donna Mattia, his wife, as security for her dowry which is 75 ducats, a house within the boundary of San Nicolo of Mandigoli, and another house situated in Chioza [Chioggia] in the parish of San Nicolo di Chioza, a stretch of meadow land and three salt works in the district of Chioza under these conditions, that in the event of any restitution of the dowry [he is] to restore to the said Donna Mattia the said 75 ducats and that she be obliged to give back the said things.

(xii) *29 April 1484. In San Iachomo de Lorio.*

Messer Zuan Chaboto in his own name and in the name of Messer Piero, his brother, gives as surety to Messer Chabriel Morexini, son of the late Messer Francesco, a piece of property of his, situated within the boundary of San Iachomo de Lorio, for 470 ducats, as it appears in an instrument done by the hand of Messer Vischonte Chaluzio, notary of the Court of Petitions, on the 26th day of the previous month, under the conditions contained in that act.

(xiii) *28 May 1484.*

Messer Cristofalo di Ornangni was called [before the court] in connection with a piece of work which Messer Zuane Cabotto has done or has had done in a property which borders on a property of the said Messer Cristofalo, situated within the boundaries of San Jacomo de Lorio, as much with a wall as a fence, as much above ground as below, as much what is already done as about what is to be done, and above all concerning the stone water channels which border on the ditches and paths of the said Messer Cristofalo's [property].

(xiv) *11 December [1484].*

I Joannes Caboto, son of Messer [blank], with my successors, make manifest in the name of God and of Christ that I do give, sell and make over to you, Messer Bernardinus de Podio, and your brothers, sons of the late Messer Thadeus, and to your successors, all that property which is a newly built house with all its possessions, within the boundary of S. Iacobus de Luprio, for 1600 ducats according to the form of the written contract.

(xv) *11 December 1484. In San Iachomo da Lorio*

Messer Zuan Bagoto [Caboto] has sold to Messer Bernardin of Pozo and to his brethren, sons of the late Messer Tadio, a dwelling house with all its possessions and appurtenances, situated within the boundary of San Iachomo da Lorio, for 1600 gold ducats, according to the agreements drawn up at the Mesetaria.

Notification made to Messer Zuan Bagoto, as father of a family of sons, December 15.

(vi) *30 December 1484. In San Nicolo and in Chioza*

Messer Zuan Chabotto, son of the late Messer Julio, by his right of possession has executed a charter drawn up and authenticated by the hand of Vischonte Caruzio, notary of the fifth district, in the year 1482 on the 30th day of October, by which charter Donna Pulissena Valier, daughter of the late Messer Nicolo, gives to the said Messer Zuan Chiabotto a house situated within the boundary of San Nicolo of Mandigoli, and a house situated in Chioza within the boundary of San Nicolo and a stretch of meadow land and three salt works situated within the boundary of Chioza under the conditions contained in the said charter.

12

JOHAN CABOTO MONTECALUNYA, VENETIAN, IN VALENCIA, 1490-3

Archivo Regional de Valencia, Archivo del Real, Epistolarum vol. 496. These documents were first made public by M. Ballesteros-Gaibrois, as appendices to his article 'Juan Caboto en España', *Revista de Indias*, vol. IV (1943), pp. 607-27. For the translations from the Aragonese originals, here printed by kind permission of Professor Ballesteros, the editor is indebted to Dr J. Molas and Mr D. W. Lomax of the School of Hispanic Studies, University of Liverpool, and to the good offices of Professor D. B. Quinn.

(i) *The King to Diego de Torres, Governor-General of Valencia* [*27 September 1492*]

Letter addressed by the king to the governor-general about the port to be constructed on the beach of this city.

To our noble and beloved Councillor, Chamberlain and Governor-General in the kingdom of Valencia, don Diego de Torre:
The King.

Chamberlain and Governor-General, we have been informed by Johan Caboto Montecalunya, the Venetian, that he arrived at this city two years ago, and during this time he has considered whether on the beach of this city a port could be constructed, and, on finding that the aforesaid port could be constructed very easily both on land and sea, he has designed and painted plans of them, and he has brought them to us; and, having seen them and heard the aforesaid Johan Caboto, it appears to us that if the said port and jetty could be constructed in the sea just as in the plan he has brought here, it would be something which would result in a great benefit for the common weal of this kingdom; and, since it seems that there is some truth in what he says, we have decided that some people who know these things should be chosen by the Lieutenant-Governor, the Jurors, and you, and that they should diligently examine whether the said Johan Caboto's statement is true as he has related it here and as it is painted on the plan which we send you by Gaspar Rull, merchant of this city, for if the aforesaid things could be done as easily as he says our will is that . . . [the remainder is broken off].[1]

(ii) *Diego de Torres to the King, 25 October 1492*

Most high and most powerful Lord.

I received a letter from Your Royal Lordship, dated the 27 of September, last, by which Your Highness ordered that the Lieutenant-General, the Jurors and I should go to inspect whether a port could be built on the beach of this city, and that we should inform you of all the things necessary for making the aforesaid port. Firstly, to see whether the seizer or beach of the port of this city is clay or mud, and of such a sort that the lie of the stones which will be worked on the same beach to make the port, may have such disposition and firmness that the said port can be built securely on them. Secondly, to see whether the depth of the aforementioned beach in the arms indicated by Johan Caboto Montecalunya, the Venetian, is sufficient, both at the beginning of the port and at its entries, in the manner which is necessary here, both for the entry of big ships, and for their stay in the said port. Thirdly, to see whether the stone which must be used for the said port can be obtained from the Cap de Cullera just as the aforesaid Johan Caboto says. Fourthly, to see if the mudscows which have to carry the said stone during the summer season when the said work must be done, will be able to navigate and to carry the said stone to the place where the aforesaid port must be built, despite the waves which beat on that shore in that season. Fifthly, to send stone-cutters to the Cap de Cullera to cut stone of the size which the said Johan Cabot will indicate, and to have a boat carry it over to the said shore and to see more or less what it will cost to put a stone in the place where the said port must be constructed;

---

[1] The document lacks a date, because the page is broken off at the end, but the same page contains a document of 1492. In the letter of the Governor-General, it is stated that this letter, which is answered by Document ii, is dated 27 September 1492. [Footnote by Ballesteros-Gaibrois.]

because on learning the depth of the place where the said port must be constructed, it will be possible to calculate how many stones will be necessary for building it, and to have some idea of what the said port and jetty will cost. Sixthly, on seeing that all the aforesaid things are going well, to see where the money can be obtained for building the said port.

And so, most excellent Sir, here we have all spoken together many times, so that [. . . illegible . . .] receiving the letter from Your Highness everything was effected by me, as being something so useful and good for their city. And there were many opinions about whether the port should be built or not and whether it would result in a benefit to the royal finances of Your Highness, and to the common good of this your city, and many have argued that the building of this port will ennoble and enrich this city and even the whole kingdom, and because the Lieutenant-General has written the opinions of everybody at length to Your Highness, I shall not need to recite them here. I shall say to Your Highness only that concerning the five first things, that is, to see about the place, seizer and clay for building the said port, and about the stone where it must be built, and to show the stone for calculating how much the said port will cost; and, moreover, I declare to Your Highness that, concerning the stone, it is of such a nature and so good for carrying and cutting that nobody could ask for so good a stone as it has been found, in price and expense, for progress in the said work. As for the sixth part, that is, to inform you where we shall be able to obtain the money from, for building the said port, we have not spoken about this hitherto. However, the bearer of this letter, Gaspar Rull, who is going with the aforesaid Venetian to Your Highness, will tell Your Highness orally some expedients for obtaining money for building the said port; when Your Majesty hears that, you will see which is most satisfactory and least burdensome for Your Majesty and least harmful for this city. Similarly, the General Treasurer and the royal financial scribe are also there, who are very knowledgeable in the affairs of this city and kingdom. From them Your Highness will be able to obtain a full relation of where the money can come from, because if the Lieutenant-General and the Jurors had to see where it had to come from, they would never agree, but only Your Highness can best see what is most satisfactory for your service and order it to be put into execution. May Our Lord prosper your life and royal estate and keep for you many more kingdoms and lordships.

From Valencia, 25 October 1493 [*sic* for 1492].[1]

Your Royal Highness' humble serf and chamberlain, who kisses your royal feet. The Chamberlain.[2]

(iii) *The King to Diego de Torres, 26 February 1493*

The text, which is printed in *Revista de Indias*, as above, is not here reproduced, since it does not mention Cabot. It shows that the harbour project was to be abandoned.

13

THE VISIT OF BARTHOLOMEW COLUMBUS TO ENGLAND, *c.* 1488–9

Fernando Colombo, *Le Historie di Cristoforo Colombo*, ed. Rinaldo Caddeo (Milan, 1930), vol. I, pp. 95–8 (first printed, Venice 1571).

But fearing lest, in the same way, the King of Castile might not agree to his undertaking, and that he might have to propose it once more to another prince, and in case much time might be lost in his so doing, he [Christopher Columbus] sent a brother of his called Bartolomeo Colon, whom he had with him, to England. This man, though boasting of no Latin learning, was practical and prudent in sea matters and was well able to make sea charts, globes, and other instruments of that profession, as his brother the Admiral had taught him. Consequently, once he had set out for

[1] 'The original clearly has III, which misled Sr Carreras, and at first, myself as well. A careful re-reading shows that the first I is erased. Document iii, of 26 February 1493, makes this clear, since it cannot be 1494, as Sr Carreras suggested, since the Monarchs were not then in Barcelona.' [Footnote by Ballesteros-Gaibrois.]

[2] 'The Chamberlain was Diego de Torres, Governor-General of Valencia.' [Footnote by Ballesteros-Gaibrois.]

England, Bartolomeo Colon followed his own destiny, which gave him into the hands of pirates, who despoiled him together with others in his ship. For which reason, and because of his poverty and the sickness which in those foreign parts assailed him cruelly, his mission, with which he was entrusted, dragged on for a long time until, having acquired a little competence from the maps which he was making, he began to make approaches to King Henry VII, father of Henry VIII who is now reigning, to whom he presented a world map on which were written these lines, which I found among his writings and which I will set down here, rather for the sake of posterity than for their elegance:

> Terrarum quicumque cupis feliciter oras
> Noscere, cuncta decens docte pictura docebit,
> Quam Strabo affirmat, Ptolemaeus, Plinius, atque
> Isidorus: non una tamen sententia quisque.
> Pingitur hic etiam nuper sulcata carinis
> Hispania zona illa, prius incognita genti,
> Torrida, quae tandem nunc est notissima multis.

And lower down he says: Pro auctore, sive pictore: Janua, cui patria est, nomen cui Bartholomaeus Columbus de Terra Rubra, opus edidit istud Londiniis anno Domini M.CCCC.LXXX, atque insuper anno octavo, decimaque die cum tertia mensis Februari.

> Laudes Christo cantentur abunde.

And because it will inform any who question [the style] Columbus de terra rubra, I may say that in the self-same way I saw some signatures of the Admiral before he acquired that rank, in which he signed himself Columbus de terra rubra.

But coming back to the King of England, I say that once he had seen the world map, and what the Admiral was offering him, he accepted the offer with good will and had him sent for. But since God had reserved him for Castile, the Admiral had gone already and returned with victory in his enterprise, which accordingly in its order will be told.

THE VOYAGES OF JOHN CABOT IN
1497 AND 1498

14

JOHN DEE'S STATEMENTS ON THE DATE OF
THE DISCOVERY OF NORTH AMERICA

From a map of the North Atlantic drawn by John Dee in 1580: British Museum, Cotton MS Aug.I.i.1. The statement printed below is extracted from matter written on the back of the map, and, as its internal evidence shows, was composed in 1578.

A brief remembrance of sundry foreign Regions, discovered, inhabited and partly Conquered by the Subjects of this Brytish Monarchie: And so the lawfull Title of our Soveraigne Lady Queene Elizabeth for the due Clayme and just recovery of the same disclosed. Which (in effect) is a Title Royall to all the Coasts and Ilands, beginning at or about Terra Florida, alongst or nere unto Atlantis, going Northerly, and then to all the most Northen Ilands, great and small, and so compassing abowt Groenland until the Territorie opposite, unto the fardest Easterly and Northern Bownds of the Duke of Moscovia his Dominions; which last Bownds are from our Albion more than half the Sea voyage to the Cathayen westerly and Northern Sea Coasts, as most evidently and at large yt is declared in the volume of Famous and Ryche Discoveries.

Circa An. 1170. 1. The Lord Madoc, sonne to Owen Gwynedd Prynce of Northwales, led a Colonie and inhabited in Terra Florida or thereabouts.

Circa An. 1494. 2. Mr Robert Thorn his father, and Mr Eliot of Bristow, discovered Newfownd Land.

Circa An. 560. 3. Brandan, the learned man, discovered very much of the western parts: but chiefly Ilands, unto one of which he gave the name Brandan his Iland. And so is called at this present.

Circa An. 1497. 4. Sebastian Caboto, sent by King Henry the

seventh, did discover from Newfownd Land so far along and abowt the Coaste next to Laborador tyll he came to the Latitude of 67½. And styll fownd the Seas open before him.

Anno 1576 et 1577. 5. The Ilands, and Broken land Easterly, and somwhat to the Sowth of Labrador were more particularly discovered and possessed A° 1576. and the last yere by Martin Frobysher Esquier: and presently is by our People to be inhabited: The Totall Content of which Ilands and parcell of Land thereabowt by our Soveraigne Queene Elizabeth is lately named Meta Incognita.

15

ROBERT THORNE THE YOUNGER ON THE DISCOVERY OF THE NEW FOUND LAND BY HIS FATHER AND HUGH ELYOT

From the Book addressed by Thorne to Dr Lee, English Ambassador in Spain, in 1527: British Museum, Cotton MS, Vit. c. vii, ff. 329–45. For consideration of other versions of this statement, see above, pp. 26–8.

[ff. 339b–340] I reason that as some sicknes[ses are] hereditarious and come [from the Father] to the Sonne: So this Inclynation or desyre of [discover]ing I inherited of my father, which with an [other] Marchaunt of Brystow named hughe Elliot [were] the discoverers of the Newfound Landes, of the w[hich] there is no dowt, (as now plainly appeareth) yf [the] mariners wolde then have bene ruled & followed the[ir] Pilots mynde, the Land of the Indians[1] from wh[ence] all the Gold commeth had bene ours: for all is one Coast, as by the Carde appeareth, and is afores[aid].

16

THE SPANISH SOVEREIGNS TO GONZALES DE PUEBLA, 28 MARCH 1496

Archivo General de Simancas, Estado Tratados con Inglaterra, leg. 2, fol. 16. Spanish text printed with translation, by Biggar, *Precursors*,

[1] Hakluyt's text spoke of 'the lands of the West Indies', which suggests a different meaning from 'the Land of the Indians'. It was Hakluyt's own amendment.

pp. 10–11. Dr Biggar was Canadian Archivist in Europe, and the above work is a Canadian official publication. Its texts of documents are drawn wherever possible from the originals and should be used in preference to the versions occurring in some earlier works. The present writer owes much to Dr Biggar, not only in common with all Cabot students, for his published work, but also for his kindness in giving copies of some of his unpublished translations.

[Tortosa, 28 March 1496] In regard to what you say of the arrival there of one like Columbus for the purpose of inducing the King of England to enter upon another undertaking like that of the Indies, without prejudice to Spain or to Portugal, if he [the king] aids him as he has us, the Indies will be well rid of the man. We are of opinion that this is a scheme of the French King's to persuade the King of England to undertake this so that he will give up other affairs. Take care that you prevent the King of England from being deceived in this or in anything else of the kind, since wherever they can the French will endeavour to bring this about. And things of this sort are very uncertain, and of such a nature that for the present it is not seemly to conclude an agreement therein; and it is also clear that no arrangement can be concluded in this matter in that country [England] without harm to us or to the King of Portugal.

17

THE PETITION OF JOHN CABOT AND HIS SONS, 5 MARCH 1496

Public Record Office, Chancery Warrants for Privy Seal, ser. II, 146. Printed by Biggar, *Precursors*, p. 6.

Memorandum that on the fifth day of March, in the eleventh year of King Henry the Seventh, the following bill was considered by the Lord Chancellor of England at Westminster:

To the kyng our sovereigne lord:

Please it your highness of your moste noble and haboundant grace to graunt unto John Cabotto, Citezen of Venice, Lewes,

Sebastyan and Soncio, his sonnys, your gracious letters patentes under your grete seale in due forme to be made according to the tenour hereafter ensuying. And they shall during their lyves pray to God for the prosperous continuance of your moste noble and royall astate long to enduer.

18

THE FIRST LETTERS PATENT GRANTED TO
JOHN CABOT AND HIS SONS, 5 MARCH 1496

Public Record Office, Treaty Roll 178, membr. 8. Latin text first printed by Hakluyt in 1582; reprinted, with English translation here reproduced, by Biggar, *Precursors*, pp. 7–10.

For John Cabot and his Sons

The King, to all to whom, etc. Greeting: Be it known and made manifest that we have given and granted as by these presents we give and grant, for us and our heirs, to our well-beloved John Cabot, citizen of Venice, and to Lewis, Sebastian and Sancio, sons of the said John, and to the heirs and deputies of them, and of any one of them, full and free authority, faculty and power to sail to all parts, regions and coasts of the eastern, western and northern sea, under our banners, flags and ensigns, with five ships or vessels of whatsoever burden and quality they may be, and with so many and with such mariners and men as they may wish to take with them in the said ships, at their own proper costs and charges, to find, discover and investigate whatsoever islands, countries, regions or provinces of heathens and infidels, in whatsoever part of the world placed, which before this time were unknown to all Christians. We have also granted to them and to any of them, and to the heirs and deputies of them and any one of them, and have given licence to set up our aforesaid banners and ensigns in any town, city, castle, island or mainland whatsoever, newly found by them. And that the before-mentioned John and his sons or their heirs and deputies may conquer, occupy and possess whatsoever such towns, castles, cities and islands by them thus discovered that they may be able to conquer, occupy and possess, as our vassals and governors lieutenants and deputies therein, acquiring for us the dominion, title and jurisdiction of the same towns, castles, cities, islands and mainlands so discovered; in such a way nevertheless that of all the fruits, profits, emoluments, commodities, gains and revenues accruing from this voyage, the said John and sons and their heirs and deputies shall be bounden and under obligation for every their voyage, as often as they shall arrive at our port of Bristol, at which they are bound and holden only to arrive, all necessary charges and expenses incurred by them having been deducted, to pay to us, either in goods or money, the fifth part of the whole capital gained, we giving and granting to them and to their heirs and deputies, that they shall be free and exempt from all payment of customs on all and singular the goods and merchandise that they may bring back with them from those places thus newly discovered.

And further we have given and granted to them and to their heirs and deputies, that all mainlands, islands, towns, cities, castles and other places whatsoever discovered by them, however numerous they may happen to be, may not be frequented or visited by any other subjects of ours whatsoever without the licence of the aforesaid John and his sons and of their deputies, on pain of the loss as well of the ships or vessels daring to sail to these places discovered, as of all goods whatsoever. Willing and strictly commanding all singular our subjects as well by land as by sea, that they shall render good assistance to the aforesaid John and his sons and deputies, and that they shall give them all their favour and help as well in fitting out the ships or vessels as in buying stores and provisions with their money and in providing the other things which they must take with them on the said voyage.

In witness whereof, etc.

Witness ourself at Westminster on the fifth day of March.

By the King himself, etc.

19

MAURICE TOBY'S ACCOUNT OF
JOHN CABOT'S FIRST VOYAGE, 1497

From a Bristol Chronicle known as the Fust MS. Extracted and printed by Biggar, *Precursors*, pp. 194–5, with bibliographical references. See also above, pp. 56–7.

1496.[1] This year on St John the Baptist's day the land of America was found by the Merchants of Bristowe in a shippe of Bristowe, called the *Mathew*; the which said ship departed from the port of Bristowe the second day of May and came home again the 6th of August next following.

20

THE *MATTHEW* OF BRISTOL IN 1503–1504

From the Bristol Customs Records in the Public Record Office.

E. 122/199, 1. Account, 19–20 Hen. VII

[20 December 1503] The bark called the Mathewe of Bristol in which Edmund Griffeth is master sailed for Ireland on this day and has in it [cargo, chiefly for Hugh Elyot].

[4 May 1504] The bark called the Mathewe of Bristol in which Edmund Griffeth is master came from Ireland on this day.

[13 June 1504] The bark called the Mathewe of Bristol in which William Claron is master sailed for Bordeaux on this day.

[12 August 1504] The bark called the Mathewe of Bristol in which William Claron is master came from Bordeaux this day.

[28 August, 1504] The bark called the Mathewe of Bristol in which William Claron is master sailed for Spain on this day and has in it [cargo for a large number of merchants including William Thorne].

---

[1] That is, the year beginning 15 September 1496, the opening date of the Bristol civic year.

John Cabot's Voyages, 1497 and 1498

21

THE EIGHTH LEGEND OF THE WORLD MAP OF 1544
(THE PARIS MAP)

Original inscription printed in both Spanish and Latin on the copy of the Map now in the Bibliothèque Nationale, Paris. Hakluyt printed a Latin version differently worded but giving the same facts, probably from another version not now extant. The Legends were also separately printed in Latin in a twenty-four-leaf pamphlet, *c.* 1544, the only known copy of which is in the Universitätsbibliothek, Munich. The translation here given is that of Beazley, *John and Sebastian Cabot.*

The Eighth Legend: This land was discovered by John Cabot the Venetian, and Sebastian Cabot his son, in the year of the birth of our Saviour Jesus Christ 1494, on the 24th of June in the morning, to which they gave the name First Land Seen [*Prima Terra Vista*], and to a large island which is near the said land they gave the name Saint John, because it had been discovered on the same day. The people of it are dressed in the skins of animals; they use in their wars bows and arrows, lances and darts, and certain clubs of wood, and slings. It is a very sterile land. There are in it many white bears, and very large stags like horses, and many other animals; and likewise there is infinite fish, sturgeons, salmon, very large soles a yard long, and many other kinds of fish, and the greater number of them are called baccallaos [codfish]; and likewise there are in the same land hawks black like crows, eagles, partridges, linnets, and many other birds of different kinds.

22

LORENZO PASQUALIGO TO HIS BROTHERS AT VENICE, 23 AUGUST 1497

From the MS *Diarii* of Marin Sanuto. Venice, Biblioteca Marciana, MSS Ital. Cl. VII, Cod. 417 (vol. 1), fol. 374v. Italian text, with translation, in Biggar, *Precursors*, pp. 13–15.

[London, 23 August 1497] That Venetian of ours who went with a small ship from Bristol to find new islands has come back and says he has discovered mainland 700 leagues away, which is the country of the Grand Khan, and that he coasted it for 300 leagues and landed and did not see any person; but he has brought here to the king certain snares which were spread to take game and a needle for making nets, and he found certain notched [or felled] trees so that by this he judges that there are inhabitants. Being in doubt he returned to his ship; and he has been three months on the voyage; and this is certain. And on the way back he saw two islands, but was unwilling to land, in order not to lose time, as he was in want of provisions. The king here is much pleased at this; and he [Cabot] says that the tides are slack and do not run as they do here. The king has promised him for the spring ten armed ships as he [Cabot] desires and has given him all the prisoners to be sent away, that they may go with him, as he has requested; and has given him money that he may have a good time until then, and he is with his Venetian wife and his sons at Bristol. His name is Zuam Talbot and he is called the Great Admiral and vast honour is paid to him and he goes dressed in silk, and these English run after him like mad, and indeed he can enlist as many of them as he pleases, and a number of our rogues as well. The discoverer of these things planted on the land which he has found a large cross with a banner of England and one of St Mark, as he is a Venetian, so that our flag has been hoisted very far afield.

23

NEWS SENT FROM LONDON TO THE DUKE OF MILAN, 24 AUGUST 1497

Milan Archives (Potenze Estere: Inghilterra). Translation in A. B. Hinds (ed.), *Calendar of State Papers, Milan*, vol. 1 (London, 1912), no. 535.

[24 August 1497] News received from England this morning by letters dated the 24th August[1]. . . . Also some months ago his

[1] This dispatch has been attributed to Raimondo de Soncino, Milanese ambassador in England. He, however, could hardly have written it, since he had landed in England only the day before. He disembarked at Dover on August 23 and was still there on the 24th (*Cal. S.P., Milan*, vol. 1, No. 536).

Majesty sent out a Venetian, who is a very good mariner, and has good skill in discovering new islands, and he has returned safe, and has found two very large and fertile new islands. He has also discovered the Seven Cities, 400 leagues from England, on the western passage. This next spring his Majesty means to send him with fifteen or twenty ships. . . .

24

RAIMONDO DE RAIMONDI DE SONCINO TO
THE DUKE OF MILAN, 18 DECEMBER 1497

Milan Archives (Potenze Estere: Inghilterra). English translation and important parts of the original Italian printed by Hinds, *Calendar of State Papers, Milan*, vol. 1, no. 552.

[London, 18 December 1497] Perhaps amid the numerous occupations of your Excellency, it may not weary you to hear how his Majesty here has gained a part of Asia, without a stroke of the sword. There is in this Kingdom a man of the people, Messer Zoane Caboto by name, of kindly wit and a most expert mariner. Having observed that the sovereigns first of Portugal and then of Spain had occupied unknown islands, he decided to make a similar acquisition for his Majesty. After obtaining patents that the effective ownership of what he might find should be his, though reserving the rights of the Crown, he committed himself to fortune in a little ship, with eighteen persons. He started from Bristol, a port on the west of this kingdom, passed Ireland, which is still further west, and then bore towards the north, in order to sail to the east, leaving the north on his right hand after some days. After having wandered for some time he at length arrived at the mainland, where he hoisted the royal standard, and took possession for the king here; and after taking certain tokens he returned.

This Messer Zoane, as a foreigner and a poor man, would not have obtained credence, had it not been that his companions, who are practically all English and from Bristol, testified that he spoke the truth. This Messer Zoane has the description of the world in a map, and also in a solid sphere, which he has made, and shows where he has been. In going towards the east he passed far beyond the country of the Tanais. They say that the land is excellent and temperate, and they believe that Brazil wood and silk are native there. They assert that the sea there is swarming with fish, which can be taken not only with the net, but in baskets let down with a stone, so that it sinks in the water. I have heard this Messer Zoane state so much.

These same English, his companions, say that they could bring so many fish that this kingdom would have no further need of Iceland, from which place there comes a very great quantity of the fish called stockfish. But Messer Zoane has his mind set upon even greater things, because he proposes to keep along the coast from the place at which he touched, more and more towards the east, until he reaches an island which he calls Cipango, situated in the equinoctial region, where he believes that all the spices of the world have their origin, as well as the jewels. He says that on previous occasions he has been to Mecca, whither spices are borne by caravans from distant countries. When he asked those who brought them what was the place of origin of these spices, they answered that they did not know, but that other caravans came with this merchandise to their homes from distant countries, and these again said that the goods had been brought to them from other remote regions. He therefore reasons that these things come from places far away from them, and so on from one to the other, always assuming that the earth is round, it follows as a matter of course that the last of all must take them in the north towards the west.

He tells all this in such a way, and makes everything so plain, that I also feel compelled to believe him. What is much more, his Majesty, who is wise and not prodigal, also gives him some credence, because he is giving him a fairly good provision, since his return, so Messer Zoane himself tells me. Before very long they say that his Majesty will equip some ships, and in addition he will give them all the malefactors, and they will go to that country and form a colony. By means of this they hope to make London a more important mart for spices than Alexandria. The leading men in this enterprise are from Bristol, and great seamen, and now they know where to go, say that the voyage will not take more than a fortnight, if they have good fortune after leaving Ireland.

I have also spoken with a Burgundian, one of Messer Zoane's companions, who corroborates everything. He wants to go back, because the Admiral, which is the name they give to Messer Zoane, has given him an island. He has given another to his barber, a Genoese by birth, and both consider themselves counts, while my lord the Admiral esteems himself at least a prince.

I also believe that some poor Italian friars will go on this voyage, who have the promise of bishoprics. As I have made friends with the Admiral, I might have an archbishopric if I chose to go there, but I have reflected that the benefices which your Excellency reserves for me are safer, and I therefore beg that possession may be given me of those which fall vacant in my absence, and the necessary steps taken so that they may not be taken away from me by others, who have the advantage of being on the spot. Meanwhile I stay on in this country, eating ten or twelve courses at each meal, and spending three hours at table twice every day, for the love of your Excellency, to whom I humbly commend myself.

London, the 18th of December, 1497

25

JOHN DAY TO THE LORD GRAND ADMIRAL

Archivo General de Simancas, Estado de Castilla, leg. 2, fol. 6. This document, the discovery of which is the most important event in Cabot research during the past hundred years, was brought to light in 1956 by the American scholar Dr L. A. Vigneras. The Spanish text was published by him in *Hispanic American Historical Review*, vol. xxxvi (1956), pp. 503–9; and his English translation appeared in 'The Cape Breton landfall: 1494 or 1497', *Canadian Historical Review*, vol. xxxviii (1957), pp. 219–28. Of his discovery Dr Vigneras has written (*HAHR*, loc. cit.): 'While we were both doing research in the Archivo de Simancas last spring, Dr Hayward Keniston, knowing that I was interested in the discovery of North America, mentioned that he had seen a document relating to English voyages in one of the first three legajos of Estado de Castilla. My first search through the three legajos yielded nothing, but a second attempt three weeks later established the fact that the document in question was folio 6, legajo 2.' Dr Vigneras has elsewhere added that the document was described on its cover as concerning an English voyage to Brazil.

Your Lordship's servant brought me your letter. I have seen its contents and I would be most desirous and most happy to serve you. I do not find the book Inventio Fortunata, and I thought that I (or he) was bringing it with my things, and I am very sorry not find it because I wanted very much to serve you. I am sending the other book of Marco Polo and a copy of the land which has been found. I do not send the map because I am not satisfied with it, for my many occupations forced me to make it in a hurry at the time of my departure; but from the said copy your Lordship will learn what you wish to know, for in it are named the capes of the mainland and the islands, and thus you will see where land was first sighted, since most of the land was discovered after turning back. Thus your Lordship will know that the cape nearest to Ireland is 1800 miles west of Dursey Head which is in Ireland, and the southernmost part of the Island of the Seven Cities is west of Bordeaux River, and your Lordship will know that he landed at only one spot of the mainland, near the place where land was first sighted, and they disembarked there with a crucifix and raised banners with the arms of the Holy Father and those of the King of England, my master; and they found tall trees of the kind masts are made, and other smaller trees, and the country is very rich in grass. In that particular spot, as I told your Lordship, they found a trail that went inland, they saw a site where a fire had been made, they saw manure of animals which they thought to be farm animals, and they saw a stick half a yard long pierced at both ends, carved and painted with brazil, and by such signs they believe the land to be inhabited. Since he was with just a few people, he did not dare advance inland beyond the shooting distance of a crossbow, and after taking in fresh water he returned to his ship. All along the coast they found many fish like those which in Iceland

John Cabot's Voyages, 1497 and 1498

are dried in the open and sold in England and other countries, and these fish are called in English 'stockfish'; and thus following the shore they saw two forms running on land one after the other, but they could not tell if they were human beings or animals; and it seemed to them that there were fields where they thought might also be villages, and they saw a forest whose foliage looked beautiful. They left England toward the end of May, and must have been on the way 35 days before sighting land; the wind was east-north-east and the sea calm going and coming back, except for one day when he ran into a storm two or three days before finding land; and going so far out, his compass needle failed to point north and marked two rhumbs below. They spent about one month discovering the coast and from the above mentioned cape of the mainland which is nearest to Ireland, they returned to the coast of Europe in fifteen days. They had the wind behind them, and he reached Brittany because the sailors confused him, saying that he was heading too far north. From there he came to Bristol, and he went to see the King to report to him all the above mentioned; and the King granted him an annual pension of twenty pounds sterling to sustain himself until the time comes when more will be known of this business, since with God's help it is hoped to push through plans for exploring the said land more thoroughly next year with ten or twelve vessels—because in his voyage he had only one ship of fifty 'toneles' and twenty men and food for seven or eight months—and they want to carry out this new project. It is considered certain that the cape of the said land was found and discovered in the past by the men from Bristol who found 'Brasil' as your Lordship well knows. It was called the Island of Brasil, and it is assumed and believed to be the mainland that the men from Bristol found.

Since your Lordship wants information relating to the first voyage, here is what happened: he went with one ship, his crew confused him, he was short of supplies and ran into bad weather, and he decided to turn back.

Magnificent Lord, as to other things pertaining to the case, I would like to serve your Lordship if I were not prevented in doing so by occupations of great importance relating to shipments and deeds for England which must be attended to at once and which keep me from serving you: but rest assured, Magnificent Lord, of my desire and natural intention to serve you, and when I find myself in other circumstances and more at leisure, I will take pains to do so; and when I get news from England about the matters referred to above—for I am sure that everything has to come to my knowledge—I will inform your Lordship of all that would not be prejudicial to the King my master. In payment for some services which I hope to render you, I beg your Lordship to kindly write me about such matters, because the favour you will thus do me will greatly stimulate my memory to serve you in all the things that may come to my knowledge. May God keep prospering your Lordship's magnificent state according to your merits. Whenever your Lordship should find it convenient, please remit the book or order it to be given to Master George.

I kiss your Lordship's hands,

JOHAN DAY

26

ENTRIES FROM THE DAYBOOKS OF KING'S PAYMENTS,
OTHERWISE KNOWN AS THE HOUSEHOLD BOOKS

Public Record Office. Some of these items have not previously been printed. In the Daybooks, entries for several days are grouped together. The dates here given are the terminal dates of the group in which an entry occurs.

(i) *E 101/414, 6*[*1 October 1495–30 September 1497*]

1497 Aug. 10–11   Item to hym that founde
                  the new Isle   x li

(ii) *E 101/414, 16*[*1 October 1497–30 September 1499*]

1498 Jan. 8–12   Item to a Venysian in Re-   lxvj s viij d
                  warde

Mar. 17–22   Item to lanslot thirkill of
             London apon a prest for his Shipp
             going towardes the new Ilande   xx li

214

Mar. 25–31   Item delivered to launcelot
thirkill going towardes the new
Ile in prest   xx li

Apr. 1–3   Item to thomas bradley &
Launcelot thirkill going to the
new Isle   xxx li

Apr. 4–6   Item delivered to thomas
bradley & launce thirkill in full
payment of cxiij li viij s   xliij li   viij s

Apr. 8–11   Item to John Cair goying to
the newe Ile in Rewarde   xl s

1499 Sept. 21–26   Item to thenbassador of
portingale   lx li   xiij s   iiij d
—   Item to the doctor of portingale   l li
—   Item to the [contracted word,
unintelligible][1] of portingale   C s

(iii) *E 101/415, 3[1 October 1499–30 September 1502]*

1501 Jan. 7–8   Item to Edward of Portingale
in Rewarde   iiij li

May 1–7   Item to Robt brigandyn[2] in
parte of payment of xlvj li xiij s
iiij d for the Rigging of ij
berkes   xx li

June 20–26   Item to an herrald of port-
ingale in Rewarde   vj li   viij s   iiij d

Sept. 26–28   Item to willm thomas of
bristoll in Rewarde   vj s   viij d

1502 Jan. 1   Item to Edwarde le portingale in
Rewarde   xxvj s   viij d

Jan. 2–7   Item to men of bristoll that
founde thisle   C s

Feb. 13–18   Item to Edward portingalle
in Rewarde   iiij li

---

[1] It may be 'protonithory'.   [2] Brigandine was Clerk of the King's Ships.

Sept. 18–23   Item to a mariner that
brought haukes   x s
—   Item to an other that brought
an Egle   vj s viij d
Sept. 25–30   Item to the merchauntes of
bristoll that have bene in the
newe founde launde   xx li

(iv)

Daybook, 1 October 1502–30 September 1505: Brit. Mus., Add. MS
7099, a transcript made *c.* 1829 by Craven Ord, is here used in default
of the book for this period, which is now missing. Ord rendered the
payments in arabic numerals.

1503 Sept. 15   To Sir Walter Herbert's servant for
bringing a brasell bow & 2 rede arowes   6s. 8d.
Nov. 17   To one that brought haukes from the
Newfounded Island   20s.
1504 Apr. 8   To a preste that goith to the new Ilande   40s.
1505 Aug. 25   To Clays goying to Richemount with
wylde catts & popyngays of the New-
found Island for his costs   13s. 4d.
—   To Portyngales that brought popyngais &
catts of the mountayne with other stuf to
the King's grace   100s.

(v) *E 36/214. T.R. Misc. King's Book of Payments* [*1 October 1505–
30 September 1509*]

1506 Feb. 15–20   Item to Griffeth Rede's servant for
bringing upe a [   ]¹ don at Penbroke by
portyngales   xx s
1507 Apr. 11   Item to oone that came oute of por-
tyngale in gold   x li

(vi) *E 36/215. T.R. Misc. King's Book of Payments, 1–9 Henry VIII*
Examined to October 1510; no entries on Bristol explorations.

¹ The omitted word is not intelligible: see Pl. V(*b*), opp. p. 134.

27

GRANT OF PENSION TO JOHN CABOT,
13 DECEMBER 1497

Public Record Office, Privy Seals, 13 Hen. VII, December. Printed by
Biggar, *Precursors*, p. 16.

Henry, by the grace of God King of England and of ffraunce and
lord of Irland, To the most reverend fadre in God John, Cardinal
archiebissop of Cantrebury, prymate of all England, and of the
apostolique see legate, our chaunceller, greeting: We late you
wite that We for certaine considerations us specially moevying
have yeven and graunted unto our welbiloved John Calbot of the
parties of Venice an annuitie or annuel rent of twenty poundes
sterling, to be had and yerely perceyved from the fest of thanun-
ciation of our lady last passed, during our pleasur, of our custumes
and subsidies commying and growing in our Poort of Bristowe,
by thands of our custumers ther for the tyme beying, at Michel-
mas and Estre by even porcions; Wherefor we wol and charge you
that under our grete seal ye do make heruppon our letters
patentes in good and effectual forme. Yeven undre our Pryve Seal
at our paloys of Westminster the xiii^th day of Decembre, The
xiii^th yere of our Reigne. [With memorandum in Latin that this
was duly done on January 28 following.]

28

WARRANT FOR PAYMENT OF JOHN CABOT'S PENSION,
22 FEBRUARY 1498

Public Record Office, Warrants for Issue, 13 Hen. VII, E. 404, Bundle
82. Printed by Biggar, *Precursors*, pp. 24–5.

Henry by the grace of God King of England and of ffraunce and
lord of Irland To the Tresourer and Chambrelains of oure
Eschequier greting:
  Where as We by oure warrant under oure signet for certain
consideracions have yeven and graunted unto John Caboote xx li.

[£20] yerely during oure pleasur to be had and perceyved by the handes of oure Custumers in oure poorte of Bristowe, and as we be enfourmed the said John Caboote is dilaied of his payement bicause the said Custumers have no sufficient matier of discharge for their indempnitie to be yolden at their accomptes before the Barons of oure Eschequier; Wherefore we wol and charge you that ye oure said Treasourer and Chambrelains that now be and hereafter shallbe, that ye, unto suche tyme as ye shall have from us otherwise in commaundement, do to be levied in due fourme ij severall tailles, every of theim conteignying x li. upon the Customers of the revenues in our said poort of Bristowe at two usuell termes of the yere, whereof oon taill to be levied at this tyme conteignying x li. of the Revenues of oure said poort upon Richard Meryk and Arthure Kemys, late Custumers of the same, And the same taill or tailles in due and sufficient fourme levied ye delyver unto the said John Caboote to be had of oure gift by way of rewarde without prest or eny other charge to be sette upon hym or any of theim for the same. And thies our letters shalbe youre sufficient warrant in that behalf. Yeven undre oure prive seal at oure manour of Chene the xxii^th day of ffebruary The xiii^th yere of oure Reigne.

29

PAYMENTS OF JOHN CABOT'S PENSION

(i) *Payment of Cabot's pension by the Bristol customers,*
25 March 1498

Public Record Office, Exchequer 122, 20/11 (View of Account, Bristol Customs, Michaelmas-Easter, 13 Hen. VII). Original Latin, with translation, printed by Biggar, *Precursors*, pp. 25–7.

[Among other items] . . . And £10 paid by them to John Calbot a Venetian, late of the town of Bristol aforesaid, for his annuity of £20 a year granted to him by our said lord the king by his letters patent, to be taken at two terms of the year out of the customs and subsidies arising and growing in the said port of the town of

Bristol, to wit, for the term of the Annunciation of the Blessed Virgin Mary [25 March 1497] falling within the time of this view, by a quittance of the said John, shown upon this view and remaining in the possession of the said collectors.

(ii) *Payment of Cabot's pension by the Bristol customers, 1498–9*

Westminster Chapter Archives, Chapter Muniments, 12243 (Roll of Accounts of the Bristol Customers for the years 1496–9). Original Latin, in fascimile, in E. Scott and A. E. Hudd (ed.), *The Cabot Roll*, (Bristol, 1897).

[Among other items] [Michaelmas, 1497–Michaelmas, 1498] And in the treasury in one tally in the name of John Cabot, £20. [Michaelmas, 1498–Michaelmas, 1499] And in the treasury in one tally in the name of John Cabot, £20.

30

RENTAL OF PHILIP GRENE IN BRISTOL, 1498-9

Extracted from 'A Bristol Rental 1498–9. The property of Mrs Chester-Master. Transcribed and edited by St Clair Baddeley', *Transactions of the Bristol and Gloucestershire Archaeological Society*, vol. XLVII (1925), pp. 123–9. This is obviously not an exact transcription, but its statements of fact appear trustworthy.

The Rental of lands and tenements of Phillip Grene in the town of Bristol and its suburbs, from the feast of St Michael Archangel in the xivth year of Henry VII until the same feast of St Michael in the following year complete.

p. 126   From John Jay for a house and belongings in Brodestrette v^{li}.

St. Nycoles Street supra bakka 8th [*sic* for St] Jacopi . . . From John Cabotta for a House p.a. xl^s.

p. 127   On the Key and Marche Strett

. . . Wm. Clerke for a ten^t. [tenement] there p.a. xiii^s and $iiij^d$.

Brodemede From John Thomas for a ten^t. with garden p.a. $viij^s$.

LONDON CHRONICLES ON THE VOYAGE OF 1498

(i) *The Great Chronicle of London*[1]

Thys yere also [September 1497–September 1498], the kyng by meanys of a venyzian which made hym sylf verray expert & kunnyng In knowlage of the cyrcuyte of the world and Ile landis of the same, as by a caart & othir demonstracions Reasonable he shewid, Cawsid the kyng to man & vytayll a Shypp at Brystow to seche for an Ile land which he said he knewe well was Rich & Replenysshid with Rych commodytees, Which shyp thus mannyd & vitaylid at the kyngis Cost dyvers marchauntis of london aventrid In (hir) small stokkys beyng In hir as chieff patron the said venesian, and In the Company of the said shypp saylid also owth of Brystow iij or iiij smale shyppis ffrawgth wyth sleygth & groos marchandysis as course cloth cappis lasis poyntis & other tryfyls And so departid ffrom Brystow In the begynnyng off maii, Of whoom in this mayris tyme Retowrnd noo tydyngisy.

. . . .

Thys yere alsoo [September 1501–September 1502] were browgth unto the kyng iij men takyn In the Newe ffound Ile land, that beffore I spak of In wylliam purchas tyme beyng mayer, These were clothid In bestys skynnys and ete Rawe fflesh and spak such spech that noo man cowde undyrstand theym, and In theyr demeanure lyke to bruyt bestis whom the kyng kept a tyme afftyr, Of the whych upon (ij) yeris passid (afftir) I sawe ij of theym apparaylyd afftyr Inglysh men In westmynstyr paleys, which at that tyme I cowde not dyscern ffrom Inglysh men tyll I was lernyd what men they were, But as ffor spech I hard noon of them uttyr oon word.

(ii) *'Cronicon regum Anglie'*[2]

This yere the kyng at the besy request and supplicacion of a Straunger venisian, which by a Caart made hym self expert in

[1] Ed. A. H. Thomas and I. D. Thornley (London, 1939), pp. 287–8, 320.
[2] British Museum, Cotton MS Vit. A xvi, f. 173. The year referred to is the civic year September 1497 to September 1498. The summer is that of 1498.

knowyng of the world, caused the kyng to manne a ship with vytaill & other necessaries for to seche an Iland wheryn the said straunger surmysed to be grete comodities. With which ship by the kynges grace so rygged went iij or iiij moo owte of Bristowe, the said straunger beyng Conditor of the said fflete. Wheryn dyvers merchauntes aswell of london as Bristow aventured goodes & sleight merchaundises, which departed from the west cuntrey in the begynnyng of somer, but to this present moneth came revir knowledge of their exployt.

(iii) *The Chronicle of Robert Fabyan as rendered by Richard Hakluyt*[1]
A note of Sebastian Gabotes Voyage of Discoverie, taken out of an old Chronicle, written by Robert Fabian, sometime Alderman of London, which is in the custodie of John Stowe, Citizen, a diligent searcher and preserver of Antiquities.[2]

This yeere the king (by means of a Venetian, whiche made himself very expert and cunning in knowledge of the circuite of the worlde and Ilandes of the same as by a Carde and other demonstrations reasonable hee shewed), caused to man and victuall a shippe at Bristowe, to search for an Ilande, which hee saide hee knewe well was riche and replenished with riche commodities. Which Ship, thus manned and victualed at the Kinges cost, divers merchants of London ventured in her small stockes, being in her as chiefe Patrone the saide Venetian. And in the companie of the saide shippe sayled also out of Bristowe three or foure small ships fraught with sleight and grosse merchandizes, as course cloth, Caps, Laces, points, and other trifles, and so departed from Bristowe in the beginning of May: of whom in this Maiors time returned no tidings.

[marginal notes:] In the 11 yere of King Henrie the VII. 1498. Note. Bristow. William Purchas, Maior of London.

·   ·   ·   ·   ·   ·   ·   ·   ·

---

[1] R. Hakluyt, *Divers Voyages* (London, 1582); repr. Hakluyt Society, ed. J. W. Jones (1850), pp. 23–4. The Fabyan Chronicle itself has not been preserved.
[2] Note that this heading is from the pen of Hakluyt, who assumes that the navigator was Sebastian Cabot. Fabyan himself speaks only of 'a Venetian', and his account evidently describes the second voyage of John Cabot in 1498. The marginal notes are also by Hakluyt.

Three savage men brought into England.

Of three savage men which hee[1] brought home and presented unto the king in the xvij yeere of his raigne.

This yeere also were brought unto the king three men, taken in the new founde Iland, that before I spake of in William Purchas time, being Maior. These were clothed in beastes skinnes, and ate rawe fleshe, and spake such speech that no man coulde understand them, and in their demeanour like to bruite beastes, whom the king kept a time after. Of the which upon two yeeres past after I saw two apparelled after the manner of Englishmen, in Westminster pallace, which at that time I coulde not discern from Englishmen, till I was learned what they were. But as for speech, I heard none of them utter one worde.[2]

(iv) *The Chronicle of Robert Fabyan as rendered by John Stow*[3]

Stow gives the extracts from the Fabyan Chronicle, then in his possession, which have been quoted above from Hakluyt's *Divers Voyages*, but with the following variations:

[Opening of the first extract] This yeere one Sebastian Gabato, a Genoa's sonne, borne in Bristow, professing himself to be experte in knowledge of the circuite of the worlde and Ilandes of the same, as by his Charts and other reasonable demonstrations he shewed, caused the King to man and victual a shippe at Bristow. . . .

[1] Again the heading is Hakluyt's, and so is the quite gratuitous assumption that the savages were brought home by the navigator of 1498.

[2] In 1600 Hakluyt reprinted the above passages in the third volume of his *Principal Navigations*, with the words 'by means of a Venetian' altered to 'by meanes of one John Cabot a Venetian'. It is evident that Hakluyt supplied the name from independent information, and did not find it in the Fabyan Chronicle.

[3] From Stow's *Chronicle* (London, 1580), p. 875. Both Stow and Hakluyt worked from the same copy of the original. There can be no doubt that it did not contain the name of Sebastian Cabot, which was supplied by both editors. Hakluyt admits as much by placing the name in the introductory heading avowedly written by himself. Stow simply interpolated from independent knowledge, without avowing the fact. This was in accordance with sixteenth-century practice in editorship. It is apparent from the general similarity of the texts that Stow's Fabyan Chronicle was substantially the Great Chronicle above quoted.

[Opening of the second extract] 1502, ann. reg. 18. This yeere were brought unto the king three men taken in the new found Ilands, by Sebastian Gabato, before named, in anno 1498. . . .

32

MARCO POLO ON CIPANGO AND THE ARCHIPELAGO

The Travels of Marco Polo, translated from the text of L. F. Benedetto by Aldo Ricci, *Broadway Travellers* (London, 1931), pp. 270-1, 276.

Chipangu is an island towards the east, in the high seas, 1500 miles from the continent. It is a very large island. The people are white, courteous, and handsome. They are idolaters. They are independent, and know no lordship but their own.

You must know that they have immense quantities of gold, because it is found on the spot in great abundance. Moreover, no one ever brings the gold away from the country, for no one goes thither from the continent, not even merchants. This is why they have as much gold as I have said.

I will tell you, too, of a great wonder concerning one of the palaces of the Lord of this island. You must know that he has a very large palace, all covered with fine gold. Just as we roof our houses and churches with lead, so this palace is all roofed over with fine gold: so the value of it is such that one can barely calculate it. Further, the floors of the chambers, of which there is a great number, are also of fine gold, over two fingers in thickness. And all the other parts of the palace, namely the halls, and the windows, are similarly adorned with gold. I assure you that this palace is of such immeasurable wealth that if anyone told the value of it, it would be past all belief.

They have pearls in abundance, of a rose colour, very beautiful, and round, and large. They are worth as much as the white ones, more indeed. In this island some of the dead are buried, and some are burnt; and those that are buried have one of these pearls put into their mouths. This is a custom of theirs. Besides pearls, they also have abundance of many kinds of precious stones. It is a rich island, so rich that no one can tell its wealth.

. . . .

You must know that the sea in which these islands lie, is called the Sea of Chin, which means the sea opposite Manji, for in the language of the islanders, Chin means Manji. This sea stretches to the east. According to the good sailors and pilots that navigate it, and who know the truth, there are 7448 islands in it, the majority of which are inhabited. I will add that in all these islands there is no tree but has a powerful and pleasant perfume, and is valuable; no less valuable, for example, than aloes-wood, and even more. There are also many precious spices of different kinds. Further, in those islands grow abundance of a kind of pepper that is as white as snow, as well as black pepper. The amount of gold and other precious things in those islands is truly prodigious. . . . Moreover, I will add that this sea, though I have said that it is called the Sea of Chin, yet is nothing but the Ocean Sea.

33

POLYDORE VERGIL ON JOHN CABOT

The Anglica Historia of Polydore Vergil, edited with a translation by Denys Hay, *Camden Series*, vol. LXXIV (Royal Historical Society, 1950), pp. 116–17. This passage, which does not appear in the printed editions of the book, is from Liber XXIV of a MS copy in the Vatican Library, written in 1512–13. The names 'Ioanne Cabot' and 'Ioanni' were inserted later in spaces previously left blank (editor's footnote, p. 116).

Hisdem temporibus rumor erat quosdam nautas nauigando speculatos esse terras in oceano Britannico antea incognitas. Res facile credebatur pro uera, fidemque faciebat, quod Hispaniae Reges saeculo nostro complures insulas prius ignotas comperissent. Quare Rex Henricus rogatus a quodam Ioanne Cabot natione ueneto rei nauticae peretissimo, unam nauem tam uiris quam armis instruxit, tradiditque ipsi Ioanni qui eas insulas uestigatum iret. Ille hoc eodem anno profectus in Hyberniam primum delatus est, Deinde in occidentem uersus uela fecit, qui ad postremum creditur nullibi alias inuenisse terras, quam in imo Oceani fundo, in quod una cum naui, descendisse putatur raptus ab ipso Oceano quoniam post eam nauigationem, nusquam amplius comparuit.

. . . .

There was talk at about this time that some sailors on a voyage had discovered lands lying in the British ocean, hitherto unknown. This was easily believed because the Spanish sovereigns in our time had found many unknown islands. Wherefore King Henry at the request of one John Cabot, a Venetian by birth, and a most skilful mariner, ordered to be prepared one ship, complete with crew and weapons; this he handed over to the same John to go and search for those unknown islands. John set out in this same year and sailed first to Ireland. Then he set sail towards the west. In the event he is believed to have found the new lands nowhere but on the very bottom of the ocean, to which he is thought to have descended together with his boat, the victim himself of that self-same ocean; since after that voyage he was never seen again anywhere.

34

STATEMENTS ON THE NAVIGATION TO NORTH AMERICA
c. 1583, BY SIR GEORGE PECKHAM, CHRISTOPHER CARLILE,
AND EDWARD HAYES

Richard Hakluyt, *Principall Navigations* (London, 1589)

(i) '*A true Report of the late discoueries* ... *by* ... *Sir Humfrey Gilbert* ... *Written by Sir George Pec[k]ham*'

[p. 714] For after once we are departed the coast of England, we may passe straight way thither, without danger of being driuen into any the countryes of our enemies, or doubtfull friends: for commonly one winde serueth to bring vs thither, which seldome faileth from the middle of Januarie to the middle of May, a benefite which the mariners make great account of, for it is a pleasure that they haue in few or none of other iourneyes. Also the passage is short, for we may goe thither in thirtie or fortie dayes at the most, hauing but an indifferent winde, & returne continually in twenty or foure & twentie dayes at the most.

(ii) '*A briefe and summarie discourse* . . . *written by captaine*
[*Christopher*] *Carlill in Aprill, 1583*'

[p. 720] . . . Secondly, that one wind suffiseth to make the passage,
where as most of your other voyages of like length, are subiect to
3. or 4. winds.

(iii) '*A report of the voyage* . . . *attempted* . . . *by Sir Humfrey
Gilbert* . . . *written by M. Edward Haies*'

[p. 685] About this time of the yere [latter half of June] the windes
are commonly West towards the Newfound land, keeping ordi-
narily within two points of West to the South or to the North,
whereby the course thither falleth out to be long and tedious after
June, which in March, Aprill & May, hath beene performed out
of England in 22 dayes and lesse. . . .

35

THE SECOND LETTERS PATENT GRANTED TO JOHN CABOT,
3 FEBRUARY 1498

Public Record Office, Warrants for Privy Seal, C. 82/173, 13 Hen. VII,
February. Printed by Biggar, *Precursors*, pp. 22–4. A Latin copy is in
P.R.O., Treaty Roll 179, membr. 1.

To the kinge

Pleas it your highnesse, of your moste noble and habundaunt
grace, to graunte to John Kabotto, Venician, your gracious letters
patentes in due fourme to be made accordyng to the tenour hereafter ensuyng, and he shal contynually praye to God for the
preservacion of your moste noble and roiall astate longe to endure.

H[en]R[icus] Rex

To all men to whom thies presentis shall come, send gretyng:
Knowe ye that we of our grace especiall and for dyvers causis us
movyng we have geven and graunten and by thies presentes geve
and graunte to our wel beloved John Kaboto, Venician, sufficiente
auctorite and power that he by hym, his deputie or deputies
sufficient may take at his pleasure vi englisshe shippes in any porte

or portes or other place within this our realme of Englond or obeisaunce, so that and if the said shippes be of the bourdeyn of cc tonnes or under, with their apparaill requisite and necessarie for the saveconduct of the seid shippes, and theym convey and lede to the londe and Iles of late founde by the seid John in oure name and by our commaundemente, paying for theym and every of theym as and if we shuld in or for our owen cause paye and noon otherwise.

And that the seid John by hym, his deputie or deputies sufficiente maye take and receyve into the seid shippes and every of theym all suche Maisters, Maryners, pages and our subiectes, as of their owen free wille woll goo and passe with hym in the same shippes to the seid londe or Iles withoute any impedymente, lett or perturbaunce of any of our officers or ministres or subiectes whatsoevir they be by theym to the seid John, his deputie or deputies and all other our seid subiectes or any of theym passing with the seid John in the seid shippes to the seid londe or Iles to be doon or suffer to be doon or attempted. Yeving in commaundement to all and every our officers, ministres and subiectes seying or herying thies our letters patentes, without any ferther commaundement by us to theym or any of theym to be geven, to perfourme and socour the seid John, his deputies and all our seid subiectes so passyng with hym according to the tenour of thies our letters patentes, any statute, acte or ordenaunce to the contrarye made or to be made in any wise notwithstanding.

36

AGOSTINO DE SPINULA TO THE DUKE OF MILAN, 20 JUNE 1498

Milan Archives (Potenze Estere: Inghilterra). Translation in *Calendar of State Papers, Milan*, vol. 1, No. 571.

[London, 20 June 1498] . . . There were three other letters, one for Messer Piero Carmeliano, one for Messer Piero Penech, and one for Messer Giovanni Antonio de Carbonariis. I will keep the last until his return. He left recently with five ships, which his Majesty sent to discover new islands.

PEDRO DE AYALA TO THE SPANISH SOVEREIGNS,
25 JULY 1498

Archivo General de Simancas, Estado Tratados con Inglaterra, leg. 2, fol. 196. Original sent to Spain with most of the words in cipher, deciphered inaccurately on receipt. Re-deciphered by G. A. Bergenroth in *Calendar of State Papers, Spain* (1862); and again, more accurately, by Biggar, *Precursors*, pp. 27–9. Biggar's text should be used; and his translation is here printed.

[London, 25 July 1498] . . . I think Your Highnesses have already heard how the king of England has equipped a fleet to explore certain islands or mainland which he has been assured certain persons who set out last year from Bristol in search of the same have discovered. I have seen the map made by the discoverer, who is another Genoese like Columbus, who has been in Seville and at Lisbon seeking to obtain persons to aid him in this discovery. For the last seven years the people of Bristol have equipped two, three [and] four caravels to go in search of the island of Brazil and the Seven Cities according to the fancy of this Genoese. The king made up his mind to send thither, because last year sure proof was brought him they had found land. The fleet he prepared, which consisted of five vessels, was provisioned for a year. News has come that one of these, in which sailed another Friar Buil, has made land in Ireland in a great storm with the ship badly damaged. The Genoese kept on his way. Having seen the course they are steering and the length of the voyage, I find that what they have discovered or are in search of is possessed by Your Highnesses because it is at the cape which fell to Your Highnesses by the convention with Portugal. It is hoped they will be back by September. I let [? will let] Your Highnesses know about it. The king has spoken to me several times on the subject. He hopes the affair may turn out profitable. I believe the distance is not 400 leagues. I told him that I believed the islands were those found by Your Highnesses, and although I gave him the main reason, he would not have it. Since I believe Your Highnesses will already have notice of all this and also of the chart or mappemonde which this man has made, I do not send it now, although it is here, and so far as I can see exceedingly false, in order to make believe that these are not part of the said islands. . . .

London, 25th July, 1498

38

PIETRO PASQUALIGO, VENETIAN AMBASSADOR IN PORTUGAL, TO HIS BROTHERS IN VENICE, 19 OCTOBER 1501

Paesi nouamente retrouati (Vicenza, 1507), lib. VI, cap. CXXVI.

[Lisbon, 19 October 1501] On the eighth of the present month arrived here one of the two caravels which this most august monarch sent out in the year past under Captain Gaspar Corterat to discover land towards the north; and they report that they have found land two thousand miles from here, between the north and the west, which never before was known to anyone. They examined the coast of the same for perhaps six hundred to seven hundred miles and never found the end, which leads them to think it a mainland. This continues to another land which was discovered last year in the north. The caravels were not able to arrive there on account of the sea being frozen and the great quantity of snow. They are led to this same opinion from the considerable number of very large rivers which they found there, for certainly no island could ever have so many nor such large ones. They say that this country is very populous and the houses of the inhabitants of long strips of wood covered over with the skins of fish. They have brought back here seven natives, men and women and children, and in the other caravel, which is expected from hour to hour are coming fifty others. These resemble gypsies in colour, features, stature and aspect; are clothed in the skins of various animals, but chiefly of otters. In summer they turn the hair outside and in winter the opposite way. And these skins are not sewn together in any way nor tanned, but just as they are taken from the animals; they wear them over their shoulders and arms. And their privy parts are fastened with cords made of very strong sinews of fish, so that they look like wild men. They are very shy and gentle, but well formed in arms and legs and shoulders beyond description. They have their faces marked like those of the Indians, some with six, some with eight, some with less marks. They speak, but are not understood by anyone, though I believe that they have been spoken to in every possible language. In their land there is no iron, but they make knives out of stones and in like manner the points of their arrows. And yet these men have brought from there a piece of broken gilt sword, which certainly seems to have been made in Italy. One of the boys was wearing in his ears two silver rings which without doubt seem to have been made in Venice, which makes me think it to be mainland, because it is not likely that ships would have gone there without their having been heard of. They have great quantity of salmon, herring, cod and similar fish. They have also great store of wood and above all of pines for making masts and yards of ships. On this account his Majesty here intends to draw great advantage from the said land, as well by the wood for ships, of which they are in want, as by the men, who will be excellent for labour and the best slaves that have hitherto been obtained. This has seemed to me worthy to be notified to you, and if anything more is learned by the arrival of the captain's caravel, I shall likewise let you know.

39

ALONSO DE SANTA CRUZ ON
THE NORTH-WESTERN DISCOVERIES

Extracts from Alonso de Santa Cruz, 'Islario General de todas las Islas del Mundo', completed in 1541. Here translated from the Spanish text (Vienna, Österr. Nationalbibliothek, MS 7195) printed by F. R. von Wieser (ed.), *Die Karten von Amerika in dem Islario General des Alonso de Santa Cruz* (Innsbruck, 1908), pp. 1-4. A slightly differing text

John Cabot's Voyages, 1497 and 1498

(Madrid, Biblioteca Nacional, MS J92) is printed and translated by Biggar, *Precursors*, pp. 183–94. The Madrid MS was published in full by Antonio Blázquez in 1918.

The Land of the Labrador

That region of which we now wish to treat is commonly called the land of the Labrador, opinions differing whether it is cut off from the continent of Engrovelandia, of which we made mention in the first part [of this MS], or whether it is all one land with the northern continent of Europe, which still awaits navigation, by reason of the harshness of that region, which is so cold that it can only be attempted in summer. Ziegler holds that this land is all continuous with Escondia, being influenced by what Antonio Gaboto said of it, who had coasted the land and northern shore even farther than the land of the Bacallaos and almost as far as Florida, that even in July there were such great floes and masses of ice on the sea, larger than their ships, which came along the coast propelled by the currents, that they could hardly keep clear of them; but that story was very confused, and one in which little trust was placed, as being the first [of its kind]. Olaus Magnus states that this land is cut off, so that according to him one could pass by it and round Escondia to go to the eastern islands, that is to say, on the eastern side of the same [i.e. of the land of Labrador]. As for the western side towards the land of the Bacallaos, it is said that two Portuguese brothers, named the Corte Reals, who went there to colonize by licence of the King of Portugal, and after whom it is also called the land of the Corte Reals, or Corteratos by the corruption of a syllable, asserted that the great main land of the West Indies, of which they occupied the extreme end, was separated from that island of the Labrador by a very large and wide sea channel, of which the pilot Antonio Gaboto, above named, also had information. It was called the land of the Labrador because a labrador [landholder] of the islands of the Azores gave notice and information about it to the King of England, when he sent in search of it Antonio Gaboto, the English pilot and father of

Sebastian Gaboto who now is Your Majesty's pilot-major. And since that time the land is frequented by the English who go there for fish, which the people of that land take in large quantities, which people they say are similar in their customs to those of Polonia, a province of Escondia, of which we spoke at the beginning of the first part. They obtain in the same way the furs of animals of great price and worth and carry thither merchandise which suits those people. It is said that the land is well peopled, with many trees and fine waters, and rivers of great volume, and with very small and very pleasant islands adjoining it along the whole coast, and with a well-stocked fishery. In the summer it has a pleasant aspect by reason of the many trees they say are there, an aspect which it does not retain in the winter on account of the heavy snowfall. The southern coast of this land, which is the part that has been hitherto explored, is a hundred and fifty leagues long, east and west, from the most easterly cape, called Cabo Gruesso to another called Cabo de las Islas. Many fine rivers spring from it, and along the coast are many islands, although uninhabited and of no value. In the western part there is a great bay with many islands. It is in the latitude of fifty-six degrees and in the eleventh climate. Its longest day is of seventeen hours and a quarter.

Island of St John: Islands of the Virgins

Adjoining the coast of the land which we have above named the Bachallaos, where the Corte Reales, the two Portuguese brothers, went to colonize, and which was first discovered by the pilot Antonio Gaboto, the Englishman, by command of the King of England, there are many islands, large and small, of all of which, to the present day, there is little knowledge because the land is very cold and of little value, and the two brothers aforesaid died there with all their men, although it is not known how, for nothing was ever heard of them from a short while after they reached that place; for which reason, and because of the small value of the land, the King of Portugal has not sought to send thither any more men or ships; but it is held to be a much better land than that of the Labrador, because it is warmer. [Continues with a confused account of a number of islands in the Newfoundland region, but without any more allusions to English discoveries.]

40

EXTRACTS FROM THE PATENT GRANTED BY THE SPANISH
SOVEREIGNS TO ALONSO DE OJEDA, 8 JUNE 1501

Archivo General de Simancas, Cédulas, no. 5. Original Spanish printed by M. Fernández de Navarrete, *Colección de los viages y descubrimientos*, vol. III (Madrid, 1829), pp. 85–8.

[Licence to Ojeda to pursue his discoveries on terms including the following:]

Firstly, that you may not touch in the land of the pearl-gathering, of that part of Paria from the coast of the Frailes and the gulf this side of Margarita, and on the other side as far as Farallon, and all that land which is called Citriana, in which you have no right to touch.

Item: that you go and follow that coast which you have discovered, which runs east and west, as it appears, because it goes towards the region where it has been learned that the English were making discoveries; and that you go setting up marks with the arms of their Majesties, or with other signs that may be known, such as shall seem good to you, in order that it be known that you have discovered that land, so that you may stop the exploration of the English in that direction.

Item: that you the said Alonso de Hojeda, for the service of their Majesties, enter that island and the others that are around it which are called Quiquevacoa in the region of the main land, where the green stones are, of which you have brought a sample, and that you obtain as many as you can, and in like manner see to the other things which you brought as specimens in that voyage.

Item: that you the said Alonso de Hojeda take steps to find out that which you have said you have learned of another gathering-place of pearls, provided that it be not within the limits above mentioned, and that in the same way you look for the gold-mines of whose existence you say you have news.

. . . .

And their Majesties, in consideration of what you have spent and the service you have done, and are now bound to do, make you the gift of the governorship of the island of Caquevacoa, which you have discovered, during their pleasure. . . . Likewise their Majesties make you gift in the island of Espanola of six leagues of land with its boundary, in the southern district which is called Maquana, that you may cultivate it and improve it, for what you shall discover on the coast of the main land for the stopping of the English, and the said six leagues of land shall be yours for ever.

BRISTOL AND THE NEW FOUND LAND

41

LETTERS PATENT TO JOÃO FERNANDES FROM THE KING OF PORTUGAL, 28 OCTOBER 1499

Lisbon, Archivo nacional da Torre do Tombo (Dom Manoel, livro XVI, fol. 39; Livro das Ilhas, fol. 63v). Portuguese text with translation in Biggar, *Precursors*, pp. 31–2.

[28 October 1499] King Emanuel, etc. To as many as shall see this grant, we make known, that João Fernandes, dwelling in our island of Terceira, has informed us that for God's service and our own he was desirous to make an effort to seek out and discover at his own expense some islands lying in our sphere of influence, and we, in view of this his praiseworthy desire and intention, not only thank him for it, but it is our pleasure and we hereby promise to grant him, as indeed we shall grant him, the governorship of any island or islands, either inhabited or uninhabited, which he may newly discover and find; and this with the same revenues, honours, profits and advantages we have granted to the governors of our islands of Madeira and the others; and for his protection and as a memorandum to ourselves we order this grant, signed and sealed by us with our seal attached, to be given to him. Given in our city of Lisbon on October 28. André Fernandes made this in the year of our Lord Jesus Christ, 1499.

42

THE PETITION OF RICHARD WARDE, THOMAS ASSHEHURST, JOHN THOMAS, JOÃO FERNANDES, FRANCISCO FERNANDES AND JOÃO GONSALVES TO HENRY VII FOR LETTERS PATENT, 19 MARCH 1501

Public Record Office, Warrants for Privy Seals, ser. II, no. 216. Printed by Biggar, *Precursors*, p. 40.

[19 March 1501] Memorandum that on March 19, in the 16th year

235

of King Henry VII, the following bill was considered by the Lord Keeper of the Great Seal of England at Westminster.

To the kyng our sovereyne Lord:

Please it your hignes of your most noble and haboundaunt grace to graunt unto your welbeloved subjectys Richard Warde, Thomas Asshehurst and John Thomas, merchauntys of your towne of Bristowe, and to John ffernandus, ffraunces ffernandus and John Gunsalus, Squyers borne in the Isle of Surrys [Azores] under the obeisaunce of the kyng of Portingale, your gracious Letters patentis under your greate seale, in due forme to be made accordyng to the tenour hereafter ensuying, and that this byll, signyd with your gracious hand, may be to the Reverend ffader in God, Henry, bysshop of Salesbury, keper of your gret seale, sufficient and immediate warrant for the making, sealying, accomplysshyng of your seyd Letters patentes; and they shall duryng ther lyves pray to God for the prosperous contynuaunce of your most noble and ryall astate.

43

LETTERS PATENT GRANTED TO RICHARD WARDE,
THOMAS ASSHEHURST, JOHN THOMAS,
JOÃO FERNANDES, FRANCISCO FERNANDES AND
JOÃO GONSALVES, 19 MARCH 1501

Public Record Office, Patent Roll 16 Hen. VII, pt. 1, membr. 20, 21; another copy, Warrants for Privy Seals, ser. II, no. 216. Original Latin, with translation, in Biggar, *Precursors*, pp. 41–59.

Pro concessione Ricardo Warde et aliis

The King to all and singular to whom our present letters patent shall come, Greeting: Be it known to you and made manifest that we, for certain considerations us moving, by the advice of our Council, have granted and given licence, as by these presents we grant and give licence for us and our heirs, as far as in us lies, to our well-beloved subjects Richard Warde, Thomas Asshehurst and

John Thomas, merchants of our town of Bristol, and to our well-beloved John Fernandez, Francis Fernandez and John Gonzales, Esquires, of the Islands of the Azores in the dominions of the King of Portugal, and to any one of them, and to the heirs, attorneys, factors or deputies of any one of them, and to them and any one of them we grant full and unrestricted authority, faculty and power to sail and transport themselves to all parts, regions and territories of the eastern, western, southern, arctic and northern seas, under our banners and ensigns, with so many and so large and such ships or vessels as may be agreeable to them and may be necessary, of whatsoever burthen any ship or vessel may be, with masters, mates, mariners, pages and other men competent, requisite and necessary for the piloting, safeguard and defence of the aforesaid ships and vessels, at the cost and charges of the said Richard and of the others aforesaid, and at such salaries, wages and pay as they may agree upon among themselves, to find, recover, discover and search out whatsoever islands, countries, regions or provinces of heathens and infidels, in whatever part of the world they may lie, which before this time were and at present are unknown to all Christians, and to set up our banners and ensigns in any town, city, castle, island or mainland by them thus newly found, and to enter and seize these same towns, and as our vassals and governors, lieutenants and deputies to occupy, possess and subdue these, the property, title, dignity and suzerainty of the same being always reserved to us. And furthermore whenever henceforth such islands, countries, lands and provinces shall be acquired, recovered and found by the aforesaid Richard and the others before-named, then we will and by these presents grant, that all and singular as well men and women of this our kingdom and the rest of our subjects, wishing and desiring to visit these lands and islands thus newly found, and to inhabit the same, shall be allowed and have power to go freely and in safety to the same countries, islands and places with their ships, men and servants, and all their goods and chattels, and to dwell in and inhabit the same under the protection and government of the said Richard and of the others aforesaid, and to acquire and keep the riches, fruits and profits of the lands, countries and places aforesaid; giving furthermore and granting to the aforesaid Richard, Thomas and John, John, Francis and John, and to any one of them, by the tenour of these presents full power and authority to rule and govern all and singular the men, sailors and other persons removing and making their way for the aforesaid purpose to the islands, countries, provinces, mainlands and places beforementioned, as well in the company of the said Richard and of the others aforesaid, as in the company of people happening afterwards to betake themselves there, both on the sea as well as in these islands, countries, mainlands and places after they have been found and recovered, and to make, set up, ordain and appoint laws, ordinances, statutes and proclamations for the good and peaceful rule and government of the said men, masters, sailors and other persons aforesaid, and also to issue proclamations to chastise and punish according to the laws and statutes set up by them in that region all and singular those whom they may find there hostile and rebellious and disobedient to the laws, statutes and ordinances aforesaid, and all who shall commit and perpetrate theft, homicide or robberies or who shall rape and violate against their will or otherwise any women of the islands or countries aforesaid. And furthermore we have granted to the aforesaid Richard, Thomas, John, John, Francis and John, their heirs and assigns, that when any islands, countries, mainlands, region or province shall henceforth be discovered by the same Richard and the others aforesaid, then it shall not be lawful for any subject or subjects of ours, during the term of ten years next and immediately following, to visit with their ships or to make their way to the same towns, countries, islands, mainlands and places, for the purpose of trading and obtaining goods, without the licence and permission of the said Richard and of the others aforesaid, their heirs and assigns, or to enter the same, or to send into the same to obtain any goods; and that after the term of the said ten years, none of our subjects shall presume to sail to or visit any mainland, island, country or place thus newly found by the said Richard and

Thomas and the others aforesaid without our licence and that of the said Richard and of the others aforesaid, on pain of the loss and forfeiture of all the goods, merchandise, commodities and vessels whatsoever daring to sail to these places thus newly discovered and to enter the same, namely, one-half of the same to be for our use, and the other half for the use of the said Richard and of the others aforesaid and of their heirs.

And furthermore of our abundant grace we have granted and by these presents grant for us and our heirs, as far as in us lies, to the aforesaid Richard, Thomas, John, John, Francis and John and any one of them, their heirs and assigns, that they and any one of them shall have power and permission to bring and transport and cause to be brought or transported merchandise and wares, gold and silver in bar, precious stones, and other goods whatsoever grown in the countries, islands and places aforesaid by them thus to be recovered and found, as well in the said ships and vessels as in other strange ships whatsoever, from the said countries, islands, mainlands and places into this our realm of England, to any port whatsoever or other place in the same, and to sell and distribute these for their own profit and advantage, any statute, act, ordinance, restriction or order made to the contrary notwithstanding.

And we, bearing in mind most especially the heavy costs and charges which are required for the performance and execution of the above, wishing therefore to do special favour in like manner to the aforesaid Richard, Thomas and the other persons mentioned, have granted and by these presents grant to the same, their heirs and assigns, that they and any one of them, their heirs and assigns aforesaid, may from time to time during the term of four years from the date of the recovery and discovery of the islands and countries aforesaid next and immediately following, land in the port or place aforesaid the merchandise and wares and other goods, loaded and carried on one vessel, of so great tonnage whatsoever she be, and which are to be brought and transported into this our realm of England, and may sell, expose and distribute these at their pleasure from time to time after any voyage during the term of the said four years, without in any way paying to us or to our heirs within our said realm of England, any customs, subsidies or other dues on the same goods, merchandise and other things aforesaid contained and carried in the said one vessel only. Provided nevertheless that with regard to the customs, subsidies, poundages and other dues to be paid on the rest of the merchandise, wares and goods on board all the other vessels, true answers, as is right, be given to us, according to the practice hitherto prevailing in this our realm of England. And furthermore we will and grant by these presents that any chief master, mate and sailor of any ship whatsoever visiting and sailing to any mainland, island, country, province and place aforesaid, may have, enjoy and receive of the goods and wares to be brought from the said islands, mainlands and countries into this our realm of England, the following customs and subsidies, namely: that any master may have, enjoy and receive on any voyage the customs and subsidies of four tons, and any mate or quartermaster the customs and subsidies of two tons, and any sailor the customs and subsidies of one ton, even though they be loaded and carried as his own goods or as the goods of any other person whatsoever; and this without any customs, subsidies, dues or duties being in any way paid or asked for the same tonnage within this our realm of England for our needs or those of our heirs.

And should it happen that any merchant or merchants of this our realm arrive at the said islands, countries and places by licence of our said subjects or without their licence, for the purpose of obtaining merchandise and wares, and should carry on business and bring goods and wares from those parts into this our kingdom, then we will and grant by these presents to the aforesaid Richard, Thomas, John, John, Francis and John, their heirs and assigns, that they, during the aforesaid term of ten years, may receive from any such merchant, the customs, subsidies and other dues having been paid that it is customary to remit to us in such case, the twentieth part of all such goods and merchandise brought and transported by the same from the said islands, countries and places into this our realm of England on any voyage during the said term of ten years, this twentieth part to be had and taken in the port in which it shall happen that the said goods are unloaded and discharged. Provided always that during the said term of ten years the aforesaid Richard and the other aforesaid, their heirs and assigns, and not any other persons, be the factors and attorneys in the said islands, mainlands and countries in behalf of any such merchants and other persons repairing there for the aforesaid cause in and for the trade carried on there for them. Provided also that no vessel charged and loaded with goods and merchandise from the said regions thus newly found, after she has been brought into any port of this our realm, be discharged of the said goods and merchandise except in the presence of the aforesaid Richard and of the others aforesaid, or of their heirs or deputies to be assigned for this purpose, or pain of the forfeiture of the said goods and merchandise, whereof one half shall be applied to our needs and the other half be given to the aforesaid Richard and to the others before-named and to their heirs. And if afterwards any strangers or other persons should presume against the wish of the said Richard and of the others before-named to sail to these said regions for the purpose of enriching themselves, and to enter the same by violence, and there to insult the said Richard and the others aforesaid or their heirs, and to conquer and expel them, or otherwise to disturb them, then we will and by the tenour of these presents give and grant power to the same subjects of ours, to expel and resist with all their force, as well by land as by sea and fresh water, these strangers, even though they be subjects and vassals of some prince in league and friendship with us, and to wage and carry on war against them, and to arrest, bind and place them in prison, there to remain until they shall have made fine and redemption to our said subjects; or otherwise to chastise and punish them according to the sober discretion of our said subjects and of their heirs.

And also by the tenour of these presents we give and grant full power to our aforesaid subjects, and to the other persons aforesaid, to make, constitute, nominate and appoint under them by their letters patent to be sealed with their seals, any captains, lieutenants and deputies whatsoever in each of the states, cities, towns and places aforesaid for the administration and government of all and singular the persons in those parts, under the rule and authority of our said subjects there dwelling, and for the due execution and administration of justice in the same, according to the tenour and import of the ordinances, statutes and proclamations aforesaid. And furthermore we have granted and by these presents grant to the aforesaid Richard, Thomas, John, John, Francis and John for the term of their lives and of the life of any one of them, the office of Admiral at sea in any of the places, countries and provinces whatsoever by them thus newly discovered and henceforth to be found and recovered; and we make, constitute, ordain and appoint by these presents the said Richard, Thomas, John, John, Francis and John and any one of them whomsoever, conjointly and separately, our Admirals in the same parts, giving and granting to them and to any one of them whomsoever, by the tenour of these presents, full power and authority to do, exercise and carry out all and singular the things which pertain to the office of Admiral, according to the law and the naval custom obtaining in this our realm of England.

And further after the aforesaid Richard Warde, Thomas Ashehurst and John Thomas and John Fernandez, Francis Fernandez and John Gonzales shall have thus found, acquired and subdued with our assistance, any mainlands, islands, countries and provinces, cities, castles, states and towns, then we will and by these presents grant to them, their heirs and assigns, that they and their heirs may have, hold and possess for themselves, their heirs and assigns all and singular, such and so great mainlands, islands, countries, provinces, castles, cities, fortresses, states, and towns as and as great as they and their agents, lieutenants and servants are able to inhabit, take possession of, hold and maintain; the same lands, islands and places aforesaid to be had and held by them, their heirs and assigns, and by any one of them whomsoever, of us and of our heirs in perpetuity by fidelity alone, without any composition or anything else being rendered or made to us or to our heirs for the same, always excepting the dignity, dominion, regality, jurisdiction and suzerainty of the same, wholly reserved to us. And furthermore we have granted to the aforesaid Richard, Thomas, John, John, Francis and John, that when the said mainlands, islands and countries thus made over to them and to their heirs aforesaid, as set forth above, have been discovered and recovered, and when they are in full possession of the same, they, their heirs and assigns may hold, possess and enjoy the same freely, quietly and peaceably, without any impediment of any sort from us or from any of our heirs whomsoever. And that none of our subjects shall in any way expel them or any one of them from and out of their possession and title to and in the said mainlands, islands and countries in any wise against their will. Promising in good faith and on the word of a king that we shall hold ratified, acceptable and stable all and whatsoever the aforesaid Richard, Thomas, John, John, Francis and John, and any of them whosoever, by way of completing the premises, shall do or shall do or shall procure to be done herein. And that neither we nor our heirs ever nor at any time in the future shall disturb, hinder or molest them or any one of them or their heirs and assigns in their right, title and possession, nor shall we permit nor cause this to be done or brought about, nor shall we cause it to be done by others our subjects, or others whomsoever, so far as in us lies; nor shall we in any way remove them, their heirs and assigns from the said mainlands, countries, provinces and places for any cause afterwards arising or happening, nor shall we cause them to be removed or expelled by our subjects.

And further of our greater special goodness and very own motion we have granted and by these presents grant for us and our heirs, as far as in us lies, to John Fernandez, Francis Fernandez and John Gonzales Esquires, of the Islands of the Azores, born subjects of the king of Portugal and to any one of them whomsoever, that

243

they and any one of them and all their children, as well born as to
be born, are for ever subjects and lieges of us and of our heirs, and
in all lawsuits, quarrels, affairs and matters whatsoever are to be
considered, treated, held, esteemed and governed as our true and
faithful lieges born within our realm of England, and not otherwise nor in any other way. And that they and all their children
aforesaid, and any one of them whomsoever, may carry on and
bring real, personal and mixed actions in all courts, places and
jurisdictions of ours whatsoever in all ways, and may use and benefit by these and may sue and be sued in the same, answer and be
answered to, defend them and be defended in all things and
everywhere as our true and faithful lieges born within our realm
aforesaid. And that they, and any one of them whoseoever, may
examine, take, receive, own, hold, possess and inherit for himself,
his heirs and assigns, in perpetuity or in any other way whatsoever,
lands, tenements, rents, reversions, services and other possessions
whatsoever, as well in full ownership as in reversion, within our
said realm of England and the other dominions and places under
our obedience, and these give away, sell, alienate and bequeath to
any person or persons whomsoever, as it may please them, freely,
quietly, lawfully and safely, and any one of them may so do at his
pleasure, as freely, fully and peaceably as any liege of ours born
within our realm of England is able and has power to do. In such a
way nevertheless that the aforesaid John and Francis Fernandez
and John Gonzales, and all their children aforesaid, pay or cause
to be paid, and each of them pays or causes to be paid, such customs, taxes and other dues for their goods, wares, merchandise and
commodities which are to be brought into our realm of England
or taken out of the same, as foreigners pay to us, or ought, or are
accustomed to pay. And that the same John and Francis Fernandez
and John Gonzales, and all their children aforesaid, from henceforward under colour or in virtue of any statute, ordinance or
grant made or to be made in our parliament or out of our parliament, be not forced, held nor compelled nor any one of them be
forced, held or compelled to pay, give, render or bring to us or to

any of our heirs, or to anyone else whomsoever, any taxes, tallages or other dues whatsoever for their lands, tenements, goods or persons, except such and so much as our other faithful lieges, born within our said realm pay, give, render or bring, or are accustomed and held to pay, give, render or bring generally for their goods, lands, tenements or persons; but that the aforesaid John and Francis Fernandez and John Gonzales, and all their children aforesaid, and any one of them, may and can have and possess all things and all other liberties, privileges, franchises and customs, and may use and enjoy them, and any one of them may so do within our said realm of England, our jurisdictions and dominions whatsoever, as freely, quietly, fully and peaceably as the rest of our lieges, born within our said realm generally hold, use and enjoy them, or ought and should hold, possess, use and enjoy them; any statute, act, ordinance, or any other cause, affair or matter whatsoever notwithstanding. Provided always that the aforesaid John and Francis Fernandez and John Gonzales, and each of them does liege homage to us, and that they and each one of them aids with lot and scot and with the other dues payable and customary everywhere in our aforesaid realm, as our lieges do who are born within our said kingdom. Provided also that the said John and Francis Fernandez and John Gonzales pay, and each of them pays to us and to our heirs so many and such customs, subsidies and other dues for their goods and merchandise as foreigners are held to pay and give to us.

And further of our greater goodness we have granted to the aforesaid Richard, Thomas, John, John, Francis and John, that they may have our present letters in our Chancery without payment to us of any fine or fee or of any fines or fees for the same letters of ours, or for any part thereof, or for our Great Seal in any way at the Exchequer of our said Chancery. And we will and grant by these presents that the most Reverend father in God, Henry, bishop of Salisbury, the Custodian of our Great Seal, by the authority of this present grant of ours, shall cause to be prepared and sealed so many and such briefs sealed with our Great Seal and directed to the custodian or clerk of our Exchequer for the discharge of the said fines and fees, as and such as may be necessary and requisite for the same without any other warrant or attendance being made before us in this matter.

In witness whereof, etc.

Witness ourself at Westminster on the nineteenth day of March.

By the king himself, and at the date aforesaid, etc.

And the customs' officers, or the collectors of the king's customs and subsidies at the port of his town of Bristol, both present and future, are ordered according to the tenour of the aforesaid letters, to allow the aforesaid Richard, Thomas, John, John, Francis and John, and any one of them whomsoever, their heirs and assigns to land at the aforesaid harbour whatsoever goods, merchandise and wares contained, loaded and carried in the said one vessel, of whatsoever burthen she be, which are brought and transported from the said islands, countries and places to be found and recovered by the same as aforesaid, to the said port of Bristol, from time to time on any voyage during the term of the said four years from the date of the recovery and discovery of the islands, countries and places aforesaid, without payment of any customs, subsidies or other dues to the said lord the king or to his heirs for the said goods, merchandise and wares, and to set out, sell and distribute these at their will, and not to molest nor oppress the said persons contrary to the tenour of the said letters.

Witness the king at Westminster on the nineteenth day of March.

And the aforesaid customs' officers, or the collectors in the aforesaid port, both present and future, are ordered according to the tenour of the aforesaid letters, to allow the aforesaid masters, mates or quartermasters and sailors of any ship whatsoever, sailing and making its way to any mainland, country or place aforesaid, and any one of them whomsoever, to have, enjoy and receive from time to time the customs and subsidies of the aforesaid tonnage in the form and manner stated above, without the payment by them or by any of them whomsoever in any way of any customs, subsidies and other dues to the said lord the king for the said tonnage in and on any voyage whatsoever, and they are not to molest nor oppress them or any one of them in any way contrary to the tenour of these said presents.

Witness the king at Westminster on the nineteenth day of March.

44

GRANT OF BOUNTY TO ROBERT THORNE, WILLIAM THORNE AND HUGH ELYOT, 7 JANUARY 1502

Public Record Office, Exchequer, Warrants for Issues, E. 404/84.

[7 January 1502] Henry by the grace of god king of England and of ffraunce and lord of Irland, To the Tresourer and Chambrelains of our Eschequier greting. Where as Robert Thorne, hugh Elyot and William Thorne of oure Town of Bristowe merchauntes of late have bought at Depe in the parties of Normandy a ship called the verdure of Depe and now named by them the Gabriell of Bristowe, of the portage of six score tonnes or therabouts, and have doo the said ship to be conveied to Bourdeaux, and there have charged her with wynes, woad and other merchaundises to be conveied fromthens to oure said Town of Bristowe, and with the same ship the said merchauntes offre to doo unto us service at alle tymes at our commaundement, In consideracion wherof and towardes theire costes and charges in that partie we have yeven and graunted unto them the summe of twenty poundes to be taken and reteigned in theire owne handes of the custumes, subsidies and othre duties to us belonging of suche wynes, woad and other merchaundises as the said ship shall bring at her next arryvall from Bourdeaux into oure said poort of Bristowe. We wol therefore . . . you that at the receipt of oure said Eschequier ye doo levye and stake out in due and sufficient forme a taille conteigning . . . said summe of twenty poundes for the said Robert

247

Thorne, hugh Elyot and William Thorne, to be levied upon the cust . . . collectde of our Custumes and subsidies in oure said poort of Bristowe of and upon the Custumes and subsidies of such . . . woad and othre goodes and merchaundises as is charged in the said ship, now at her furst arryvall in our said poort as is. . . . And that taill soo in due forme levied ye delyver unto the said merchauntes for their sufficient discharge of the said summe . . . . prest or other charge to be sette upon them or eny of them for the same. And thies oure lettres shalbe youre sufficient warrant and discharge in that behalf. Yeven undre oure Previe Seale at our manour of Richemount the vijth day of January the xvijth yere of oure Reigne.

45

PAYMENT TO THOMAS THORNE, 4 MAY 1502

From the Bristol Customs Records in the Public Record Office.

E. 122/20, 14. View of Account, 17 Hen. VII,
Michaelmas–Easter [*1501–2*]

[Among various payments to be deducted] xx^{li} by them paid by j tally levied at the aforesaid rate on the iiijth day of May in the xvijth year of the aforesaid King on behalf of Thomas Thorne and on seeing this duly shown.

46

GRANT OF PENSIONS TO FRANCISCO FERNANDES AND JOÃO GONSALVES, 26 SEPTEMBER 1502

Public Record Office, Warrants for Issues, E. 404/84, 1. Printed by Biggar, *Precursors*, pp. 91–2.

Henry, by the grace of God King of England and of ffraunce, and lord of Irland, To the Tresourer and Chambrelains of oure Eschequier, greting: Where as We by our letters undre oure prive seal bering date at oure manour of Langley the xxvi[th] day of septembre, the xviii[th] yere of oure Reigne [1502], gaf and graunted unto oure trusty and welbeloved subgiettes, ffraunceys ffernandus and John Guidisalvus, squiers, in consideracion of the true service which they have doon unto us to oure singler pleasure as Capi-taignes into the newe founde lande, unto eithre of them ten poundes yerely during oure pleasure to be had and perceyved of the Revenues of oure Custumes commyng and growing within oure poort of Bristowe, by the handes of the customers there that now be and hereafter shalbe, at the festes of Estre and Michaelmas, by even porcions, And forasmoche as Richard Meryk and Arthure Kemys, late Custumers in oure said poort of Bristowe, have paide unto the said ffraunceys ffernandus and John Guidi-salvus twenty poundes for oon hool yere ended at the fest of Saint Michell tharchaungell last past [29 September 1503], for the which they have no maner of discharge to be alleged at theire accomptes before the Barons of oure Eschequier, Wherfore we wol that ye in due and sufficient fourme doo to be levied for thesaid ffraunceys ffernandus and John Guidisalvus a taille or tailles conteignying the said summe of xx li. upon Richard Meryk and Arthure Kemys, late Custumers in oure said poort, of the revenues of thesame, And furthermore we wol that ye fromhens-forth from tyme to tyme and yere to yere, doo to be levied severall tailles conteignyng thesaid summe of xx li. upon the Customers of oure said poort that nowe be and herafter shallbe, unto the tyme ye shall have from us otherwise in commaundement by writing, And thesaid taille or tailles in due and sufficient fourme levied upon thesaid Custumers at the festes beforesaid, we wol that ye delyvere unto thesaid ffraunceys ffernandus and John Guidisalvus, or unto the bringer herof in theire names, to be taken of oure gyfte by way of rewarde without preste or eny othre maner of charge to be set upon them or eny of them for thesame, And thies oure letters shalbe youre sufficient warrant in that behalf. Yeven undre oure prive Seal at oure Citie of London the vi[th] day of Decembre, the xix[th] yere of oure Reigne [1503].

LETTERS PATENT GRANTED TO HUGH ELYOT,
THOMAS ASSHEHURST, JOÃO GONSALVES AND
FRANCISCO FERNANDES, 9 DECEMBER 1502

Public Record Office, Patent Roll 18 Hen. VII, p. 2, membr. 29–30.
Latin text first printed by T. Rymer, *Fœdera*, vol. xiii (London, 1712),
pp. 37–42; reprinted, with translation, by Biggar, *Precursors*, pp. 70–91.

Of Licence to discover unknown Land

The king to all and singular to whom the present letters shall
come, Greeting: Be it known to you and made manifest that we,
for certain considerations us moving, by the advice of our
Council, have granted and given licence, as by these presents we
grant and give licence for us and our heirs, as far as in us lies, to our
well-beloved subjects Hugh Elyot and Thomas Asshehurste, merchants of our town of Bristol, and to our well-beloved John
Gonzales and Francis Fernandez, Esquires, of the islands of the
Azores, born under the dominion of the king of Portugal, and to
any one of them whomsoever, and to the heirs, attorneys, factors
or deputies of any one of them, and to them and to any one of
them whomsoever, we grant full and free authority, faculty and
power to sail and transport themselves to all parts, regions and
territories of the eastern, western, southern, arctic and northern
seas, under our banners and ensigns, with so many and so large and
such ships or vessels as may be agreeable to them and may be
necessary, of whatsoever burthen any ship or vessel may be, with
masters, mates, mariners, pages and other men competent, requisite and necessary for the piloting, safe-conduct and defence of the
aforesaid ships and vessels, at the cost and charges of the said Hugh
and of the others aforesaid, and at such salaries, wages and stipends
as they may agree upon among themselves, to find, recover,
discover and search out any islands, countries, regions or provinces
whatsoever of heathens and infidels in whatsoever part of the
world placed, and to set up our banners and ensigns in any city,
town, castle, island or mainland by them thus newly found, and to

enter and seize the said cities, towns, castles, islands and mainlands for us and in our name, and as our vassals and governors, lieutenants and deputies to occupy, possess, and subdue these, the property, title, dignity and suzerainty of the same being always reserved to us. Provided always that they in no wise occupy themselves with nor enter the lands, countries, regions or provinces of heathens or infidels first discovered by the subjects of our very dear brother and cousin the king of Portugal, or by the subjects of any other princes soever, our friends and confederates, and in possession of which these same princes now find themselves. And furthermore whenever henceforth these islands, countries, lands and provinces shall be acquired, recovered and found by the aforesaid Hugh and the others named, then we will by these presents that all and singular, as well men as women, of this our realm, and the rest of our subjects wishing and desiring to visit these lands and islands thus newly found, and to inhabit the same, may and shall have power to go freely and in safety to the said countries, islands and places with their ships, men and servants and with all their goods and chattels, and to dwell in and inhabit the same under the protection and government of the said Hugh and of the others aforesaid, and to acquire and obtain the riches, fruits and profits of the lands, countries and places aforesaid.

Giving furthermore and granting to the aforesaid Hugh, Thomas, John and Francis and to any one of them, by the tenour of these presents, full power and authority to rule and govern all and singular the men, sailors, and other persons removing and making their way to the islands, countries, provinces, mainlands and places aforesaid for the aforesaid purpose as well in the company of the said Hugh and of the others aforesaid, as in the company of others happening afterwards to betake themselves there, both on sea as well as in each of these countries, mainlands and places, after they have been found and recovered; and to make, set up, ordain and appoint laws, ordinances, statutes and proclamations for the good and peaceful rule and government of the said men, masters, sailors and other persons aforesaid, and also to issue proclamations, and to chastise and punish according to the laws and statutes set up by them in that region all and singular those whom they may find there hostile and rebellious and disobedient to the laws, statutes and ordinances aforesaid and all those who shall commit and perpetrate theft, homicide or robbery, or who shall rape and violate any women of the islands or countries aforesaid against their will or otherwise.

And also we have granted to the aforesaid Hugh, Thomas, John and Francis, their heirs and assigns, that when any islands, countries, mainlands, region or province shall be henceforth discovered by the said Hugh and others aforesaid, then it shall not be lawful for any subject or subjects of ours, during the term of forty years next and immediately following, to visit with their ships or to make their way to the said towns, countries, islands, mainlands and places for the purpose of trading and obtaining goods, without our royal licence and that of the said Hugh and of the others aforesaid, their heirs and assigns, or to enter the same, or to send to the same to obtain any goods. And after the term of the said forty years, that none of our subjects shall presume to sail to or visit any mainland, island, country or place thus newly found by the same Hugh and Thomas and the others aforesaid, without our aforesaid licence and that of the said Hugh and of the others aforesaid, on pain of the loss and forfeiture of all the goods and merchandise, commodities and vessels whatsoever venturing to sail to these places thus newly discovered and to enter the same, namely: one half to be for us and the other half for the said Hugh and the others aforesaid and for their heirs.

And furthermore of our abundant grace we have granted and by these presents grant for us and our heirs, as far as in us lies, to the aforesaid Hugh, Thomas, John and Francis, and to any one of them whomsoever, their heirs and assigns, that they and any one of them may and can bring and transport and cause to be brought or transported merchandise, wares, gold and silver in bar, precious stones, and other goods whatsoever, being the produce of the countries, islands and places aforesaid by them thus to be recovered and found, as well in the said ships and vessels, as in other strange ships whatsoever, from the said countries, islands mainlands and places into this our realm of England, to any port whatsoever or other place in the same, and these sell and distribute for their own profit and advantage, any statute, act, ordinance or provision made or passed thence to the contrary notwithstanding.

And we, bearing in mind most especially the heavy costs and charges which are necessary for the performance and execution of the above, wishing therefore to do special favour on that account to the aforesaid Hugh, Thomas and to the other persons mentioned, have granted, as by these presents we grant, to the same, their heirs and assigns, that they and any one of them whosoever, their heirs and assigns aforesaid, may, from time to time during the period of five years from the date of the recovery and discovery of the islands and countries aforesaid next and immediately following, land in the port or place aforesaid merchandise, wares and other goods, loaded and freighted on one vessel alone, of so great tonnage whatsoever it be, which are to be brought and transported into this our realm of England, and these sell, expose and distribute at their pleasure from time to time on any voyage during the period of the said five years without in any way paying to us or to our heirs within our said realm of England, any customs, subsidies or other duties upon the same goods, merchandise and other things aforesaid contained and loaded in the said one vessel alone. Provided nevertheless that with regard to the customs, subsidies, poundages and other payments for the rest of the merchandise, wares and goods on board all the other vessels, true answers as is right be given to us in conformity with the practice hitherto observed in this our realm of England.

And furthermore we will and grant by these presents that any master, mate and sailor of any ship whatsoever visiting and sailing to any mainland, island, country, province and place aforesaid, may have, enjoy and receive of the goods and wares to be brought from the said islands, mainlands and countries into this our realm of England the following customs and subsidies, namely: any master may have, enjoy and receive in any voyage the customs and subsidies on four tons; and any mate or quartermaster the customs and subsidies on two tons; and any sailor the customs and subsidies on one ton, even though they be loaded and charged as his own goods, or as the goods of any other person whomsoever. And this without any subsidies, customs, dues or duties being in any way paid or asked for the same tonnage within this our realm of England for our needs or those of our heirs.

And should it happen that any merchant or merchants of this our realm should arrive at the said islands, countries and places under licence of our said subjects, or without their licence, for the purpose of obtaining merchandise or wares, and should make a business of bringing goods and wares from those parts into this our kingdom, then we will grant by these presents to the aforesaid Hugh, Thomas, John and Francis, and to their heirs and assigns, that they, during the aforesaid period of forty years may receive from any such merchant, after payment to us of the usual customs, subsidies and other moneys due to us in such case, the twentieth part of all such goods and merchandise to be brought and taken by the same from the said islands, countries and places into this our realm of England on any voyage during the said period of forty years; this twentieth part to be obtained and taken in the port in which it shall happen that the said goods are unloaded and discharged. Provided always that the aforesaid Hugh and the others aforesaid, their heirs and assigns, and not any others whatsoever are henceforward the factors and attorneys in the said islands, mainlands and countries for any such merchants and other persons repairing there for the aforesaid cause during the said period of forty years in and for the trade carried on there by them. Provided also that no vessel loaded and freighted with goods and merchandise from the said regions thus newly found, after it has been brought into any port of this our kingdom, shall be discharged of these goods and merchandise except in the presence of the aforesaid Hugh and of the others aforesaid, or of their heirs or deputies assigned for this purpose on pain of the forfeiture of the said goods and merchandise, of which one half shall be for us and the other half to be given to the aforesaid Hugh and the others before-named and to their heirs.

And if in future any strangers or other persons should presume against the wish of the said Hugh and the others beforenamed to sail to those parts for the purpose of enriching themselves, and to enter the same by violence, and there to insult the said Hugh and the others aforesaid or their heirs, and to expel and subdue them or otherwise to disturb them, then it is our wish and by the tenour of these presents we give and grant power to our said subjects to expel, resist and with all their force carry on and wage war, as well by land as by sea and on fresh water, against these strangers, even though they be subjects and vassals of any prince in league and friendship with us, and to arrest, bind and imprison them, there to remain until they shall have made fine and redemption to our said subjects, or otherwise to chastise and punish them according to the sober discretion of our said subjects and of their heirs.

And also by the tenour of these presents we give and grant full power to our aforesaid subjects and to the other persons aforesaid to make, constitute, nominate and appoint under them, by their letters patent to be sealed with their seals, any captains, lieutenants and deputies whomsoever in each of the states, cities towns and places of the said islands, provinces, countries and places aforesaid, for the administration and government of all and singular the persons in those parts, under the rule and authority of our said subjects there dwelling, and for the due execution and administra-tion of justice in the same, according to the tenour and effect of the ordinances, statutes and proclamations aforesaid.

And furthermore we have granted and by these presents grant to the aforesaid Hugh, Thomas, John and Francis, for the term of their lives and of the life of any one of them, the office of Admiral at sea in any of the places, countries and provinces whatsoever by them thus newly discovered, and henceforth to be found and recovered; and we make, constitute, ordain and appoint by these presents the said Hugh, Thomas, John and Francis and any one of them, conjointly and separately, our Admirals in the same parts, giving and granting them and any one of them by the tenour of these presents full power and authority to do, exercise and carry out all and singular the things which pertain to the office of Admiral, according to the law and naval custom practised in this our realm of England.

And further after the aforesaid Hugh, Thomas, John and Francis shall thus have found, acquired and subdued any mainlands, islands, countries and provinces, cities, castles, states and towns by our assistance, then it is our wish and by these presents we give power to them, their heirs and assigns, to have hold and possess for themselves, their heirs and assigns, all and singular such and so great mainlands, islands, countries, provinces, castles, cities, fortresses, states and towns, as and as great as they and their agents, lieutenants and servants are able to inhabit, take possession of, hold and maintain; the said lands, islands and places aforesaid to be had and held by them, their heirs and assigns, and by any one of them, of us and of our heirs in perpetuity by fidelity alone, without any fee or anything else being rendered or made to us or to our heirs for the same always excepting the dignity, dominion, regality, jurisdiction and suzerainty of the same, wholly reserved to us.

And furthermore we have granted to the aforesaid Hugh, Thomas, John and Francis that they, their heirs and assigns aforesaid, may enjoy, hold and possess the said mainlands, islands and countries thus conceded to them and to their heirs aforesaid as set forth above, after these have been discovered and receovered and when they are in full possession of the same, freely, quietly, peaceably, without any impediment of any sort from us or our heirs whomsoever. And that none of our subjects shall in any way expel them or any one of them from and out of their possession and title to and in the said mainlands, islands and countries in any way whatsoever against their will; promising in good faith and on the work of a king that we shall hold ratified, acceptable and stable all and whatsoever the aforesaid Hugh, Thomas, John and Francis, and any one of them whosoever, by way of completing the premises, shall do or shall procure to be done herein. And that neither we nor our heirs at any time in the future shall ever disturb, hinder or molest them or any one of them or their heirs and assigns in their right, title and possession, nor shall we permit this to be done, nor cause it to be done by others our subjects or others whomsoever, as far as in us lies; nor shall we in any way remove them, their heirs and assigns from the said mainlands, countries, provinces and places for any cause afterwards arising or happening, nor shall we cause them to be removed or expelled by our subjects. Provided always that should it happen that the said Hugh, Thomas, John and Francis or any one of them, their heirs or assigns, or any one of these find, search out or recover in the future any places, islands, lands, regions, provinces or countries which heretofore have not been found discovered, searched out and recovered by others our subjects or by any of their heirs and assigns having authority from us in that region by other letters patent of ours under our Great Seal, then it is our wish and by these presents we grant for us and our heirs to the aforesaid Hugh, Thomas, John and Francis, and to any one of them, their heirs and assigns, that they and any one of them whosoever may and shall have power to enter, hold, administer and peaceably and securely to inhabit and cause to be inhabited and to occupy at their free will the aforesaid islands, countries, provinces and other places with their ships, men, servants and chattels whatsoever, without hindrance or impediment from us or our heirs or from any others our lieges whomsoever. And that none of our other subjects shall dare to sail or to frequent any island, land, region, country and province or place thus newly found by the same Hugh, Thomas, John and Francis, or to enter the same, for the purpose of acquiring or securing the fruits, wares and merchandise produced in the same, without obtaining our royal licence and the special one of the aforesaid Hugh, Thomas, John and Francis, on pain of the loss and forfeiture of all goods, merchandise, commodities, and ships whatsoever venturing to sail to and enter these places thus newly found by the same, namely: one half of these to be for us and the other half for the said Hugh, Thomas, John and Francis, their heirs and assigns.

And although by other letters patent of ours dated the nineteenth day of the month of May [*sic pro* March] in the sixteenth year of our reign [1501], we have given and granted to our well-beloved Richard Warde, John Thomas and John Fernandez, and to the aforesaid Hugh Eliot,[1] Thomas Asshehurst, John Gonzales and Francis Fernandez, their heirs, attorneys, factors or deputies, and to any of them whomsoever, power and authority to sail to all parts, regions and boundaries of the sea in order to find and recover and discover the islands, countries and provinces mentioned, and to pursue and carry out each of the other things contained and specified in the same letters according to the tenour and effect thereof; nevertheless we are unwilling that the same Richard Warde, John Thomas, and John Fernandez or any one of them, their heirs or assigns, should in any way enter, or that any one of them should enter or go near any of the countries, islands, lands, places or provinces found, recovered or discovered anew in the future under the authority and licence of any of these our present letters, unless they shall have first obtained leave from the aforesaid Hugh, Thomas Asshehurst, John Gonzales and Francis.

And in case the said Richard Warde, John Thomas and John Fernandez, or any one of them, or their heirs or assigns, may wish, determine and decide to make their way to these islands, countries, regions and other places aforesaid with their ships and goods in order to acquire wares in the said islands, countries and other places aforesaid, or to send and depute thither any person or persons, that they and any one of them whosoever shall be obliged from time to time to pay, furnish and sustain all and every the costs and charges to be arranged at each voyage with the aforesaid Hugh, Thomas Asshehurst, John Gonzales and Francis,

---

[1] Eliot's name is evidently inserted in error.

258

namely: any of them according to the amount of his share, as they may agree among themselves, as often as they shall undertake any voyage of this kind and make their way from this our realm to the countries and other places to be acquired and recovered as aforesaid. And furthermore since among the other things set out in the above-mentioned articles, we have granted to the aforesaid Hugh, Thomas Asshehurst, John Gonzales and Francis that they and any one of them whosoever, their heirs and assigns, can and may conduct and transport into this our realm of England, as often as they please, during a period of five years, one vessel, of whatsoever burthen she be, loaded and freighted with all kinds of goods, merchandise and wares produced in the countries, islands, provinces, lands and places whatsoever aforesaid, without paying to us any customs, subsidies and other dues for the same, and freely dispose thereof; we now bearing in mind the praiseworthy intention which the aforesaid Hugh, Thomas Asshehrust, John Gonzales and Francis entertain and practise to the honour and utility and contentment of this our realm, and considering their great costs and heavy charges, as well as the dangers both to their person as to their goods and chattels whatsoever, which to all appearances they are about to incur in such a difficult, tempestuous, dangerous and distant maritime undertaking, of our abundant grace, have granted and given licence for us and our heirs to the aforesaid Hugh, Thomas Asshehurst, John Gonzales and Francis, and to any one of them whomsoever, their heirs and assigns, and to any one of these whomsoever, that they and any one of them whosoever may and can conduct and transport into this our kingdom, jurisdictions and territories, as often as it may please them, a second vessel of one hundred and twenty tons burthen, loaded and freighted with goods, commodities, jewels, gold and silver and other wares and merchandise produced in the countries, islands, provinces and other places by them thus henceforth newly to be recovered, during a period of five years from the date of the recovery of the islands and countries aforesaid next and immediately following, and there discharge her, and deal as they wish with the goods, commodities, merchandise, jewels and other things above stated, and the same shall be permitted and allowed to their heirs and assigns, and to any one of them whomsoever, freely and securely, without in any way paying to us any customs, subsidies or other dues for the same or any portion of the same. And this without any impediment, exaction, objection, annoyance or hinderance whatsoever from us or from our officers or servants whomsoever.

And furthermore since among other things contained and set forth in our letters patent dated at Westminster on the said nineteenth of May [i.e. March], in the sixteenth year of our reign [1501], we, for certain considerations us moving, having granted to the aforesaid John Gonzales and Francis, that they should be for ever subjects and lieges of us and of our heirs, and in all lawsuits, quarrels, matters and affairs whatsoever should be held, considered, treated and governed as our true and faithful lieges born within this our realm of England, and not otherwise nor in any other manner; and that the same John Gonzales and Francis and all their children should pay or cause to be paid, and any one of them whosoever should pay or cause to be paid such customs, taxes and other dues for their goods, wares, merchandise and commodities brought into this our realm of England or carried out of this our said realm of England, as foreigners pay or are bound or accustomed to pay to us; and that the said John Gonzales and Francis should pay and either of them should pay to us and our heirs as many and as large customs, subsidies and other dues for their goods and merchandise as foreigners are bound to pay and deliver to us. We therefore for certain reasons us now moving, being unwilling that the aforesaid John Gonzales and Francis should be charged the customs and subsidies payable to us as foreigners for their goods, merchandise and wares as above stated, but wishing to shew them and each of them a further favour, of our special grace have given and granted and by these presents give and grant licence for us and our heirs to the aforesaid John Gonzales and Francis, that they and either of them, their heirs or the heirs of either of them pay such customs, subsidies and other dues for the goods, wares merchandise and commodities whatsoever to be brought into this our realm of England or to be taken out of the same realm, as pay or are bound and accustomed to pay others our lieges born within our realm of England, our said letters patent made thence to the contrary notwithstanding. Provided always that the aforesaid John Gonzales and Francis under colour or cover of this concession or privilege of ours shall not introduce into our kingdom under their own names the goods of others as their own goods, on pain of the confiscation of the goods so introduced and of the loss of our aforesaid privilege; although express mention of the true annual value of the above or of the other gifts or concessions made by us before this time to the said Hugh Elyot, Thomas Aysshehurst, John Gonzales and Francis is in no wise set out in these presents, or any statutes, acts or ordinances or restrictions made, published, ordained or provided thence to the contrary, or any other circumstance, cause or matter whatsoever in any way notwithstanding.

And again of our further favour we have granted to the aforesaid Hugh, Thomas Asshehurst, John Gonzales and Francis our present letters patent in our Chancery without payment to us of any fine or fee or of any fines or fees for the same or any part thereof or for our Great Seal in any way at the Exchequer of our said Chancery.

And we will and grant by these presents that the most Reverend father in God, William, bishop of London, custodian of our Great Seal, by the authority of this our present grant, shall cause to be prepared and sealed as many and such briefs, sealed with our Great Seal, and directed to the custodian or clerk of our Exchequer, for the discharge of the said fines and fees as and such as may be necessary and requisite for the same, without any other warrant or attendance being made before us in this matter.

In witness whereof, etc.

Witness ourself at Westminster on the ninth of December.

By the King himself and at the date, etc.

48

PAYMENT OF PENSION TO JOÃO GONSALVES AND
FRANCISCO FERNANDES, 1503–4

From the Bristol Customs Records in the Public Record Office.

E. 122/20, 12. View of Account, 19 Hen. VII,
Michaelmas–Easter [1503–4]

[Among other payments] . . . And pay to John Gonsalus and to
ffranciscus fernandus, esquires, for their annuity at the rate of xx^{li} a
year, at the present time by the acquittance shown, x^{li}.

49

THE COMPANY ADVENTURERS TO
THE NEW FOUND LANDS, 1506

Public Record Office, Early Chancery Proceedings, Bundle 247, No.
51. Internal evidence in Nos. 48–50 of the same Bundle fixes the date of
this document as 1506, about October.

Thes be the parcelles that William Clerk of London, merchant,
hath delyvered in wares and merchandises and payd in redy mony
att dyvers tymes to hewghe Eliott of Brystow, merchant:

Item, the said william Clerk payd by the
commandement of the said hewghe to molyns,
ropemaker of Bristowe . . . . xl^s

Item, paid to the same ropemaker by the
commandement of the same hewghe . . . xl^s

Item, paid to the same hewghe in hys owne
proper person in gowlde . . . . . . x^{li}

Item, receyvyd by the hondes of the same hewgh
of the said William Clerk in sylver . . . vj^{li}

Item, receyvyd also of the same william Clerk
v crownys of the sone . . . . . xx^s x^d

Item, delyvered to the same hewghe to [two]
peaces of poledavys for sayles . . . . xxxj^s

Item, payd for the same hewghe to Bartylmew Rede, late Alderman of london   xx

Item, payd for the same hewghe to the Company adventurers in to the new fownde ilondes .   xx^{li}

Item, payd for the same hewghe in Redy mony and by his commandement to William Thorne .   iiij^{li} x^s

Item, delyvered to the same hewghe in Naylys, poledavys, fflower, pypys of Bere, and pypys and redy mony that the same hewghe recyvyd by my commandement of phillipp ffox of Bristow, Berebruer .   .   .   .   .   .   vj^{li} xiij^s

Item, to be allowed of the same hewghe for ffreyght .   .   .   .   .   .   xxij^{li} xvj^s

Item, in redy mony payd to the same hewghe and to other persons by hys commandement .   xxj^{li} xvj^s

Item, for the lostes [? for 'costes'] that the same hewghe causyd the said William to have in the viage for the Company Aventurers preparyd into the new fownd londes .   .   .   .   iiij^{li} xv^s

Item, for the mony that the said hewghe receyvyd of dyvers maryners by my commandement .   iiij^{li} xv^s

Item, for xvj Tone and thre hoggesheddes that the said hewghe left unladyn in A schepe callyd the michell .   .   .   .   .   .   xviij^{li} viij^s vj^d

Summa totalis cxliiij^{li} xviij^s viij^d

50

LITIGATION BETWEEN HUGH ELYOT AND FRANCISCO FERNANDES

Public Record Office, Early Chancery Proceedings, Bundle 135, No. 76.

Bill of Complaint of Francisco Fernandez

To the most Reverend fader in god, my lorde of Cantrebury, Chaunceler of Englond.

Mekly besecheth your goode and gracious lordship your continuel Oratour ffraunces ffernandus Esquier, that where on hugh Elyot of Bristowe merchaunt commenced an accion of dette of c^{li} before the maire and Constables of the constable court of Bristowe, which c^{li} is not dewe unto the seid hugh by your seid Oratour, as it appereth by indentures made betwyxt the seid hugh and your seid Oratour; this notwithstonding, the seid hugh of his malicious mynde will not declare upon the seid accion to thentent that your seid Oratour shuld not be maynprised but only to remayne in prison ayenst all right and good conscience; And for asmuch as your seid Oratour will make dewe proofe before your seid lordship that no peny of the seid C^{li} is dewe unto the seid hugh, but that the seid hugh is indetted unto your seid Oratour in clx [or lx]^{li}, in consideracion wherof, that your seid Oratour is without remedie by the cours of the common lawe of this lande, therfor that it wolde pleas your seid lordship, the premisses considered, to grant a corpus cum causa diretto to the seid mare and Constables of the same Court, and a sub pena ayenst the seid hugh, commandyng them by the same to brynge the bodie with the cause of arreste of your seid Oratour before the Kyng in his Chauncerie at a certeyne day by your lordship to be lymitted, ther to be examyned of and upon the premisses, and forthermore to be admonyshed as right and conscience requyreth, and this at the reverence of God and in the . . . of charite.[1]

---

[1] The bill is undated but subsequent to 1503, after which date the Lord Chancellor was Archbishop of Canterbury (William Warham), as stated in the bills. Up to 1503 the Lord Chancellor was also Archbishop of Canterbury, but was Cardinal in addition (John Morton), and was always so addressed in bills of that period.

THE NORTH WESTERN VOYAGE OF SEBASTIAN CABOT

51

GRANT OF PENSION TO SEBASTIAN CABOT, 3 APRIL 1505

Public Record Office, Exchequer, K.R. Memoranda Roll, 20 Hen. VII. First printed by A. P. Newton, 'An Early Grant to Sebastian Cabot', *English Historical Review*, vol. xxxvii (1922), pp. 564–5.

Pro Sebastiano Caboot

Henry by the grace of God King of England and of France and lord of Irland. To the Tresourer and Barons of our Eschequer greting. Where we by oure othre lettres of prive seal bering date of thes presents have comaunded the custumers and collectours of oure custumes in our Town and poort of Bristowe, in consideracion of the diligent service and attendaunce that our well-beloved Sebastian Caboot Venycian hath doon unto us in and aboute the same, to content and paye unto hym an annuytie of ten pounds sterlings to be taken and yerely percyved during our pleasure by the hands of our said custumers & collectours in our said poort of the revenues coming and growing yerely of our said custumes there, that is to say at the fest of Saint Michell tharch-angell fyve pounds and at the fest of thannunciation of our blissed lady fyve pounds by even porcions, the first fyve pounds to be payde at the fest of thannunciation of oure lady next before the date herof as in oure said lettres is conteigned more at large. We therfor woll and charge you that in thaccompte or accompts which the said custumers and collectours be in yilding or shall yilde unto us of theire said office ye duly allowe acquite and discharge them of the said yerely annuitie of x li. according to oure graunt afore rehersed, any matier of cause you moeving to the contrary notwithstanding. Yeven undre our prive Seal at our manour of Grenewiche, the iij^de day of Aprill the xx^th yere of our Reigne.

PETER MARTYR'S FIRST ACCOUNT OF
SEBASTIAN CABOT'S VOYAGE

Peter Martyr of Anghiera, *De Orbe Novo Decades*, Dec. III (Alcalá, 1516), lib. vi, f. 52.

Here we must philosophize somewhat, most blessed father, and digress from cosmography to the causes of Nature's secrets. All men with one accord assert that the seas flow to the westward as rivers flow down from mountains. On that account I am drawn into doubt as to the destination of these waters, which by rotation and continual attraction flow from the east as though pressing to the west, whence they are never to return; neither may the west be the more filled thereby, nor the east emptied. If we shall say they tend to the centre by the nature of heavy things, and shall hold the centre to be the equinoctial line, as many affirm, what centre shall be said to be so capacious and able to receive so many waters? Or what circumference shall be found wet? They who have searched those coasts find no likely reason; many think there are great openings in a hidden corner of that great land to the west of the island of Cuba, which land we have said to be eight times greater than Italy: which openings may receive these swift waters, and thence discharge them to the westward, whence they may return to our east. Others say [the waters go] to the north. Some hold that this gulf in the great land is closed, and that the land trends to the north on the far side of Cuba so that it embraces those northern lands which the frozen sea surrounds beneath the pole, and that all its shores are continuous; whence they believe those waters to be diverted by the opposition of that great land, as with rivers one may see they are turned by their banks. But this is unsound. For those who have tried the frozen coasts and afterwards have gone to the west say that those waters flow likewise to the west, not swiftly however, but gently with a continual passage. A certain Sebastian Cabot has examined those [frozen coasts], a Venetian by birth but carried by his parents whilst yet a child into the island of Britain, they going thither as the habit is of Venetians, who in the pursuit of trade are the guests of all lands. He equipped two ships at his own cost in Britain, and with three hundred men steered first for the north, until even in the month of July he found great icebergs floating in the sea and almost continuous daylight, yet with the land free by the melting of the ice. Wherefore he was obliged, as he says, to turn and make for the west. And he extended his course furthermore to the southward owing to the curve of the coastline, so that his latitude was almost that of the Straits of Gibraltar and he penetrated so far to the west that he had the island of Cuba on his left hand almost in the same longitude with himself. He, as he traversed those coasts, which he called the Bacallaos, says that he found the same flow of the waters to the west, although mild in force, as the Spaniards find in their passage to their southern possessions. Therefore it is not only probable but necessary to conclude that between these two lands hitherto unknown lie great straits which provide a passage for the waters flowing from east to west, which I judge to be drawn round by the attraction of the heavens in their rotation round the earth, but not to be blown out and sucked in again by the breathing of Demogorgon, as some have supposed because perhaps they have been led to connect it with the flow and the ebb [of the tides]. Cabot himself called those lands the Baccallaos because in the adjacent sea he found so great a quantity of a certain kind of great fish like tunnies, called bacallaos by the inhabitants, that at times they even stayed the passage of his ships. He found also the men of those lands clothed in skins and not anywhere devoid of intelligence. He says there are great numbers of bears there, which eat fish. For the bears plunge into the midst of a shoal of those fish, and falling upon them with their claws grasping the scales draw them to shore and eat them; on which account, he says, the bears are less dangerous to men. Many say that they have seen copper ore in places in the hands of the inhabitants. I know Cabot as a familiar friend and sometimes as a guest in my house; for, having been summoned from Britain by our Catholic King after the death of the older Henry, King of Britain, he is one of our councillors, and is daily expecting shipping to be provided for him wherewith he may reveal this secret of Nature hitherto hidden. I believe he will depart on that quest in the month of March in the coming year 1516. What things shall follow, Your Holiness shall learn from me, if it is given to me to live. Spaniards are not lacking who deny that Cabot was the first finder of the Baccallaos and do not allow that he went so far westwards. Now I have said enough of the straits and of Cabot.

53

PETER MARTYR'S SECOND ACCOUNT OF
SEBASTIAN CABOT'S VOYAGE

Summario della Generale Istoria dell' Indie Occidentali, Libro Primo della *Historia dell' Indie Occidentali* (Venice, 1534), f. 65.

There are those who think that the said waters always flow near the shores and coasts of the said land ... and then turn northwards, where none knows anyone yet who has found where the land ends, which, it is thought, is joined to Europe. But this last opinion conflicts with the voyage made by the very prudent and practical navigator Sebastian Cabot the Venetian, who when a child was taken to England by his father, and on the latter's death, being very rich and of an enterprising mind, thought that, as Christopher Columbus had done, so he too wished to discover some new part of the world. And at his own expense he equipped two ships and in the month of July set sail between the west and the north, and sailed so far that with the quadrant he observed the pole star to be elevated 55 degrees, where he found the sea full of large masses of ice which drifted hither and thither, and the ships were in great danger of colliding with them. In that region the nights are not like ours, for the interval between the setting and the rising of the sun was clear, as at home in summer until the twenty-fourth hour.

And by reason of the said ice he was obliged to turn back and make his way along the coast which runs at first for a while in the southerly direction, [and] then turns west, and because in that part he found a great number of very large fish, which swim in shoals near the shores, and understood from the inhabitants that they called them Baccalai, he called this the Land of the Baccalai. Having had some communication with these inhabitants, he found them of good intelligence, with their bodies covered with the skins of various animals. In this place and for the remainder of the voyage which he made back along this coast towards the west, he said that he always found the waters running westwards towards the gulf that, it had been reported, the said land makes. I will not omit a sport which the said Sebastian Cabot mentions having seen with all his companions, to their great delight, namely that many bears which are found in that country came to hunt these codfish in this fashion: near the shores are many tall trees, the leaves of which fall into the sea, and the cod come to feed on them in shoals. The bears, which eat nothing but these fish, stand in ambush on the shore, and when they see the approach of the shoals of these fish, which are very large and shaped like tunny, they rush into the sea, linked with another of their kind, and striking their claws under the scales, do not let them go and try to pull them on shore; but the cod which are very strong, turn round and plunge into the sea, so that, these two creatures being grappled together, it is a great sport to see now the one under the water and now the other on top, splashing the foam into the air; and in the end the bear pulls the cod ashore and eats him. For this reason it is thought that such a large number of bears are no detriment to the men of the country.

54

PETER MARTYR AND THE DATE OF
SEBASTIAN CABOT'S VOYAGE

Peter Martyr of Anghiera, *De Orbe Novo Decades*, Dec. VII (Alcalá, 1530), f. xcii b. The 1530 edition was the first to contain the Seventh Decade, which had been written in 1524.

Let us return to that country from which we have digressed: either the Bacchalaos discovered by Cabot from England sixteen years ago [*anno abhinc sexto decimo*], or the Bacchalais, of which more elsewhere; these lands I suppose to be contiguous.

55

MARCANTONIO CONTARINI'S REPORT ON SEBASTIAN CABOT'S VOYAGE

Vienna, Österreichische Staatsbibliothek, MS 6122 (Codex Foscarini), ff. 15, 17. Italian text first printed in *Raccolta Colombiana*, Parte III, vol. 1 (1892), p. 137; reprinted with translation in Biggar, *Precursors*, pp. 182–3.

Marcantonio Contarini, 1536. Report read in the Senate [of Venice].

Sebastian Cabot, the son of a Venetian, who went into England with the Venetian galleys with the desire of discovering countries, ... had two ships from Henry, King of England, father of the present Henry, who has become a Lutheran and worse, and with 300 men navigated so far that he found the sea frozen. . . . Whence it was necessary for Cabot to turn back without effecting what he intended, but with a resolve to return to that project at a time when the sea should not be frozen. He found the King dead, and his son cared little for such an enterprise.

56

THE MANTUAN GENTLEMAN'S DISCOURSE ON SEBASTIAN CABOT'S VOYAGE

Giovanni Battista Ramusio, *Primo Volume delle Navigationi et Viaggi* (Venice, 1550), ff. 398–403.

These are the greatest changes and variations of voyages which the spice trade has made in the space of 1500 years, of which having written as much as I have been able to extract from books ancient and modern and from persons who have been there in our times, it seems fitting for me not to grow weary in any way, but to relate a great and admirable discourse which I heard some months ago, together with the excellent architect M. Michele di San Michele in the comfortable and delightful house of the excellent

Messer Hieronimo Fracastoro, called Caphi, situated near Verona on the top of a hill which overlooks the entire Lake of Garda. The which discourse my mind does not suffice to write down exactly as I heard it, because it would need an intelligence and memory other than mine, but I will endeavour summarily and, as it were, by points to relate as much as I may remember. In this place Caphi then, having gone to visit the said excellent Messer Hieronimo, we found him accompanied by a Mantuan gentleman, a very great philosopher and mathematician, who then showed an instrument made on a celestial movement newly discovered, the name of which person out of respect to him is not mentioned; And having discoursed together for a long time about this new movement, to distract their minds somewhat they had a large globe brought in, giving details of all the world, on which this gentleman began to speak, saying that all studious men were greatly obliged and indebted to their serene highnesses the Kings of Portugal of a hundred years ago, in that they had spent infinite treasures, not in any war against Christians but in discovering new lands which had been hidden for so many centuries, . . . And having made a pause, turning to us he said: 'Do you not know in this connexion of going to find the Indies by the north west, what has already been done by a Venetian citizen of yours, who is so worthy and experienced in things pertaining to navigation and cosmography that in Spain there is not now his equal, and his virtue has caused him to be set over all the pilots who sail to the West Indies, so that without his licence they cannot make the voyage, and for this reason he is called the Pilot-Major?' And replying to us, who did not know this, he went on to say that, finding himself some years ago in the city of Seville, and desiring to learn of these voyages of the Castilians, it was told him that there was a very valiant Venetian who had the charge of such voyages, named Signor Sebastian Cabot, who could make sea charts with his own hand and knew the art of navigation better than anyone else. 'Unexpectedly I met this man and found him a most amiable and courteous person, who was very kind to me and showed me many things, and amongst others a large map of the world with the navigations set forth, both of the Portuguese and the Castilians. And he told me that, his father having left Venice many years ago and having gone to England to trade, he took him with him to the city of London, when he [Sebastian] was rather young, but not before he had learnt his humanities and the sphere. His father died at the time when news came that Signor Don Christophoro Colombo the Genoese had discovered the coast of the Indies, and it was much spoken of in the court of King Henry VII, who then reigned, where they said it was a thing rather divine than human to have found that way never before known to go to the East where the spices are produced. "Whence there was born in me [said Sebastian Cabot] a great desire and an eagerness of heart that I should do some signal deed also, and knowing by reason of the sphere that if I sailed by way of the north west I should have a shorter road to find the Indies, I at once communicated my thought to his majesty, who was very pleased and equipped for me two caravels with all things needful, and it was, I believe, in 1496 at the beginning of summer. And I began to sail towards the north-west, thinking not to find land until I came to Cathay, and from thence to turn towards the Indies. But at the end of some days I discovered land, which ran to the north, which greatly displeased me; and then going along the coast to see if I could find some gulf which turned, it fell out that having gone as far as 56 degrees under our pole, seeing that there the coast turned eastwards, and despairing of finding a gulf, I turned back to examine again the same coast from that region towards the equinoctial, always with the purpose of finding a passage to the Indies, and came as far as that part now called Florida. And, my victuals being short, I decided to return to England, where, on my arrival, I found great disturbances, of the people in rebellion and of a war with Scotland. There was no further thought of sailing to those parts, for which reason I came to Spain, to the Catholic King and to Queen Isabella, who having heard what I had done received me and made good provision for me, arranging for me to sail along the coast of Brazil, in order to explore it, on which voyage I found a very great and wide river, now called La Plata. I wished to navigate it and ascended it more than 600 leagues, finding it always most beautiful and inhabited by multitudes of people, who in wonderment ran to see me, and into which an incrediable number of tributaries run. I made afterwards many other voyages, which I pretermit, and at last finding myself old I wished to rest, so many experienced and valiant young sailors having come to the fore; and now here I am with this charge that you know of, enjoying the fruits of my labours." This is what I learned from Signor Sebastian Cabot.'

57

RAMUSIO'S NOTES ON SEBASTIAN CABOT'S VOYAGE

Giovanni Battista Ramusio, *Terzo Volume delle Navigationi et Viaggi* (Venice, 1556).

[fol. 4] Up to the present day we are not clear if it [i.e. New France] is joined with the land of the province of Florida and of New Spain, or if it is all split up into islands, and if by that way it is possible to go to the province of Cathay; as was written to me, many years ago, by Signor Sebastian Cabot our Venetian, a man of great and rare experience in the art of navigation and in the science of cosmography: who had sailed beyond that land of New France at the expense of King Henry VII of England. And he told me how, having gone on for a long time towards the west and a quarter north along the islands situated by the side of the said land, at the latitude of $67\frac{1}{2}$ degrees under our pole, on the 11th of June, and finding the sea open and without any obstacle, he firmly believed that by that way he could pass towards Eastern Cathay, and he would have done it if the ill-will of the master and sailors, who were mutinous, had not compelled him to turn back.

[fol. 417] Of that land [i.e. the Baccalaos] Signor Sebastian Cabot, our Venetian, had great knowledge, who at the expense of King Henry VII of England traversed all the said coast as far as 67 degrees, but owing to the cold was forced to turn back.

GOMARA'S ACCOUNT OF SEBASTIAN CABOT'S VOYAGE

Francisco Lopez de Gomara, *La historia general de las Indias* (Saragossa, 1552), f. xx.

The Bacallaos

There is a great tract of land and coast which is called Bacallaos, and its greatest latitude is forty-eight and a half degrees. The people there call a species of large fish bacallaos, of which there are so many that they impede ships in sailing. And he who brought news of that land was Sebastian Cabot the Venetian, who equipped two ships in England, where he had lived since he was a child, at the cost of King Henry VII, who desired to trade in the spice region as did the King of Portugal; others say at his own cost. And he promised King Henry to go by the north to Cathay, and to bring thence spices in a shorter time than the Portuguese did by the south. He went also to learn what sort of land the Indies were to inhabit. He took three hundred men and went by way of Iceland to the cape of Labrador until he reached fifty-eight degrees, although he himself says much more, relating that there were in the month of July such cold and so many pieces of ice that he dared not go farther; and that the days were very long and almost without night, and the nights very clear. It is a fact that at sixty degrees the days are eighteen hours long. Cabot then seeing the cold and strangeness of the land set his course towardes the west, and refreshing himself at the Bacallaos he followed the coast as far as thirty-eight degrees and returned thence to England. Bretons and Danes have been also to the Bacallaos, and Jacques Cartier the Frenchman was there twice with three galleons, once in 1534, and again in 1535, and examined the land with a view to peopling it from forty-five to fifty-one degrees. They say that they are peopling it or will do so, as being a good land like France, since it is open to all and especially to those who shall first occupy it.

ANDRÉ THEVET'S ACCOUNT OF
SEBASTIAN CABOT'S VOYAGE

André Thevet, *Les Singularitez de la France Antarctique, autrement nommé Amérique* (Paris, 1558), f. 148 b.

Coasting then with Florida on our left, because of the wind which was contrary, we approached very close to Canada and to another country that is called Baccalos, to our lasting great regret and disadvantage, on account of the extreme cold, which troubled us for the space of eighteen days: so far does this land of Baccalos project into the open sea from the direction of the north, in the form of a point, for quite two hundred leagues, in a latitude from the equator of forty-eight degrees only. This point has been called that of the Baccales by reason of a kind of fish which is found in the adjacent sea, which fish they name Baccales, between which point and the Cape del Gado there are various inhabited islands, difficult at all times to approach because of the plentiful rocks with which they are surrounded; and they are named the islands of Cortes. Others do not think they are islands, but a mainland connected with this point of Baccalos. It was discovered in the first place by Sebastian Babate [Cabot], an Englishman, who persuaded Henry the Seventh, King of England, that he would go easily by that way, towards the north, to the country of Cathay, and that by these means he would find spices and other things, just as the King of Portugal did in the Indies; in addition to which he proposed to go to Peru and America to people those countries with new inhabitants and establish there a new England. Which project he did not execute: the truth is that he put quite three hundred men on land, in the direction of Iceland[1] towards the north, where the cold killed almost the entire company, although it was in the month of July.

[1] 'Irlande' in original, but the meaning must be Iceland.

60

GALVÃO'S ACCOUNT OF SEBASTIAN CABOT'S VOYAGE

Antonio Galvão, *Tratado* (Lisbon, 1563). Galvão's text with translation, ed. C. R. D. Bethune (Hakluyt Society, 1862), pp. 87–9.

In the year 1496 a Venetian named Sebastian Cabot, being in England and having information of such a new discovery as this [i.e. of Columbus] was, and seeing by a globe that the islands above mentioned were almost in the same latitude as, and much nearer to, his country [England] than to Portugal or Castile, he explained the matter to King Henry VII, wherewith the king was so well pleased that he ordered two ships to be equipped. He [Cabot] sailed in the spring with three hundred companions, set his course to the west until he sighted land in forty-five degrees of north latitude, and went on by that land to sixty degrees, where the days are eighteen hours long and the nights are very clear and bright. They found great cold there and many icebergs, so that they had no bottom in seventy, eighty and a hundred fathoms, but found great cold, by which they were discommoded. And so from thence finding the coast to turn to the east, they passed along it on the other tack discovering every bay, river [and] creek to see if it passed to the other side, and so went on, diminishing the latitude, to thirty-eight degrees, whence they returned to England. Others say that he reached the cape of Florida, which is in twenty-five degrees.

61

CHAUVETON'S ACCOUNT OF SEBASTIAN CABOT'S VOYAGE

Urbain Chauveton (trans. and ed.), *Histoire nouvelle du nouveau monde ... Extraite de l'italien de M. Hierosme Benzoni Milanois* (Geneva, 1579), p. 141.

In the year 1507 there was a Venetian pilot, named Sebastian Gabotto, who undertook at the cost of Henry VII, King of

England, to search for some passage to go to Cathay by the north (par la Tramontane). He discovered the point of Baccalaos (which the mariners of Brittany and Normandy to-day call the Coast of Codfish), and higher still, as far as sixty-seven degrees from the Pole, but the cold and the great ice-masses, with which this northern sea is covered, compelled him to give up, and to return without doing anything.[1]

62

RICHARD EDEN'S NOTE ON SEBASTIAN CABOT'S VOYAGE

Richard Eden, preface to his translation from Peter Martyr, *The Decades of the newe worlde or west India* (London, 1555), sig. cl.

These regions are cauled Terra Florida and Regio Baccalearum or Bacchallaos of the which yow may reade sumwhat in this booke in the vyage of the woorthy owlde man yet lyving Sebastiane Cabote, in the vi. booke of the thyrde Decade. But Cabote touched only in the north corner and most barbarous parte hereof, from whense he was repulsed with Ise in the moneth of July.

63

RIBAULT'S REFERENCE TO THE CABOT DISCOVERY

Jean Ribault, *The Whole and true discovery of Terra Florida* (London, 1563), sig. A ii–iii. Revised text from B.M., Sloane MS 3644, ff. 111–21, ed. H. P. Biggar in *English Historical Review*, vol. xxxii (1917).

Whereas in the yeare 1562 it pleased God to move your grace to chose and appoynt us to discover and vieu a certen long coste of the West Indea, from the hed of the lande called la Florida, drawing towardes the northe parte untill the hed of Britons, distant from the said hed of la Florida 900 leagues, or therabout, to the

---

[1] Chauveton adds at the end of this passage: 'Som. de Pierre Mart', meaning presumably that the account is summarized from Peter Martyr. See G. P. Winship, *Cabot Bibliography* (1900), pp. 32, 83–4.

ende that we might certifie you and make true reporte . . . it were nedefull to shewe howe manye from tyme to tyme have gon about to fynd owt this great land, to inhabite there, who nevertheles have alwaies failed and byn put by of there intention and purpose, some through feare of shipwracke, and some by great wyndes and tempestes that drove them backe, of the which ther was one a verry famyous strainger Sebastian Cabot, an excellent pilote, sent thither by the King of England, Henery the vij^th, anno 1498, and many others, who never could attayne to any habytation or take possession there of one only fote of ground.

64

SIR HUMPHREY GILBERT'S ACCOUNT OF SEBASTIAN CABOT'S VOYAGE

Gilbert, *A Discourse of a Discoverie for a new Passage to Cataia* (London, 1576; written before 1566), sig. D3.

Furthermore, Sebastian Gabota, by his personall experience, and travell, hath set foorth, and described this passage, in his Charts, whiche are yet to bee seene, in the Queenes Majesties privie Gallerie, at White hall, who was sent to make this discoverie by King Henrie the seaventh, and entred the same fret [strait]: affirming, that he sailed very far Westward, with a quarter of the North, on the Northside of Terra de Labrador, the eleventh of June, until he came to the Septentrional latitude of $67\frac{1}{2}$ degrees and finding the Seas still open, said, that he might, and would have gone to Cataia, if the Mutinie of the Maister & Mariners, had not ben.

65

RICHARD WILLES ON SEBASTIAN CABOT'S MAPS AND DISCOVERIES

Richard Willes, *The History of Travayle in the West and East Indies* (London, 1577).

[fols. 231b–232] Wel, graunt the West Indies not to continue continent unto the Pole, graunt there be a passage betwyxt these two landes, let the goulph lye neare us than commonly in cardes we fynde it set, namely, betwyxt the 61. & 64. degrees north, as Gemma Frisius in his Mappes and Globes imagineth it, and so left by our countriman Sebastian Cabote, in his table, the which my good Lorde your father [i.e. the Earl of Bedford] hath at Cheynies, and so tryed this last yeare by your Honours servaunt as hee reporteth, and his carde and compasse doe witnesse. . . .

[fols. 233–233b] The fyrste objection is of no force, that generall table of the worlde set foorth by Ortelius or Mercator, for it greatly skilleth not, being unskylfully drawen for that poynt: as manifestly it may appeare unto any one that conferreth the same with Gemma Frisius universal mappe, with his round quartered carde, with his globe, with Sebastian Cabota his table, and Ortelius Generall Mappe alone, worthily preferred in this case before all Mercator and Ortelius other doinges: for that Cabota was not only a skilful sea man, but a long travailer, & such a one as entred personally that streiete, sent by King Henry the seventh to make this aforesaid discovery, as in his owne discourse of navigation you may reade in his carde drawen with his owne hands, the mouth of the north-westerne streict lieth neare the 318 Meridian, betwixt 61. and 64. degrees in elevation, continuying the same breadth about 10. degrees west, where it openeth southerly more and more, untyll it come under the tropike of Cancer, and so runneth into Mar de Zur, at the least 18 degrees more in breadth there, then it was where it fyrst began: otherwise I coulde as well imagine this passage to be more unlykely then the voyage to Moscovia, and more impossible then it for the farre situation and continuance thereof in the frosty clime: as nowe I can affyrme it to be very possible and most lykely in comparison thereof, for that it nether coasteth so farre north as the Moscovian passage doth, nether is this steicte so long as that, before it bowe downe southerly towardes the Sonne agayne.

66

GEORGE BESTE'S ACCOUNT OF
SEBASTIAN CABOT'S VOYAGE

George Beste, *A true discourse of the late voyages of discoverie* (London, 1578), p. 16.

Also, the valor of the English men, did first of all discover and finde out all that part of America, whiche nowe is called Baccalaos: for Sebastian Cabot, an Englishe man, borne in Bristow, was by commandment of Kyng Henry the seaventh, in Anno 1508, furnished with shipping, munition, and men, and sayled all along that tract, pretending to discover the passage to Cataya, and went alande in many places, and brought home sundry of the people, and manye other things of that Countrey, in token of possession, beeing (I say) the firste Christians that ever there sette foote on land.

Also, the sayde Englishman Cabot, did first discover at the procurement of the King of Spayne, all that other porte of America, adjoyning nexte beyond Brasill, lying aboute the famous River called Rio de la plata.

67

SEBASTIAN CABOT'S MAPS AND PAPERS, 1582

Richard Hakluyt, *Divers Voyages* (London, 1582); reprinted by Hakluyt Society (1850), p. 26.

This much concerning Sebastion Gabotes discoverie may suffice for a present cast: but shortly, God willing, shall come out in print, all his owne mappes and discourses, drawne and written by himselfe, which are in the custodie of the worshipfull master William Worthington, one of her Majesties Pensioners, who (because so worthie monumentes shoulde not be buried in perpetuall oblivion) is very willing to suffer them to be overseene and published in as good order as may be, to the encouragement and benefite of our Countriemen.

68

SEBASTIAN CABOT IN 1512

British Museum, Add. MS 21481 (Household Book of Henry VIII), f. 92.

Anno iiij° primo die Maii [1 May 1512] Item to Sebastyan tabot for making of a Carde of gascoigne and Guyon, in Rewarde, xxvj⁵ viii^d.

69

KING FERDINAND TO SEBASTIAN CABOT, 13 SEPTEMBER 1512

Seville, Archivo General de Indias, est. 139, caj. 1, leg. 5, lib. iv, fol. 19 v. Spanish text with translation in Biggar, *Precursors*, pp. 115–16.

[Logrono, 13 September 1512] The King: Sebastian Cabot. You are already aware how the reverend father in Christ, the Bishop of Palencia, my chief chaplain and one of my Council, and Lope Conchillos, my secretary and one of my Council, spoke to you on my behalf in the city of Burgos in regard to the navigation to the Indies and the Island of the Bacallaos [codfish], and it was agreed between you and them that on my writing to Lord Willoughby, your Captain, to allow you to come to court, you would come at once. I am now writing to him as you will see by the enclosed paper, asking him to allow you to come. Wherefore I beg you and charge you that, on Lord Willoughby giving you the said permission, you come wherever I may be, in order that on your coming a proper agreement may be drawn up in regard to the matters whereof the said Bishop of Palencia and Secretary Conchillos spoke to you; and do not delay, for in this you will do me a service. From Logrono, 13 September 1512. I the King. By order of His Highness, Lope Conchillos. Countersigned by the Bishop of Palencia.

The Cabot Voyages and Bristol Discovery

70

SEBASTIAN CABOT'S NEGOTIATIONS WITH VENICE, 1522

Venice, Archivio di Stato, Capi del Consiglio di X, Lettere. Translation by Rawdon Brown, *Calendar of State Papers, Venice, 1502–6* (1869), No. 607.

Gasparo Contarini to the Council of Ten

According to your letter, of 27th September, I ascertained that Sebastian Cabot was at the court, and where he dwelt. I sent to say that my secretary had a letter for him from a friend of his, and that if he chose he might come to my residence. He told my servant he would come. He made his appearance on Christmas eve. At dinner time I withdrew with him, and delivered the letter, which he read, his colour changing completely during its perusal. Having finished reading it, he remained a short while without saying anything, as if alarmed and doubtful. I told him that if he chose to answer the letter, or wished me to make any communication in the quarter from whence I had received it, I was ready to execute his commission safely. Upon this he took courage, and said to me, 'Out of the love I bear my country, I spoke heretofore to the ambassadors of the most illustrious Signory in England, concerning these newly discovered countries, through which I have the means of greatly benefiting Venice. The letter in question concerned this matter, as you likewise are aware; but I most earnestly beseech you to keep the thing secret, as it would cost me my life.'

I then told him I was thoroughly acquainted with the whole affair, and mentioned how Hironimo the Ragusan had presented himself before the tribunal of their Excellencies the Chiefs, and that the most secret magistracy had acquainted me with everything and forwarded that letter to me. I added, that as some noblemen were dining with me, it would be inconvenient for us to talk together then, but that should he choose to return late in the evening we might more conveniently discuss the subject

282

together at full length. So he then departed, and returned at about 5 p.m., when, being closeted alone in my chamber, he said to me:

'My Lord Ambassador, to tell you the whole truth, I was born at Venice, but was brought up in England, and then entered the service of their Catholic Majesties of Spain, and King Ferdinand made me captain, with a salary of 50,000 maravedis. Subsequently his present Majesty gave me the office of Pilot Major, with an additional salary of 50,000 maravedis, and 25,000 maravedis besides, as a gratuity, forming a total of 125,000 maravedis, equal to about 300 ducats.

'Now it so happened that when in England some three years ago, if I mistake not, Cardinal Wolsey offered me high terms if I would sail with an armada of his on a voyage of discovery. The vessels were almost ready, and they had got together 30,000 ducats for their outfit. I answered him that, being in the service of the King of Spain, I could not go without his leave, but if free permission were granted me from hence, I would serve him.

'At that period, in the course of conversation one day with a certain friar, a Venetian, named Sebastian Collona, with whom I was on a very friendly footing, he said to me, "Master Sebastian, you take such great pains to benefit foreigners, and forget your native land, would it not be possible for Venice likewise to derive some advantage from you?" At this my heart smote me, and I told him I would think about it. So, on returning to him the next day, I said I had the means of rendering Venice a partner in this navigation, and of showing her a passage whereby she would obtain great profit; which is the truth, for I have discovered it.

'In consequence of this, as by serving the King of England I could no longer benefit our country, I wrote to the Emperor not to give me leave to serve the King of England, as he would injure himself extremely, and thus to recall me forthwith. Being recalled accordingly, and on my return residing at Seville, I contracted a close friendship with this Ragusan, who wrote the letter you delivered to me; and as he told me he was going to Venice, I unbosomed myself to him, charging him to mention this thing to none but the Chiefs of the Ten; and he swore to me a sacred oath to this effect.'

I bestowed great praise on his patriotism, and informed him I was commissioned to confer with him and hear his project, which I was to notify to the Chiefs, to whom he might afterwards resort in person. He replied that he did not intend to manifest his plan to any but the Chiefs of the Ten, and that he would go to Venice after requesting the Emperor's permission, on the plea of recovering his mother's dowry, concerning which he said he would contrive that I should be spoken to by the Bishop of Burgos and the Grand Chancellor, who are to urge me to write in his favour to your Serenity.

I approved of this, but said I felt doubtful as to the possibility of his project, as I had applied myself a little to geography, and bearing in mind the position of Venice, I did not see any way of effecting this navigation, as the voyage must be performed either by ships built in Venice, or else by vessels which it would be requisite to construct elsewhere. Venetian-built craft must necessarily pass the gut of Gibraltar to get into the ocean; and as the King of Portugal and the King of Spain would oppose the project, it never could succeed. The construction of vessels out of Venice could only be effected on the southern shores of the ocean, or in the Red Sea, to which there were endless objections. First of all, it would be requisite to have a good understanding with the Great Turk. Secondly, the scarcity of timber rendered shipbuilding impossible there. Then again, even if vessels were built, the fortresses and fleets of Portugal would prevent the trade from being carried on. I also observed to him that I did not see how vessels could be built on the northern shores of the ocean, that is to say from Spain to Denmark, or even beyond, especially as the whole of Germany depended on the Emperor; nor could I perceive any way at all for conveying merchandise from Venice to these ships, or for conveying spices and other produce from the ships to Venice. Nevertheless, as he was skilled in this matter, I said I deferred to him.

He answered me: 'You have spoken ably, and in truth neither with ships built at Venice, nor yet by the way of the Red Sea, do I perceive any means soever. But there are other means, not merely possible but easy, both for building ships and conveying wares from Venice to the harbour, as also spices, gold, and other produce from the harbour to Venice, as I know; for I have sailed to all those countries, and am well acquainted with the whole. Indeed, I assure you that I refused to accept the offer of the King of England for the sake of benefiting my country, for had I listened to that proposal, there would no longer have been any course for Venice.'

I shrugged my shoulders, and although the thing seems to be impossible, I nevertheless would not dissuade him from coming to the feet of your Highness (without, however, recommending him), because possibility is much more unlimited than man often imagines; added to which, this individual is in great repute here. He then left me.

Subsequently, on the evening of St John's Day, he came to me in order that I might modify certain expressions in the Ragusan's letter, which he was apprehensive would make the Spaniards suspicious. It was, therefore, remodelled, and written out again by a Veronese, an intimate of mine.

When discussing a variety of geographical topics with me, he mentioned, among other things, a very clever method observed by him, which had never been previously discovered by any one, for ascertaining by the needle the distance between two places from east to west, as your Serenity will hear from himself if he comes.

After this, continuing my conversation with him concerning our chief matter, and recapitulating the difficulties he said to me, 'I assure you the way and the means are easy. I will go to Venice at my own cost. They shall hear me; and if they disapprove of the project devised by me, I will return in like manner at my own cost.'

He then urged me to keep the matter secret.

Valladolid, 31st December 1522.

THE PLANS FOR THE EXPEDITION OF 1521

From the MS Records of the Drapers' Company of London (1514–50), pp. 167–70, 175–6. Printed by Biggar, *Precursors*, pp. 134–8.

[1 March–9 April 1521]

An answer made to serten of the kinges counsell as consernyng the kinges
shippes to be occupyed

The first day of Marche here assembled my lord the maire, Sir Laurence Aylmer, M. Monoux, M. Milborn, M. Bayly, & M. Wylkynson, aldermen, M. Carter, M. Clerk, & M. Vaughan, Wardens & of the Counsell, M. Hawkyns, M. Cremor, M. Gaine, M. Rudston, M. Askue, M. Gentyll, M. Perpount, M. White, M. Champyon, M. Sadler, & M. Dolphyn, and at the said assembley yt was agreed that the Wardens wᵗ M. Rudston, M. Perpount & M. Dolphyn shall common wᵗ the Wardens of other aunncyaunt ffeliships to knowe what aunswere were best to be made to M. Wynkfield & M. Broun, of the kynges counsell, concernyng the kinges shippys. And the same day, aftir assembley made at ffrere Austyns by wardens of dyvers companys, and aggreed all aftir one mynd, we made our aunswere in wrytyng & delyvered yt into the said counsell by thassent of this hows, the tenour where of is this that foloweth:

The aunswere of the Wardens of Drapers of London unto the reporte of Sir Robert Wynkfeld and Sir Wolston Broun, knyghtes, and of our Soverayn lord the kinges moste honorable counsell, ffirst where it hathe pleased the kinges highnes of his most gracious zele, good mynd, and tendre favour towardes his merchaundes of London had, as by the reporte of the foresaid Sir Robert and Sir Wolston unto the said Wardens lately made, ffor the whiche moste gracious zele, good mynd and tendre favour, all we ben naturally bounden to pray to God for his moste gracious and prosperous contynuance in good helth and long lyf. And as toching the taking or receyving of one of the kinges shipps, we say we have noo auctorite to bynd our hole company and ffeliship

286

unto any suche charge. And also that in our company we but fewe Aventurors, saving onely in to fflaunders, where unto requireth noo grete shipps. ffurthermore we say that if it be the kinges pleasur to caws to be manned, rygged, appareled and vitayled suche a ship as the company shall think convenient, that than we, the said wardens, shall applye us to labour our said company for to freght and laid the said ship to the best of our powers, having suche a reasonable price of ye freght, as other shipps hath in lyke viage & lading. Also we think it is dowtfull that any English ship shalbe suffered to laid in Spayn & in other countres, by reason of such actes & statutes there made, after suche lyke maner as be made in Englond for gascon wyn & colles wood from Burdeux.

. . . . . .

The xi day of Marche here assembled M. Monoux, M. Milborn, M. Bayly & M. Wylkynson, Aldermen, M. Carter, M. Clerk, M. Vaughan, Wardens, the hole counsell, the lyverey & the hole body of the ffeliship, ryche & poure, and at the said assembley was redd openly unto them the Articles folowing, directed unto us by the Wardens of the Mercers from the kinges Counsell and to x other craftes of the moste Aunciant, in thies woordes, that is to say:

Certen nomber of shippes to be appoynted to go unto the new fownd lande

ffirst the king & my lord Cardinall & the Counsell thynketh aswele for his honour as for the generall welth of this his Realm that there be appoynted a certayn noumbre of ships to be prepared for a viage to be made into the newefound Iland.

And his gracious pleasur is, that it be opened unto the generaltie of merchauntes adventurers & to certayn companys to knowe there benevolent myndes there in.

And the demaund that is required of you is to furnyshe v shipps aftir this maner: The kinges Grace to prepare them in takyll, ordenaunce and all other necessaries at his charge, And also the king to bere the adventour of the said shipps, And the merchauntes & companys to be at the charge of the vitayling and

287

mennys wages of the same shipps for one hole yere, and the shipps not to be above vj^{xx} ton a pece. And also it is the kinges pleasur that this Citie of London shalbe as hede Reulers for all the hole realm, for asmany Cites and Townes as be mynded to prepare any shipps forwardes for the same purpos & viage, as the Town of Bristowe hath sent up there knowlege, that they wyll prepare ij shipps; And if ye be mynded to doe as afore is resyted, his gracious pleasur is that x yere after, there shall no nacion have the trate but you.

And to have respyte for there custom xv monthes & xv monthes, and the said Wardens to make aunswere in wryting of the premisses aforesaid bitwen this & Wednysday next commyng.

The premisses considered, the Maister, Wardens & Counsell endeverd them furthwith w^t the best wordes, exortacion and diligence, to knowe the benivolent mynd of every man there assembled at that tyme, and also commaunded them that than were absent to come bifore my lord the maire and them the next morowe aftir. Soo that all there graunts amownted to a small somme. And my lord & maisters seying that, made there aunswer in form folowing, that is to say:

Answer made to byl sent by the Wardens of Mercers

The aunswere of the Wardens of Drapers of London w^t thassent & consent of the moste parte of all there company, unto a byll lately sent unto them by the Wardens of the Mercers of London consernying the appoyntement of v shipps to be prepared towardes the Newefound Iland.

ffirst the foresaid Wardens & company of Drapers supposen and say, that if our Soverayne lord the kinges highnes, the Cardinalles grace and the kinges moste honorable counsell were duely & substauncially enformed in such a maner as perfite knowlege myght be had by credible reporte of maisters & mariners naturally born w^t in this Realm of England, having experience, and exercised in and abowt the forsaid Iland, aswele in knowlege of the land, the due course of the seey, thiderward & homeward,

288

as in knowlege of the havenes, roodes, poortes, crekes, dayngers & sholdes there uppon that coste and there abowtes being, that than it were the lesse joperdy to aventur thider than it is nowe, all though it be ferther hens than fewe English maryners can tell.

And we thynk it were to sore aventour to joperd v shipps w^t men & goodes unto the said Iland uppon the singuler trust of one man, callyd as we understond, Sebastyan, whiche Sebastyan, as we here say, was never in that land hym self, all if he makes reporte of many thinges as he hath hard his ffather and other men speke in tymes past.

And also we say that if the said Sebastyan had bene there and were as connyng a man in & for thoos parties as any man myght be, having non other assistauntes of maisters & maryners of Englond, excercised & labored in the same parties, for to guyd there shipps & other charges than we knowe of, but onely trusting to the said Sebastyan, we suppos it were no wysdom to aventur lyves & goodes thider in suche maner, what for fere of syknes or dethe of the said Sebastian, or for desevering of the said v shipps by nyght or by day, by force of tempestes or otherwyse, one from an other owt of syght, for than it shuld be gretely to dowte wheder ever thes v shipps shuld mete ayen in company or nay, for the said Sebastian connot be but in one ship, than the other iiij^{or} shipps & men standes in grete perell, for lak of connyng maryners in knowlege of thoos parties, and to ordre & guyd them; and soo the vitaylles and mennys wages shalbe spent in vayn, and they glad to retorn homeward w^t small comforte, for it is said among maryners in old proverbe: he salys not surely that salys by an other mannys compas.

Also we say that it is not possible that the said v shippes, besides there Balast, may receyve the vitaylles to suffice so many men for one hole yere, soo that we think verely that in this adventour can be percevyed any advauntage or profeit to growe unto any man, but rather losse and damage, besides the gretest joperdy of all, whiche is mennys lyves.

Than aftir that this our Aunswere and the Aunswers of x other crafts were debated & resoned among them all at Saynt Thomas of Akers, they agreed to send furth the Governour and iiij^{or} Wardens of divers misters unto my lord Cardynall w^t this commyssion folowing:

Here aftir foloweth the Articles that the commissioners sent to my lord Cardynall from the Wardens of xj companys to be spoken in the behalf of the said Wardens.

ffyrst the foresaid Wardens sayen that there companys be wyllyng to accomplishe the kinges desire and pleasur in furnysshing of ij shippys accordingly, and they suppos to furnyssh the thryd, soo that one may bere w^t an other indifferently of xj ffelishippes assembled w^t the Aldermen of the same, And also uppon certayn articles to them to be graunted by the kinges highnes & his honorable Councell.

And the said wardens desyre to have longer repyte for a full aunswere therein to be yeven.

The said commissioners brought aunswere fro my lord Cardynall that the king wold have the premisses to goo furth and to take effect. And there uppon my lord the maire was send for to speke w^t the king for the sam matier, so that his grace wold have no nay there in, but spak sharpely to the maire to see it putt in execucion to the best of his power.

ffor the same purpose the xxvj day of Marche my lord the Maire commaunded the hole company of all this fraternite to assemble bifore bym at the Drapers hall, where was w^t grete labour & deligence & many divers warnynges, graunted first & last ij^c marces, presentyd by a byll to the maire, the ixth day of Aprill in this manner:

ij^e marcks grauntyd towart maryners wages & rygging of shippes to the new found land

The Maiser and Wardens of Drapers of London in the names of all there company graunten of there benevolent myndes to pay towardes maryners wages and vitayling of certayn shippes for one viage to be made by the grace of God into the Newfound Iland ij^c marces under suche condicion as shalbe articled bitwen the kinges moste Noble counsell and the Adventurers of the said cite of London unto the foresaid Iland, the names of the payers & their severall sommes for the said ij^c marces appereth in the iijd leef following.

. . . . . .

Here aftir foloweth the Names of them that graunted to pay unto the charges of the viage to be made into the newefound Iland ij^c marcs.[1]

[1] Documents 70 and 71 have been included, not for their evidence on the project of 1521, but for their bearing on Sebastian Cabot's expedition of 1508–9.

THE CARTOGRAPHY OF THE VOYAGES

THE CARTOGRAPHY OF THE VOYAGES

by R. A. SKELTON[1]

I

THE LANDS of the north-west Atlantic, to which the voyages discussed in this volume were directed, are represented in a number of extant maps from the early years of the sixteenth century. These maps have been the subject of an extensive literature, some of which is cited in the bibliographical note at the end of this Appendix. In the following pages an attempt is made to analyse the delineations given by cartographers and to relate them to the voyages and geographical concepts from which these delineations sprang.

A strict discipline and much caution in interpreting the early maps are necessary if we are not to place on them too heavy a burden of proof for the reconstruction of historical events, particularly when (as often) they are unsupported by textual documents. Only a small proportion of the maps produced in the first decades of the sixteenth century have survived. Soncino writes of a world map and a globe made by John Cabot,[2] but neither Cabot's nor any English maps of his time have been preserved. Although John Day had in Spain 'the copy of the land discovered' by Cabot in 1497, we can now only guess at its character from the imperfect and corrupted tracing of the 'English coast' in La Cosa's map of 1500. Of the copious output of the Portuguese workshops in this period, only a handful of works are now known. As in the fifteenth century, evidence of Portuguese and English discoveries is to be found in maps of Italian authorship.

---

[1] Some passages in this are reproduced from a paper read at the Congress of the History of the Discoveries, Lisbon, September 1960. Bibliographical details of the works cited briefly in footnotes are given in the list of References at the end.

[2] See above, pp. 209–10.

The Italian maps are of particular interest in that they bring together elements, information and ideas from various sources. As eclectic compilations, they are at two or more removes from the original pilots' logbooks or sketches; as works of the study, they often graft new materials on a traditional stock derived from older prototypes. Dominant among such prototypes, in this period, was the representation of the Old World established about 1490 by Henricus Martellus Germanus, a cartographer associated with the Florentine map-engraver Francesco Rosselli.[1] A printed map by Martellus, reflecting Toscanelli's views on the extension of Eurasia and on the width of the western ocean, undoubtedly served as the model for Behaim's globe of 1492; and its influence can be traced in the map-production of widely separated centres and in the cosmographical ideas of Columbus and John Cabot.

The designer of a world map might have at his disposal, besides this traditional 'base-map' of the Old World, certain materials derived directly or indirectly from discovery. Among these were doubtless pilots' sketches of the type exemplified by John Day's 'copy of the land' discovered in 1497 and by Columbus's little sketch-map of north-west Hispaniola drawn in December 1492—the only extant document of this kind from the fifteenth century. Columbus's running survey was good; but his draft, however correct in outline and proportion, lacks all the data (notably scale of miles or latitudes) necessary for relating the coasts depicted to other discoveries or to the framework of a world map. The cartographer who incorporated such materials into a world map had to convert the leagues and miles logged or recorded by the explorer into degrees, by an accepted conversion factor. He must also form an opinion, to be graphically expressed in his map, concerning the location of a discovered coast on the earth's surface, both absolutely and in relation to other disjunct discoveries or known lands. If his map embraced the full 360 degrees of the earth's circumference, it must offer, and illustrate, a hypothesis of the longitudinal extension of the landmasses and the oceans.[2]

[1] Almagià (1940) and (1951).   [2] See Fig. 4.

Cartography of the Voyages

The unexplored regions lying between or beyond the sectors of known or discovered coastline had therefore to be supplied by a map-maker from conjecture, theory or tradition. In using an early map as testimony to the course of an exploratory voyage, it is essential to distinguish between those parts of the design attributable to such processes and those parts which are drawn from authentic records of experience.

Few of the original maps from the decade after 1500 are dated either explicitly or from good internal evidence. In most cases we can only arrive at a *terminus a quo*, that is, a date after which the map must have been made, from the positive information which it contains. The maps cannot in consequence be arranged in a precise chronological series; indeed the representations even in dated maps may go back to lost sources considerably earlier. The chain of communication leading to affinities of design or nomenclature between one map and another is generally hidden from us; nor may we assume (as the treatment of some commentators implies) that a cartographer was cognizant of all previous work. To group or classify maps on a basis of common features is nevertheless a legitimate and profitable exercise. Only by this method can we isolate some characteristic delineations and geographical concepts and attempt to associate them with the voyages which are chronicled in the documents presented in this volume.

II

Of the voyages which may have reached North America before that of John Cabot in 1497, no indisputable cartographic record exists. The landfall said by John Day to have been made by the men of Bristol is shown on no map. The delineation of the Antillia group in Italian charts of the fifteenth century has been held by Dr Armando Cortesão[1] to indicate a pre-Columbian Portuguese discovery of America; the arguments against this view, which has not won general acceptance, have been stated by Admiral Samuel Morison.[2]

[1] Cortesão (1954).   [2] Morison (1940).

297

The only map which unambiguously illustrates John Cabot's voyage of 1497—and (with less certainty) his voyage of 1498 also —is that of Juan de La Cosa dated 1500, now preserved in the Museo Naval, Madrid.[1] Although corruptions in the place names and some generalization of the outlines point to the work of a copyist who had not direct access to original materials, the map appears to be in one hand throughout; and its content is consistent with a compilation date of 1500 or a little earlier. As Mr G. R. Crone has shown,[2] the map is constructed in two clearly differentiated sections: an older model (pre-Vasco da Gama) served for the Old World, while the New World is drawn—on a larger scale—from recent discoveries, completed by conjectural or theoretical interpolation. A continuous coastline stretches from Greenland to Central America, uninterrupted by any strait or channel.

The section of the North American coast trending E–W and marked by English flags, with its generally accepted assimilation to the discoveries of John Cabot in 1497, is discussed by Dr Williamson above (pp. 72–82). This tract of coast has been variously identified by students of the map: as the south coast of Newfoundland (with part of Nova Scotia), as the south coast of Labrador, as the east coast of Labrador, and even as the coast of Greenland.[3] John Day's letter exemplifies the means by which a sketch-chart of the voyage, perhaps with a rutter or list of places and distances, may have come into La Cosa's hands. Apart from the terminal latitudes given for Cabot's coasting,[4] none of the details in Day's letter is inconsistent with W. F. Ganong's identification of La Cosa's 'English coast' with the south coast of Newfoundland, from a landfall in Nova Scotia to Cape Race, 'the cape nearest to Ireland'.[5] The section of E–W trending coast-line,

[1] See Pls. I, II.   [2] Crone (1953), pp. 84–5.
[3] These various interpretations, with bibliographical references, are listed by Ganong (1929–37), I, 143–4, and by Nunn (1946), pp. 3–4.
[4] See above, pp. 68–9.
[5] Ganong (1929–37), I, 144–63. But Ganong's specific identifications of names or features on the map with real features of this coast sometimes appear too ingenious to carry complete conviction.

which reappears in later Italian maps, is a cartographic feature which may be taken as indicating an origin (if at several removes) in Cabot's 1497 voyage and its delineation by La Cosa.

The Paris Map of 1544, ascribed to Sebastian Cabot, and its testimony regarding the landfall and course of the 1497 voyage have also been examined by Dr Williamson (pp. 24–6, 57–9, 63–4). This map may be identified as the printed world map for which Sebastian in 1541 signed a contract at Seville with two 'German' printers;[1] and his responsibility for the map, which was formerly disputed, can now be accepted. That Sebastian inserted in the map some details from his own experience or recollection need not be doubted; but it would be rash to conclude that its representation of the lands of the north-west Atlantic reflects his considered judgment on their geography. This part of the map, including Labrador and Greenland, is in fact a close copy of the debased version derived by the Norman cartographers of Dieppe from a Portuguese prototype of the 1530's, at the end of an evolutionary process to be described below.[2]

If any cartographic evidence for the course of John Cabot's ships in 1498 exists, it can be sought only in the coastline drawn by La Cosa, in a general WSW direction, from the *Mar descubierta por inglese* to the latitude of Cuba.[3] To the eye of the present writer the delineation has a conventional appearance (though this may perhaps be put down to the generalising tendency of the copyist's hand), and it seems curious that, if La Cosa disposed of an original source for these outlines, it apparently furnished him with no names. Nevertheless many students have associated this delineation with the voyage of 1498, identifying certain details of it with real geographical features (the Delaware, Cape Cod, Long Island, the Hudson River, Florida). It may be conceded that, if La Cosa is here recording the results of a voyage, that voyage is much more

[1] J. Toribio Medina, *El veneciano Sebastián Caboto al servicio de España* (1908), vol. I, pp. 554–65; cited by Almagià (1958), pp. 58, 63.

[2] The Paris Map shows a particularly close affinity to the mappemonde of 1541 by N. Desliens.

[3] See Fig. 1.

likely to be John Cabot's of 1498 than any other; but, beyond this, dogmatism is unjustified.[1]

Some support, by analogy, for the hypothesis that in this section of coastline, notwithstanding its lack of nomenclature, the cartographer has drawn on experience is offered by his delineation of the north coast of Venezuela and the isthmus of Panama. Here, as Dr Williamson points out,[2] comparison with the modern chart reveals a correctness of outline so striking that it can only be derived from discovery; yet the drawing bears no names along this coast, and no expedition is recorded to have traversed it before La Cosa's map was drawn.[3]

We may note that La Cosa's map seems to reproduce no information, or scarcely any, from recent Portuguese sources. The southern coast of Africa is drawn from the voyage of Bartolomeu Dias in 1487–8, or from a map illustrating it; and the discoveries of Vasco de Gama in 1498–9 and of Cabral in 1499–1500 are unrepresented.[4]

III

It must be asked what light is thrown by La Cosa's map on its author's views about the relationship of the continents and (consequently) on his identification of the western discoveries. Since the lands in the East and in the West extend, respectively, to the extreme right- and left-hand edges of the parchment, it is crucial to determine whether the cartographer has set out to represent the full 360 degrees of the earth's circumference in longitude. In studying this and other early world maps which have no

[1] Some Portuguese historians suppose Miguel Corte Real (or an unchronicled Portuguese expedition) to have coasted as far south as Florida; but this is hardly more than conjecture, supported only by the supposed representation of Florida in the Cantino map.

[2] See above, pp. 108–9 and Fig. 3.

[3] Nunn cites this delineation in support of his contention that the La Cosa map was drawn after 1508. Nunn (1934), p. 27.

[4] Unless the 'island discovered by the Portuguese' marked in the South Atlantic represents Brazil. Crone (1953), p. 84. Also as noted above (p. 76), Portuguese ships are shown in the Indian Ocean.

longitudinal graduation, attempts have been made to construct a scale of longitude on the basis of a single known measurement, by taking (for instance) the length of the Mediterranean as 41 degrees, as Ravenstein did.[1] The validity of this method is however very doubtful if it is applied to world maps in which, by the very circumstances of their construction, overall uniformity of scale was not only impossible but, in many cases, probably not attempted.[2] We have therefore no grounds on which to determine whether, as a world map, the design was intended to embrace 360 degrees of longitude. If this was the cartographer's intention, then his Eastern Asia and the continental land depicted on the western side of the North Atlantic were, in his view, continuous, and John Cabot had reached the coasts of China.[3]

Such an interpretation of La Cosa's map, speculative as it may seem, finds some support in the affinity between his delineation of the lands of the north-west Atlantic and that presented in a group of world maps drawn or engraved in Italy between 1506 and 1511. These are, in chronological sequence: the world map drawn at Venice by Giovanni Matteo Contarini and engraved by Rosselli at Florence in 1506[4] (with some woodcut derivatives of similar character); the printed world map drawn by Johan Ruysch and included in the editions of Ptolemy published at Rome in 1507 and 1508; a map of the North Atlantic in an anonymous MS atlas in the British Museum (Egerton MS 2803), believed to have been drawn at Naples by Vesconte Maggiolo about 1510; and the world map in a MS atlas of 1511

[1] Ravenstein, *Martin Behaim* (1908). This practice seems somewhat unhistorical, even if, by the end of the fifteenth century, the Ptolemaic length of 62° for the Mediterranean had been reduced to about 50° by some cartographers, under the influence of the portolan charts. In some of his world maps Henricus Martellus uses the greater figure, in others the lesser.

[2] Ganong (1929–37), III, 185 (and elsewhere).

[3] Cf. Fig. 4. Dr Williamson comments: 'I think that La Cosa's design is meant to show that the question is open. Why else does he cut off eastern Asia beyond the Ganges and show no Asiatic names on his North America? He could have had results of the 1498 voyage, with doubts raised by them.'   [4] Pl. VIII.

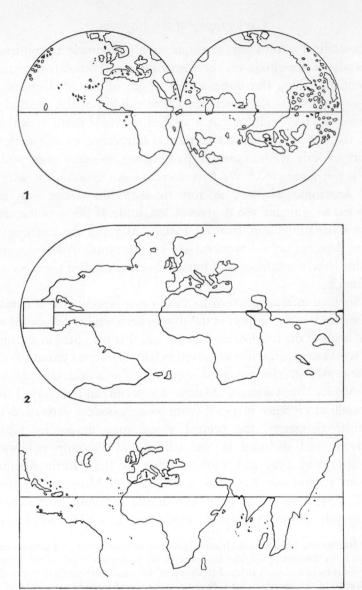

Fig. 4. Comparative outlines of six world maps, 1492–1508
     1. Behaim, 1492   4. King-Hamy, *post*-1503
     2. La Cosa, 1500   5. Waldseemüller, 1507
     3. Cantino, 1502   6. Ruysch, 1508

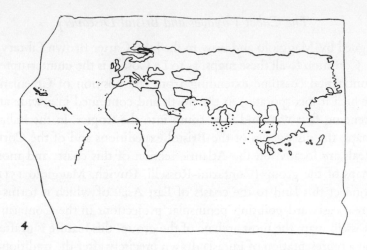

4

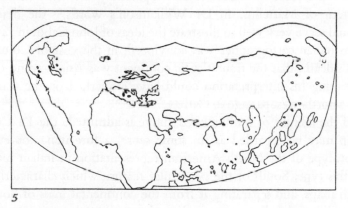

5

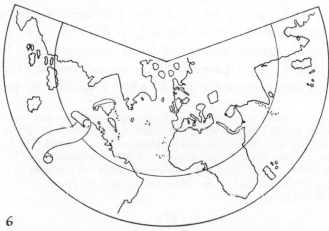

6

signed by Maggiolo and now in the John Carter Brown Library.[1]

Common to all these maps, as to La Cosa's, is the uninterrupted continental coastline extending from the position of Greenland (which it incorporates) in the north and continued in a wide arc trending first west and then south into the tropics. In the Italian maps, the discoveries of the Bristol expeditions and of the Corte Reals are located on the Atlantic section of this coast; and most maps of the group (Contarini-Rosselli, Ruysch, Maggiolo 1511) connect this land to the coasts of East Asia, of which it forms a great eastward-pointing peninsular projection. In the Contarini-Rosselli map, the most archaic of the group, this feature is grafted on a representation of Eurasia drawn precisely after the traditional pattern of Martellus. In Dr Williamson's words,[2] 'the design would serve very well to illustrate the ideas of John Cabot in 1497. This Italian cartographer was convinced, in the year of Columbus's death, that the transatlantic continent was Asia; and no one accepting his interpretation could have embarked on the search for a north-west passage to Cathay.'

If the affinity of outline cited above is admitted, the La Cosa map may be regarded as (in some sense) a forerunner or even prototype of the North American representation in Italian maps of this type. South of the peninsular feature which characterizes such maps, and separating it from the continental mass of South America, the Italian cartographers show a broad sea passage, 50 degrees wide, within which lie the Caribbean islands, with Cipangu further to the west. Nothing like this is seen in La Cosa's map; but the general similarity of design lends some colour to the suggestion that the vignette of St Christopher covering Central America may point to the area in which a westerly sea passage

---

[1] The only known impression of the Contarini-Rosselli map was acquired in 1923 by the British Museum, which has published it in facsimile (1924); see Plate VIII. Ruysch's map has been frequently reproduced and studied. The Egerton atlas was reproduced by E. L. Stevenson in 1911. Maggiolo's atlas of 1511 (together with the other works in this group) has been the subject of studies by G. Caraci, including one (in English) in *Imago Mundi*, vol. II (1937), pp. 37–54.

[2] See above, p. 142.

VIII. Contarini-Rosselli world map, 1506. Designed by G. M. Contarini, Venice, and engraved by Francesco Rosselli, Florence

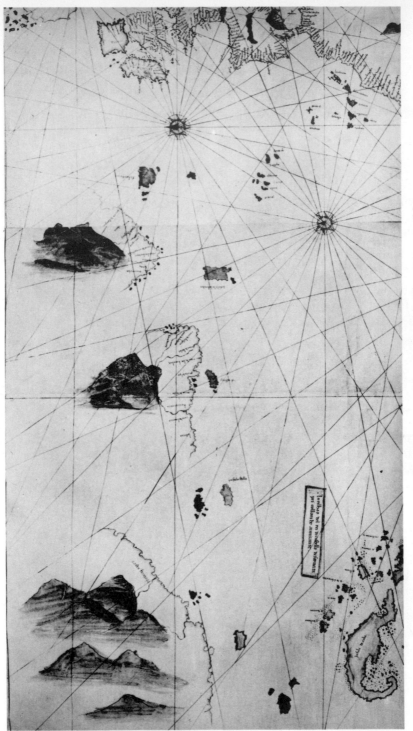

IX. The North Atlantic, in the anonymous Oliveriana world map

might be found, and where it was in fact sought by Columbus on his fourth voyage.[1] Thus La Cosa does not positively assert the continuity of the Spanish discoveries along the South American mainland with his delineation of the Atlantic coasts of North America.

While the outline of the north-western lands adopted by these Italian cartographers may recall that of La Cosa, it is to be noted that the Italian maps reproduce none of La Cosa'a nomenclature. They are of course not primary records of exploration, but academic exercises in the incorporation of new discoveries into an older world pattern. The channels by which authentic information of Cabot's expeditions could have come into La Cosa's hands are now well attested; but we can only guess at the routes, doubtless indirect, by which such information was conveyed from England or Portugal to the centres of map-production in Italy. To these general statements one exception may doubtfully be admitted. The world map by Johan Ruysch, a Dutch cosmographer resident in Rome, was engraved for the Rome editions of Ptolemy (1507 and 1508) edited by Marcus Beneventanus of Verona.[2] The commentary by Beneventanus appended to the 1508 edition contains a biographical note on Ruysch: 'Joannes vero Ruschi Germanus ... dixit: se nauigasse ab albionis australi parte: & tam diu quo ad subparallelum ab sub æquatore ad boream sub gradibus .53. peruenit: & in eo parallelo nauigasse ad ortus littora per angulum noctis atque plures insulas lustrasse.'[3] Ruysch thus claimed that, from a port of southern England, he had sailed to latitude 53° N and thence westward along this parallel 'through the angle of the night to the eastern shores',[4] discovering some

[1] Nunn's use of this argument to assign the La Cosa map to a date after Columbus's fourth voyage strains credulity. Nunn (1934), p. 26.

[2] On Ruysch, see J. Keuning, 'XVIth century cartography in the Netherlands', *Imago Mundi*, vol. IX (1952), p. 38; and references there given.

[3] Ptolemy, *Geographia* (Rome, 1508), sig. a3.

[4] Professor E. G. R. Taylor comments (in a private letter): ' "Angle of the night" ... is an astrological expression, and means that the traveller went over the western rim of the celestial horizon, after which he was travelling (it was considered) from west to east under the earth. Strictly speaking, it would mean that they got beyond 90° W (and reached Asia).'

islands. This voyage must have taken place before the summer of 1506, when the map was probably already in draft.[1] When and with whom Ruysch sailed is unknown; but in any case his experience (if the story is to be credited) left no mark on his world map, which is simply a compilation from Italian cartographic sources not difficult to identify. The peninsular projection of North-East Asia reaching across into the North Atlantic is common to Ruysch and to Contarini-Rosselli, and may with little doubt be considered a type-feature originating in Rosselli's workshop.[2] On this Ruysch grafts the representations of Greenland and of Labrador-Newfoundland seen in another group of Italian maps (to be discussed later) and derived from Portuguese and English sources. Thus Ruysch's 'half-moon' outline of 'Terra Nova', although connected to the mainland by an isthmus, at once recalls the almost identical outline found in such maps as the Italian atlas in the British Museum (Add. MS 31316) and—less strikingly—that in the Portuguese 'Cantino' map. For this region, most of Ruysch's nomenclature seems to present merely debased Portuguese forms.[3] His map cannot be taken as evidence of any discoveries not otherwise, or earlier, recorded by cartographers.

None of the maps referred to above admits the possibility of a strait or seaway between Greenland and Terra Nova. If there had been a voyage in this direction in 1498, their authors had no knowledge of it.

One more Italian map, somewhat different in character from those discussed above, deserves mention in relation to La Cosa's representation of the coasting by John Cabot in 1497. The world map (undated, perhaps of *c.* 1508–10) in the Biblioteca Oliveriana, Pesaro, draws the south coast of the feature representing Terra Nova with an east-west trend which may be taken to derive from

---

[1] Harrisse (1900), p. 57.

[2] As Harrisse divined, twenty-three years before the Contarini-Rosselli map came to light. Harrisse (1900), p. 61.

[3] E.g. 'Baia de Rockas', for Baia de Rosas.

La Cosa or La Cosa's source or a copy.[1] Yet (as Harrisse pointed out)[2] both the outline and the nomenclature of this east-west coastline are plainly those of the *east* coast of Labrador-Newfoundland, as presented in the Portuguese maps to be considered below. The influence of La Cosa might explain how this section of coast came to be turned through a right angle by the Oliveriana cartographer—a notable instance of confused compilation from disjunct materials. When we also find, in the Oliveriana map, La Cosa's hooked form for Cuba and an island name (Groga y) recalling one of La Cosa's (C. grago), the suspicion of affinity is strengthened. The north-eastern promontory of Asia however also reappears in the Oliveriana map as a peninsular feature drawn in the extreme north-west. The Portuguese 'Cantino' map of 1502 (discussed below) and its derivatives show a peninsular fragment of land in the approximate position of Florida, and this may perhaps be the origin of the representation in the Oliveriana map, with a shift northward and eastward and some modification of outline. Since the right-hand section of the Oliveriana map is missing, we cannot tell how the cartographer related the lands in the west to the east coast of Asia.

IV

The cartographic record of the *post*-Cabot voyages from Bristol and Lisbon is best considered by analysis of the several delineations of the north-west Atlantic found in Portuguese and Italian maps of the early sixteenth century. These manuscript maps illustrate, with varying degrees of authenticity, the results of the Portuguese and English voyages of discovery.

The *Portuguese maps* to be taken into account are:

The anonymous 'Cantino' planisphere (Biblioteca Estense, Modena), whose completion at Lisbon can be securely dated to September 1502;[3] and its derivative, the planisphere of Nicolo de Caveri (Bibliothèque Nationale, Paris), which may have been drawn three to four years later.

---

[1] See Plate IX. [2] Harrisse (1900), pp. 54–5. [3] See Plate IV.

307

The so-called 'Kunstmann I' map of the North Atlantic by Pedro Reinel; undated, post-1503.[1]

The anonymous Kunstmann III map of the Atlantic; undated, probably post-1506.[2]

The anonymous Kunstmann IV world map; similar to Kunstmann I, and ascribed by Dr A. Cortesão to Jorge Reinel, c. 1519.

Map of the North Atlantic in the so-called 'Miller' atlas (Bibliothèque Nationale, Paris); anonymous and undated; probably by Pedro and Jorge Reinel, c. 1519.

The planispheres drawn by Diogo Ribeiro in Spain between 1525 and 1530.

Anonymous atlas in the Biblioteca Riccardiana, Florence; ascribed by Dr A. Cortesão to Gaspar Viegas, c. 1537.

Atlas by João Freire dated 1546 (Huntington Library, California).

The *Italian maps* of special significance are:

The 'King-Hamy' planisphere (Huntington Library); anonymous and undated, post-1503.

Map of the North Atlantic in an atlas in the British Museum (Add. MS 31316, f. 5); anonymous and undated; probably by the same author and of about the same date as the King-Hamy map.[3]

Planisphere by Vesconte Maggiolo (Biblioteca Federiciana, Fano); drawn at Genoa and dated 15.4 (i.e. 1504?).

The anonymous Kunstmann II map of the Atlantic; undated, post-1506.

The Oliveriana planisphere (Biblioteca Oliveriana, Pesaro); undated, c. 1508–10.[4]

Planispheres by Vesconte Maggiolo drawn at Naples in 1516 (Huntington Library)[5] and at Genoa in 1527 (Biblioteca Ambrosiana, Milan).[6]

Planisphere by Girolamo da Verrazano, 1529 (Vatican Library).

[1] See Plate XII. The manuscript maps known as Kunstmann I, II, etc. are preserved in the Bayerische Staatsbibliothek, Munich; they take their name from the plate numbers in F. Kunstmann's *Atlas zur Entdeckungsgeschichte Amerikas* (1859), in which they were first reproduced.

[2] See Plate XIII.

[3] See Plates X, XI. The attribution of these two works to the same author has been made by Comandante A. Teixeira da Mota.

[4] See Plate IX.   [5] See Plate XIV.

[6] The Maggiolo map of 1516, which has never been reproduced, is in poor condition. To the courtesy of Cdr Teixeira da Mota I owe photographs of it and a reading of the 'Labrador' legend, established by Dr A. Cortesão and Dr H. C. Schulz in 1955 with a chemical re-agent and ultra-violet light. Both maps have been studied by G. Caraci (1958), with tracings and lists of place names.

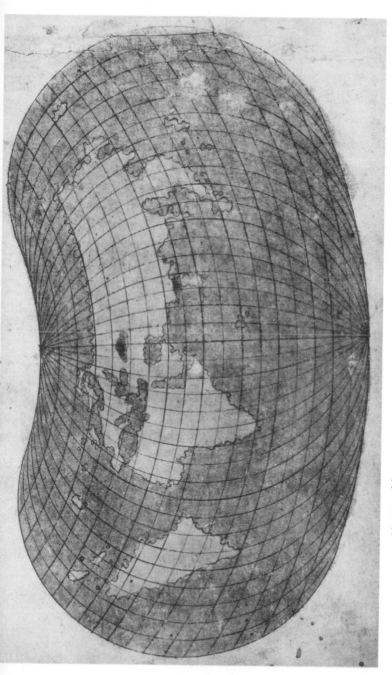

X. World map in an anonymous Italian atlas in the British Museum

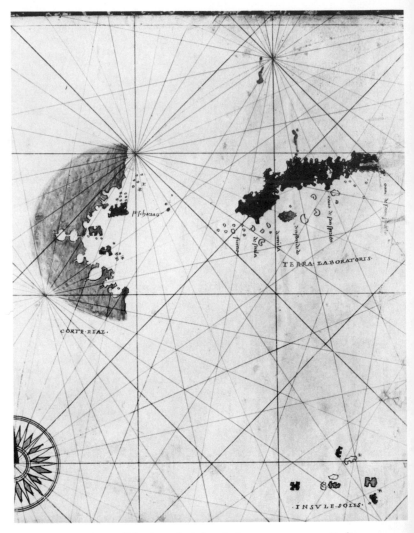

XI. Chart of the North Atlantic in an anonymous Italian
atlas in the British Museum

It is convenient to begin with the representation of Greenland. The Cantino map gives a detailed drawing of the east coast only, with an apparently conventional outline for the west coast. A legend ascribes the discovery to Portugal; and this type for Greenland, which is found in other Portuguese maps (Kunstmann I, III and IV), is reasonably derived from the Corte Real voyage of 1501. The early Portuguese mapmakers consistently drew Greenland as a peninsula; the Cantino map and Kunstmann III, following a cartographic tradition of the fifteenth century, plainly depict it as a westward extension of Asia. This representation had had a long history.[1] In its later evolution, exemplified in the world map of the Ptolemy printed at Ulm in 1482, Greenland appears as a peninsular tongue of land to the north of Norway. The Cantino map places Greenland to the west of Iceland, as seen in the early fifteenth-century maps of Claudius Clavus and even in the Medici Atlas of 1351. In a legend off Greenland the Cantino cartographer cites 'the opinion of cosmographers' in support of his delineation of Greenland as a 'promontory of Asia'. It seems more probable that his authority was a recent printed source than an older manuscript document; and his transference of Greenland westward may be interpreted as a reconciliation of the Corte Real data with the peninsular representation found in the Ulm Ptolemy and in other printed maps.

A variant delineation of Greenland (also as a peninsula), although doubtless of Portuguese origin, appears in some Italian works (the Oliveriana, and Maggiolo 1516 and 1527), but in no early Portuguese maps. Here both the east and the west coasts of southern Greenland are drawn with precision; this led the Danish scholar A. A. Bjørnbo to see in the Oliveriana planisphere the 'true Corte Real map' of Greenland, on the presumption that it illustrated the discoveries of the two Corte Real expeditions of 1500 and 1501.[2]

[1] Nansen (1911), vol. II, pp. 248–79; Bjørnbo (1912), pp. 89–152.
[2] Bjørnbo (1910), p. 314.

In the earliest of the Italian maps however Greenland has an altogether different form, suggesting another source, not Portuguese. These maps (King-Hamy, Add. MS 31316, Kunstmann II) draw Greenland as an elongated island, its longer axis extending east-west.[1] They have Corte Real place names for the east coast; and they all name the land 'Terra Laboratoris' (or a variant of this). No map of Portuguese authorship before the much later Kunstmann IV, of *c.* 1519, gives this name; and in no Portuguese map of any date is Greenland shown as an island.

The insular representation of Greenland has suggested a connection with the Bristol voyages of 1501 onward.[2] The Privy Purse records for 1502-5 in fact refer to the land found by 'men of Bristoll' variously as 'Thisle', 'the new Ilande', 'the Newfound Island'. Dr Williamson rightly observes that 'the phrase "the isle" must not be construed too literally';[3] and no documents tell us what land was reached by the Bristol expeditions in 1501-5. But (as will be seen) the nomenclature and legends of maps drawn in Italy, and later in Spain, provide positive evidence that their makers—even if only conjecturally—identified Greenland as an objective of these voyages; and the association of the island-delineation in the oldest of these maps creates a strong presumption of a common origin for the outline and the nomenclature.

The connection of João Fernandes with Greenland, in the minds of the early cartographers, is attested not only by the name 'Terra Laboratoris' and by the statement of Santa Cruz in his *Islario* of 1541;[4] it is placed beyond reasonable doubt by the map-legends transcribed below:

Maggiolo, 1516: Terra noua de pescaria inuenta de laboradore de re de anglitera tera frigida

---

[1] The orientation is of course magnetic. Rotation of the map anti-clockwise brings the geographical meridian, in this region, into the vertical. See Winter (1937), pp. 65-6.

[2] Bjørnbo (1912), pp. 174-5.

[3] Williamson, *Voyages of the Cabots* (1929), pp. 66-7, 207-8.

[4] See above, pp. 100-1.

Kunstmann IV [*P. Reinel*], *c. 1519*: DOLAVRADOR terram istam
portugalenses viderūt atamē nom intraverunt

Wolfenbüttel B [*Ribeiro?*], *c. 1525*: TIERA DEL LABRADOR laqual fue
descubierta por los Yngleses dela uila de bristol e por q̄ el
q̄ dio el lauiso della era labrador de las islas de los acares le
quido este nōbre

Ribeiro, 1529 (*Vatican*): TIERA DEL LABRADOR la qual descubrieron
los Ingleses dauilla de bristol en la qual no allarō cosa de
nēhū provecho

Ribeiro, 1529 (*Weimar*): Esta tierra descubrierō los Ingleses no ay
en ella cosa de prouecho TIERA DEL LABRADOR

Verrazano 1529: TERRA LABORATORIS questa terra fu discoperta da
inghilesi

With the exception of the only map drawn in Portugal,
all these legends refer to a discovery by the English and (in two
cases) by the men of Bristol. The legend in Maggiolo's map of
1516—the earliest in the series—seems to ascribe the discovery to
the *labrador* João Fernandes, apparently under the English flag.
But in the world map of Maggiolo's 1511 atlas already examined,
drawn from a different prototype, the two most northerly penin-
sulas of the New World are named respectively 'Terra de los
ingresy' and 'Terra de lauoradore de rey de portugall'.

At what date and in what service João Fernandes made the
Greenland landfall thus commemorated is therefore left uncertain
by the map-evidence. The map-legends however do not forbid
the hypothesis, originally put forward (as 'no more than a guess')
by Nansen and more recently revived by Admiral Morison, that
Fernandes, on the authority of King Manuel's charter of October
1499, sailed to Greenland with Pedro de Barcelos in 1500 and that
on his return, learning of Gaspar Corte Real's similar charter, he
transferred his base of operations from Lisbon to Bristol in search
of fresh support.[1]

We may note (without attaching much significance to the

[1] Nansen (1911), vol. II, pp. 357–8; Morison (1940), pp. 64–8.

association) that among the Corte Real nomenclature of the Oliveriana map in this region are two 'labrador' names: 'cauo larbadore' (on the Greenland coast) and 'Insula de labardor'. The latter name is placed by the cartographer on a large island which has the shape and position of the Antillia of fifteenth-century charts.

VI

The map-makers of the early sixteenth century could choose between four possible interpretations of Greenland: as an eastward extension of Asia, as a westward extension of Asia, as a southward extension of lands round the Pole, as an island.[1] Implicit in each of these representations, except the first, is the concept of a broad seaway to the west of Greenland, heading northward or north-westward. This feature, identifiable with Davis Strait, is found in two of the earliest Portuguese maps (Cantino, with Portuguese flags on both shores, and Kunstmann III) and in the Italian maps which show Greenland as an island.

For the relationship of Greenland to the lands to the westward, a different representation—also of Portuguese origin—appeared quite early.[2] It is first seen in the Atlantic chart signed by Pedro Reinel and known as Kunstmann I,[3] and it was copied in nearly all subsequent Portuguese (and some Italian) maps to the middle of the century. In this version, a line of coast extends from Cape Farewell (the southernmost point of Greenland) in a WNW direction to the extremity of the map and is separated from Labrador by a narrow strait running west or WNW. In the world maps drawn in Spain by the Portuguese Diogo Ribeiro, between 1525 and 1530, the head of this strait is closed, making it a gulf; this delineation, by way of later Portuguese works, was adopted by the Dieppe cartographers, and so we find it in Sebastian Cabot's map of 1544.

Pedro Reinel's delineation implies a common and continuous

---

[1] These versions are analysed in Taylor (1930), pp. 79–81 and Fig. 8.
[2] Winter (1937), pp. 62–5.   [3] Pl. XII.

south coast for Greenland and Baffin Land. This hypothesis, graphically illustrated in Kunstmann I, seems to be reflected in a passage of the letter written by Pietro Pasqualigo from Lisbon on 18 October 1501: '. . . The crew of the caravel believe that the land alluded to [Labrador] is mainland, and that it is joined to the land which was discovered last year in the north [Greenland] . . . but they were unable to reach it [Greenland], for the sea was frozen over.' Other reasons for supposing that Pedro Reinel was here interpreting the results of a Portuguese voyage will be examined below.

The Labrador-Newfoundland coast was drawn with striking conservatism by the Portuguese, from the Cantino cartographer in 1502 and Pedro Reinel a few years later to João Freire in 1546.[1] The stylized and geometrical outline found in the early Italian maps (King-Hamy, Add. MS 31316 and Kunstmann II) is merely a simplification of the more detailed Portuguese one. The representation of this coast throughout the first half of the sixteenth century stems from a common stock, and such variations—in design or nomenclature—as may be noted in individual maps reflect only differences in rendering a common source, and not differences of content due to the accretion of new information.

The cartographic evidence for these general statements, and for the more precise identification of the coastline thus drawn, must be sought in:

(1) the orientation and latitudinal extension given to this coast in the maps,
(2) its outline and principal features,
(3) its nomenclature.

The 'oblique' (or geographical) meridian drawn in Kunstmann I off the coast in question indicates a magnetic declination of about two points west for this region (corresponding to the value quoted by John Day from John Cabot). If the map is rotated through this angle, the Labrador-Newfoundland coast is seen to

---

[1] João Freire's outline is modified only to admit Cartier's discovery of Belleisle Strait.

313

lie NNW-SSE, a fair approximation to its real trend. The northerly and southerly limits of the coastline represented can be determined from those maps which have latitude scales, as shown in the following table:

	Caveri	Kunstmann I	King-Hamy	Kunstmann III	Maggiolo 1516	Kunstmann IV	Maggiolo 1527	Ribeiro 1529	Riccardiana	True latitude (geographical)
Limit of land to north-west	—	62°	63°	63°	—	61°	—	—	—	—
'I. de fortuna' (?Button Is.)	56°	61°	61°	56°	66°	60°	61°	59°	62°	60° 45'
Cape Race	48°	51°	48°	48°	52°	48°	50°	48°	51°	46° 38'

(All these northerly latitudes, except in the last column, are read on the magnetic meridian.)

For the coast between Cape Race and 'I. de fortuna' (that is, the section drawn in detail and with names), two of these nine maps give a latitude difference of 8 degrees, one gives 10 degrees, three give 11 degrees, and the other three (respectively) 12, 13, and 14 degrees. Allowing for problems of compilation and adjustment, and discounting 'scatter', it is reasonable to accept 11 degrees as a mean. The actual difference (measured on the geographical meridian) is about 14 degrees, that is, an extension of roughly the same order as that shown by most of the maps.

Professor E. G. R. Taylor has demonstrated the conformity of the actual coastline from Belleisle Strait to Cape Chidley, when replotted on a magnetic meridian, with the delineation of the Newfoundland-Labrador coast by João Freire in 1546.[1] Her diagrams are (with her permission) reproduced opposite (Fig. 5). Professor Taylor concluded that an unchronicled Portuguese expedition must have reached the entrance of Hudson Strait before 1546. But, as we have seen, João Freire merely reproduced the outline established long before and derived from a common Portuguese prototype at least as early as the Cantino map and

[1] Taylor (1939), p. 49.

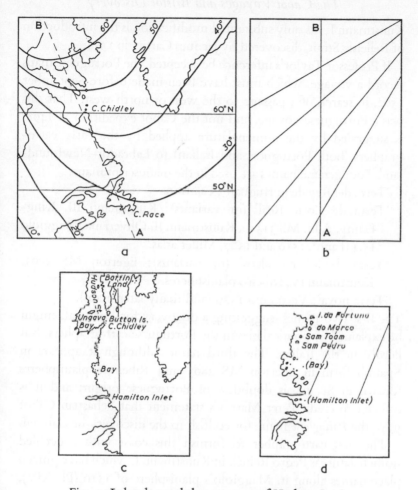

Fig. 5. Labrador and the entrance of Hudson Strait
charted by compass (after E. G. R. Taylor, 1939)
(a) Magnetic deviation, 1937
(b) Oblique meridians through points on line A–B
(c) Modern outline replotted on a magnetic meridian
(d) The coast from C. Race to
C. Chidley in the atlas of João Freire, 1546

Kunstmann I; his only substantial modification is the introduction of Belleisle Strait, discovered by Jacques Cartier in 1534.

If Professor Taylor's inference be accepted, the Portuguese maps record a voyage, which must have been made before September 1502, in search of a passage to the west or north-west. That this was a Portuguese voyage, and not the Cabot expedition of 1498, is suggested by the nomenclature applied by the early cartographers (both Portuguese and Italian) to Labrador-Newfoundland. Four general names are used in the manuscript maps:

'Terra del Rey de portuguall': Cantino.

'Terra de Corte Real' (or variants): Kunstmann III, King-Hamy, Add. MS 31316, Kunstmann II, Oliveriana, Maggiolo 15.4 (Fano), 1516 and 1527, Miller atlas.

'Terra de los baccalaos' (or variants): Egerton MS 2803, Kunstmann IV, Ribeiro planispheres.

'Terra nova': Verrazano 1529 (and many later maps).

The first two names, suggesting a discovery for Portugal, might be explained by political bias in the Portuguese cartographers, but hardly in the Italian. The third name, although it appears in Spanish form in Egerton MS 2803 and Ribeiro's planispheres (drawn in Spain), is doubtless of Portuguese origin; and it is difficult to credit Peter Martyr's statement that Sebastian Cabot gave the *Portuguese* name for codfish to the discovery he claimed.

The first cartographer to furnish this coast with a detailed nomenclature is Pedro Reinel, in Kunstmann I, which has eighteen place names along it. Maggiolo's planisphere of 1516 (Pl. XIV), which draws this region from a good Portuguese prototype, gives twenty-five names—more than any Portuguese map before the Miller atlas of *c.* 1519 (which has twenty-eight). The names in all three maps derive from the same stock, and appear to have been conferred by a Portuguese expedition. Maggiolo's map of 1516 provides significant testimony to this. Among the nine names in this map which are not in the Miller atlas we note 'abaya do padran'—a name here found for the first time in any extant map—at a point which may be identified as Nain Bay. The

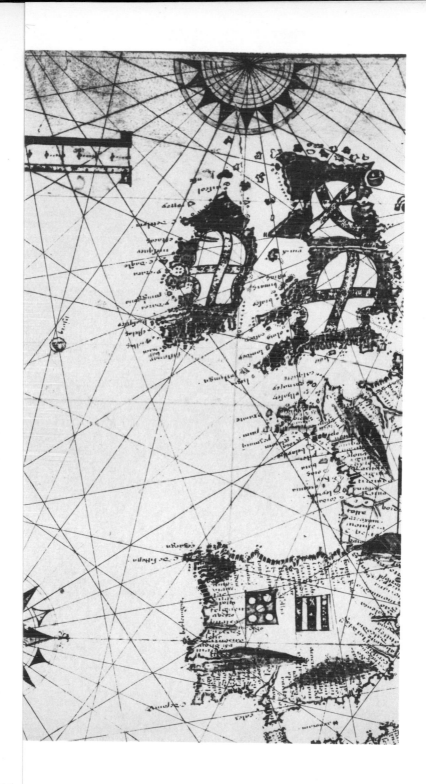

padrão was the stone pillar set up at any conspicuous feature by Portuguese explorers from Diogo Caõ onward; and this name could have been bestowed only by a Portuguese commander claiming discovery. The Oliveriana planisphere has a mutilated name of similar derivation, also presumably taken from a Portuguese source: 'ponta del pa[dram]'.

The only documented Portuguese voyages to the region, that is, in search of a north-west passage, at this early date are those of the Corte Reals; and it is unlikely that any others were undertaken from Portugal after the Cape route to India came into regular use. Most writers have concluded that the exploration of the Labrador-Newfoundland coast recorded in these maps is to be credited to the Corte Reals, and that the scholars, such as H. P. Biggar, who have used the map nomenclature to reconstruct their course were justified in doing so.[1]

This conclusion has recently been challenged by Professor Arthur Davies, who uses the place names of Kunstmann I as evidence for John Cabot's course in 1498, and identifies this voyage as the expedition to the north-west described by Sebastian Cabot to Peter Martyr in or before 1515.[2] The early explorer's practice of naming features after the church festival or saint's day on which they were discovered is well authenticated; but this evidence, if unsupported by documents, calls for the most critical application in establishing, by its use, the course of a voyage. When the seven names of saints or festivals adduced by Professor Davies from Kunstmann I are tested from the Portuguese kalendars of the *Regimento do Astrolabio e do Quadrante*,[3] only two names are found to point unambiguously to a single date for each: 'R. de sam francisquo' (October 4) and 'B. de conceiçam' (December 8).

These two names, with their associated dates, may indeed be reasonably held to support Professor Davies's hypothesis that the

---

[1] H. P. Biggar, *Voyages of the Cabots and of the Corte Reals* (1903).

[2] Davies (1955).

[3] The only two surviving copies, the so-called *Regimento de Munich* and *Regimento de Evora*, are assigned to the approximate dates of (respectively) about 1509 and about 1518. Their kalendars differ in detail from one another.

nomenclature on this coast must have been bestowed by an expedition which wintered there; and he infers that it could not have been the Corte Real expeditions of 1500–2, which—according to the documents we have—were back in Lisbon by October. Yet the maps present reasons which are fatal to the supposition that the nomenclature derives from an English discovery. First, the appearance, among these names, of that of a purely Portuguese saint, St Iria (or Eiria), which can hardly have been used by—or perhaps even known to—Englishmen or Italians.[1] Second, the occurrence of names derived from the Portuguese *padrões* in maps from the same stock as Kunstmann I, as noted above. Third, the extreme improbability that a Portuguese cartographer would have preferred names from an English source (if indeed he had them) to names from Portuguese expeditions, whose presence on this coast is attested by other evidence; this must be equally true of the outline. Placed in the balance against these considerations, the names called by Professor Davies to witness to the date of the discoveries will not bear the weight of proof laid on them; and we must either concede (with W. F. Ganong) that 'there are surely reasons for the occurrence of saints' names on early maps besides dates of discovery',[2] or suppose that the names on this coast were bestowed by a Portuguese expedition which wintered there.

The land behind the Labrador-Newfoundland coastline is drawn by these cartographers in a form intended to express their ignorance or uncertainty of what lay beyond—certainly not as the west coast of an island. Their representation thus appears to leave open the question whether this land was to be considered to have a

---

[1] This obscure seventh-century saint (Virgin and Martyr) was apparently not well known even in Portugal and Italy, if we may judge from the corruptions which her name suffered at the hands of later cartographers: santa ana (Miller atlas), s.ta zecara (Maggiolo 1516). According to the *Grande Enciclopedia Portuguesa–Brasileira*, her cult was confined to some Portuguese dioceses only. Harrisse (1900) misreads the name in Kunstmann I as Santa Cyria. Santa Iria's festival is on October 20.

[2] Ganong (1927–37), I, 159. Ganong (IV, 178) gives other instances of 'the complete breakdown of the liturgical test' and its 'anomalous results' when confronted with external evidence for the chronology of a voyage.

connection with Asia or with an unknown intervening land mass. Only two of the early Portuguese maps continue its south coast to the western edge of the parchment, although in too vague and speculative a drawing to allow us to read it confidently as a record of discovery. Kunstmann I however shows a feature which may well represent Cabot Strait, between Newfoundland and Cape Breton, with (beyond it) a Portuguese flag and two small islands, one of which is named. If this reflects a Portuguese discovery, it does not seem necessary to associate it (as Ganong did)[1] with the voyages of João Alvares Fagundes and therefore to date the map as late as 1520; a Corte Real report need not be excluded.[2] Kunstmann III has coastlines running both southward and westward from 'Cabo de Cōcepicion', without detail or names. The line drawn towards the west, which looks like an addition, may express an alternative hypothesis by the cartographer, or his knowledge of a map similar to La Cosa's.

The earliest Portuguese world maps and Atlantic charts do not explicitly convey their makers' judgment on the relationship of the lands in the west to the continent of Asia,[3] although there is evidence of other kinds that the Portuguese cartographers considered that the western discoveries were not—were indeed remote from—the coast of Cathay. Thus the inset of Martin Waldseemüller's world map of 1507[4] is the earliest map to show, without the least room for doubt, eastern Asia and the whole of America as two distinct continents, separated by a broad ocean in which is sited Cipangu. The northern edge of North America and the western coasts of both Americas and of the isthmus linking them

---

[1] Ganong (1929–37), II, 137–8.

[2] In a different context Ganong (I, 163–4), discussing the Cantino map, suggests that the indentation drawn on the south-west coast of Newfoundland represents Placentia Bay and that the Portuguese flag shown at this point may indicate the place at which the Corte Reals, coming on John Cabot's mark, ceased their 'survey' although their exploration may have continued westward. This seems rather fanciful. Kunstmann IV, which generally follows Kunstmann I, adds a significant legend on the west side of Cabot Strait (where Pedro Reinel has a Portuguese flag): 'tera q̄ foy descoberto por bertōmes'.

[3] Cf. Fig. 4.   [4] And his globe gores of the same year. See Plate VI.

are drawn in straight lines, indicating that they were as yet un-explored. Here (in Dr Williamson's words),[1] 'we have an aca-demic geographer of western Germany expressing the dominant truth of the connection of the two Americas and their separation from Asia by an ocean not yet named the Pacific, ten years after the return of John Cabot from his first voyage. If Waldseemüller could obtain by 1507 the information which he welded into this conception, it seems evident that the exploring captains of Western Europe must have had it some time earlier.'

Waldseemüller's map, by cutting off North America at about 50° N, admits the theoretical possibility of a north-west passage navigable in open water round it. We now have to examine the traces which the earliest voyages in search of this passage have left on other maps.

VII

In many of the early Portuguese and Italian maps the Labrador-Newfoundland coast is turned at its northernmost point ('I. de fortuna') and extended a considerable distance in a generally north-westerly direction (on a magnetic bearing) before petering out. Corrected for variation, this represents an approximate westerly trend. The limit of north latitude at which the coast ends, in the maps with latitude scales, is shown in the table on page 314 above. The strait, of which this coastline forms the southern shore, is represented with an orientation, position, and relationship to adjacent lands, corresponding to those of Hudson Strait. The drawing, although devoid of names, is positive enough to suggest that its source was an exploring voyage rather than hypothesis. It is natural to associate it with the Portuguese exploration to which the outline and nomenclature of Labrador itself are due; and in his globe of about 1537 Gemma Frisius did so explicitly.[2]

[1] See above, p. 143.
[2] See Plate VII. The only known pair of globes (terrestrial and celestial) by Gemma Frisius, formerly preserved in the Anhalter Landesmuseum, Zerbst, was destroyed during the war. From this Bjørnbo (1912) published a clear reproduc-tion, and Ganong (1929–37) tracings, of the north-western regions. In 1951 an

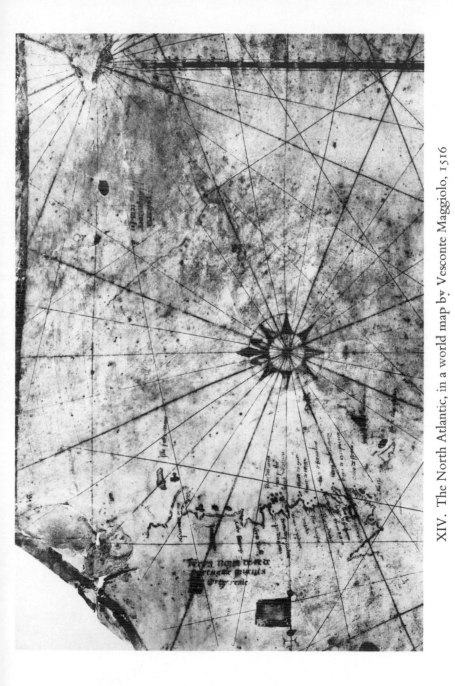

XIV. The North Atlantic, in a world map by Vesconte Maggiolo, 1516

The legend at the eastern end of the strait on this globe refers to a Portuguese attempt to pass this way to the Indies: 'Fretum arcticum siue triū fratrū per quod lusitani ad orientem & ad Indos & moluccas nauigare conati sunt'. Another and longer legend refers, somewhat confusedly, to Gaspar Corte Real's supposed attainment of the coast of Cathay.[1]

There was, however, an English expedition which apparently penetrated the strait, namely, that described by Sebastian Cabot to Peter Martyr between 1512 and 1515 and to Ramusio in 1551. As Dr Williamson has shown, the balance of documentary evidence points to 1508–9 as the date of this voyage.[2] If his interpretation is correct, we cannot expect to find traces of the voyage in any maps produced before 1509 or (apart from minor details) in maps of later date drawn in substance from prototypes which had been developed before 1509. These two classes embrace all the maps so far considered; and the globe of Gemma Frisius is in fact the earliest surviving cartographic work to illustrate Sebastian's voyage, or his account of it.

As shown above (pp. 166–70), Gemma Frisius incorporates in his design all the principal geographical facts that can be extracted from Sebastian's reported narratives: the strait, two or three degrees wide, leads westward nearly under the Arctic Circle (that is, in 65° or 66° N) and broadens into a wide gulf trending to the west, the south shore of which is labelled 'Terra per britannos inuenta'. We can only guess at Gemma's sources and at the channels by which his information came to Louvain, since Peter Martyr's printed versions of the story do not furnish all the data required for the delineation on the globe, which correspond

example of the terrestrial globe was discovered in Florence, and this is now in the Globusmuseum, Vienna; see Haardt (1952). The celestial globe bore the date 1537; the terrestrial is undated. The imperial privilege for the two globes, of which Haardt prints a translation, is dated 2 February 1536 and shows that at this date the terrestrial globe was not yet completed; it was perhaps published with the celestial in 1537. Gemma had already, by 1530, published a pair of globes, now lost.

[1] These legends are printed by Taylor (1930), p. 275.
[2] Introduction, chapters VII, VIII.

closely enough with those in Ramusio's account published nineteen years later. Here nevertheless, in a far more developed form than the embryonic figuration of a strait drawn in the Portuguese maps (presumably from a Portuguese voyage), we have the first cartographic illustration of the north-west expedition described by Sebastian Cabot, on which he appears to have reached the entrance of Hudson Bay.

The representation by Gemma Frisius came into currency by its repetition in Mercator's world map of 1538 and globe of 1541, in the maps of Sebastian Münster from 1540, and in the world maps of Gemma himself.[1] Whether Sebastian Cabot's information, directly or indirectly obtained, lay behind Gemma's delineation of the North West Passage, or whether Sebastian adopted this delineation into his own maps as a convenient expression of his views, we cannot say. It is nevertheless plain that Gemma's globe and the works derived from it enable us to visualize the representation of the passage in the lost world map or maps by Sebastian seen or described in England by Gilbert, Chytraeus, Willes, Hakluyt and Purchas. Willes indeed, coupling together the 'Mappes and Globes' of Gemma Frisius and the 'table' of Sebastian, implies that they depicted the passage in the same way.[2]

The map drawn by Sebastian Cabot in England after 1548 must have presented a very different version of the north-western regions from that in the Paris Map of 1544, which he had prepared in Spain. Its character is discussed above by Dr Williamson (pp.

---

[1] For lost cartographic works by Gemma Frisius, see L. Bagrow, *A. Ortelii catalogus cartographorum*, I (1928), 97–9. They include a pair of globes prepared in or before 1530 and a world map printed in 1540. Taylor (1930, p. 94) adds a reference to a map printed in 1549. The 1540 map was doubtless the model for the smaller world map added by Gemma to his editions of Peter Apian's *Cosmographia* from 1544; this is the only surviving world map from his hand.

[2] Professor Taylor (1930, pp. 78, 256) supposes the 'two globes of Gerardus Mercator's best making', which John Dee brought back from Louvain in 1547 and presented to Trinity College, Cambridge, to be those of Gemma Frisius, in the engraving of which Mercator had participated. The presence of Gemma's globes in England is also attested by the ledgers of Plantin, who exported a pair to London in April 1568.

158–9, 165–6), and it will be enough to summarize here the notices of it by early writers.[1]

From Hakluyt (writing in 1584) we learn that the map was 'cut', that is engraved, by Clement Adams;[2] Purchas in 1625 also ascribes it to Adams and gives the date 1549, which is confirmed by the earlier testimony of Chytraeus. By 1566 there were maps by Sebastian Cabot in 'the Queenes Majesties privie Gallerie at Whitehall', where Gilbert saw them; in 1569 the German traveller Nathan Kochhaff, *alias* Chytraeus, examined one at Oxford and transcribed nineteen of its legends;[3] and in 1577 Willes described the map belonging to the Earl of Bedford at Chenies. Hakluyt in 1584 wrote of 'the copye ... sett oute by Mr Clemente Adams' which was 'in many merchantes houses in London'.[4] It is uncertain, but appears probable, that the copies described by Chytraeus and Willes were from the same blocks or plates as those seen at Whitehall by Gilbert and Hakluyt.

The Whitehall copies of the map were twice recorded in the seventeenth century. They were still there when Purchas wrote in 1625 (although he refers only to one map); they are listed (in the plural, as 'Sebastian Gabots Maps') among the printed maps in an inventory of the Royal map collection made soon after 1660;[5] and they were presumably lost—with most of the other maps there

---

[1] The early references are assembled by G. P. Winship, *Cabot Bibliography* (1900), pp. 17–18.

[2] I see no reason to doubt (with Harrisse) that 'cut' here means engraved. Although Ortelius records, by Sebastian Cabot, 'universalem tabulam, quam impressam aeneis formis vidimus', there was little copper-plate engraving in England before 1550, and it seems probable that Adams's map was woodcut. Another possibility is that the plates of the Paris map were sent from the Netherlands to England, and there altered by Adams in accordance with Sebastian's draft or instructions.

[3] Chytraeus, who was a professor of classics, complains of the lack of elegance in the Latinity of the legends. The variants between the printed legends of the Paris Map and the transcripts of Chytraeus and Hakluyt are discussed by Winship (*op. cit.*, pp. 22–6) and Almagià (1958, pp. 59–60). See also above, pp. 25–6, 207.

[4] 'Discourse of Western Planting'. Taylor, *Hakluyts* (1935), p. 296.

[5] R. A. Skelton, 'The Royal map collections of England', *Imago Mundi*, vol. XIII (1956), pp. 181–3.

listed—in the fires which destroyed the Palace of Whitehall in 1691 and 1698.

No example of this map, which was cited as a source and authority by the Elizabethan promoters of enterprises for the North West Passage, has survived. Its influence is doubtless to be discerned in the cartographic works produced as propaganda for these enterprises by Gilbert, Dee and Lok.

References

ALMAGIÀ, R. 'I mappamondi di Enrico Martello e alcuni concetti geografici di Cristoforo Colombo', *La Bibliofilia*, vol. XLII (1940).

—— 'On the cartographic work of Francesco Rosselli', *Imago Mundi*, vol. VIII (1951), pp. 27–34.

—— *Commemorazione di Sebastiano Caboto nel IV centenario della morte* (1958).

BJØRNBO, A. A. 'Die echte Corte-Real-Karte', *Petermanns Mitteilungen*, vol. LVI (1910), pp. 313–15.

—— 'Cartographia Groenlandica', *Meddelelser om Grønland*, vol. XLVIII (1912).

CARACI, G. 'La produzione cartografica di Vesconte Maggiolo ed il Nuovo Mondo', *Memorie geografiche*, vol. IV (1958), pp. 221–89.

CORTESÃO, A. *Cartografia e cartógrafos portugueses dos séculos XV e XVI* (1935).

—— *The nautical chart of 1424* (1954).

—— and TEIXEIRA DA MOTA, A. *Portugaliae Monumenta Cartographica*, vols. I–IV (1960).

CRONE, G. R. *Maps and their Makers* (1953).

DAVIES, A. 'The last voyage of John Cabot and the rock at Grates Cove', *Nature*, vol. CLXXVI (1955), pp. 996–8.

GANONG, W. F. 'Crucial maps in the early cartography and place-nomenclature of the Atlantic coast of Canada', *Transac-*

tions of the *Royal Society of Canada*, ser. 3, vols. XXIII–XXXII (1929–37).

HAARDT, R. 'The globe of Gemma Frisius', *Imago Mundi*, vol. IX (1952), 109–10.

HARRISSE, H. *La découverte et évolution cartographique de Terre-Neuve* (1900).

MORISON, S. E. *Portuguese voyages to America in the fifteenth century* (1940).

NANSEN, F. *In Northern Mists* (1911).

NUNN, G. E. *The Mappemonde of Juan de la Cosa* (1934).

—— *The La Cosa Map and the Cabot Voyages* (1946).

TAYLOR, E. G. R. *Tudor geography 1485–1583* (1930).

—— 'Hudson's Strait and the Oblique Meridian', *Imago Mundi*, vol. III (1939), 48–52.

WINTER, H. 'The pseudo-Labrador and the oblique meridian', *Imago Mundi*, vol. II (1937), 61–73.

Note. Mr. Bernard G. Hoffman's map-study entitled *Cabot to Cartier* (Toronto, 1961) came into the writer's hands after final proofs of this paper had been passed.

INDEX

Adams, Clement, 322–4
Agramonte, Juan de, 148, 164
Ailly, Pierre d', 5, 7, 177–8
Albertus Magnus, 5
Alcaçovas, Treaty of, 14
America, a new continent, 106, 119–20, 122, 135, 143–4; concept of in maps, 319–20
Anglo-Portuguese relations (1499), 116
Antillia, 7, 8, 9, 21, 297, 312
Asia, westward passage to, 7–8, 10, 45, 47–8, 51, 68, 87, 89, 99, 105–6, 142, 208, 209–10
Asshehurst, Thomas, 125, 132, 137, 235–47, 250–61
Atlantic, interest in, 3–4; English trade in islands, 14 16; winds, 62–3, 99–100, 225–6
Ayala, Pedro de, 23–4, 30, 38–9, 86, 89, 98, 228–9; analysis of his letter of 1498, 103–4
Azores, 9, 15

Baccalaos, 22, 147–8, 231–3, 267, 268–9, 274, 275
Bacon, Roger, 5
Ballesteros-Gaibrois, M., 39
Barcelos, Pedro de, 116–17, 311
Barlow, Roger, 26
Bastidas, Rodrigo de, 111
Behaim, Martin, globe of, 8–9; see also Maps
Beneventanus, Marcus, 305
Beste, George, 159, 160, 280
Biddle, Richard, 96, 172
Biggar, H. P., 66, 98, 203
Bjørnbo, A. A., 309
Bobadilla, Francisco de, 112
Borough, Stephen, 171–2
Bradley, Thomas, 92, 215
Brasil, Island of, 10, 20–1; reported discovery of, 30, 38, 60, 68, 71, 82–3, 187–8, 188–9, 213, 228

Brigandine or Brickenden, Robert, 215
Bristol, relations with Iceland, 13–14, 18, 175–7; trade with Madeira, 15, 187; knowledge of Atlantic, 15–16, 17–18; Atlantic voyages of 1480–1, 19–23, 187–8, 188–9; and Island of Brasil, 43, 60, 82–3, 127, 213, 228; voyages of the 1490's, see John Cabot; voyages of 1501–6, ch. VIII passim, 215–16, 220–3; syndicates for discovery, 124–32; Company Adventurers to the New Found Land, 134, 161; patent of 1501, 125–6, 235–47; patent of 1502, 132–3, 250–261; and Sebastian Cabot, 161–2; plan of, Pl. III; map evidence for voyages, 297, 310–11
Brown, Rawdon, 34, 66, 96

Cabot, John, 23; origins, 33–4, 191; Venetian naturalization, 33, 190–1; ? in 1494, 24–6; early life, 33–4, 37–44, 191–2, 192–5, 210; as a merchant, 37–8, 210; arrival in England, 37–44, 48–9, 203; Ayala's testimony, 38–9; Caboto Montecalunya at Valencia, 39–42, 196–9; and Columbus, 40–2; in Lisbon and Seville, 42, 98–9; his project, 45–53; house at Bristol, 47, 103, 219; letters patent, 1496, 49–51, 133, 203–5; voyage of 1496, 54, 213; voyage of 1497, 54–83, 206–14, 295–9, 306–7, 313; problems of landfall and coasting, 66–7; return reported, 84–5, 206; pension, 86–7, 102, 213, 217–19; his conception of the discovery, 88–9, 207–11; intentions, 1497 8, 87–9, 220–3; magnificence, 89–90; patent of 1498, 91, 226–7; voyage of 1498: preparations, 91–4, 224–5; the ships, 91–2; analysis of evidence, 95–101; events and possibilities, 101–13,

327

Index

Index

letters patent, nature of, 49–50
liturgical test for dating discoveries, 317–18
Lloyd (Thloyde), John, 19–20, 21, 187
Lucar, Emanuel and Cyprian, 27

Madeira, trade with, 15, 17, 187
magnetic declination, 313–14, Fig. 5
Mantuan Gentleman, The, 152–3, 160, 270–3
map evidence, nature of, 59–60, 67
maps and globes, classification, compilation, and dating of, 296–7; Dieppe maps, 299, 312; Italian maps, 296–9, 308–12; Portuguese maps, 307–9, 312–19; anonymous maps: B.M. Add. MS 31316, 308–10, 313, Pls. X, XI; Cantino planisphere, 122–3, 129, 139, 300 n., 306–8, 312–16, 319 n., Pl. IV, Fig. 4; Caveri (formerly known as Canerio) planisphere, 139, 307; 'copy of the land' sent by John Day, 65, 81, 295–296, 298; B.M. Egerton MS 2803, 301–6, 316; King-Hamy world map, 121, 308–10, 313, 316, Fig. 4; Kunstmann II, 121, 140–1, 308–10, 313, 316; Kunstmann III, 139–40, 308–9, 312, 316, 319, Pl. XIII; Kunstmann IV, 121, 308–11, 316, 319 n.; Medici atlas (1351), 309; Miller Atlas (c. 1519), 308, 316; Oliveriana world map, 121, 139, 306–9, 311–12, 316–17, Pl. IX; Paris (1544), see Sebastian Cabot; Riccardiana atlas, 309; Wolfenbüttel, 120; named cartographers' maps: Behaim, Martin (globe 1492), 8–9, 296, Fig. 4; Bianco, Andrea, 14; Cabot, John, 47, 81, 87, 88–9, 142, 209–10, 212, 228–9, 295; Cabot, Sebastian (1544), 24–5, 57–9, 63, 83, 158, 159, 207, 278, 279, 299, 312, 322, (1549), 158, 322–4; Claudius Clavus, 14, 309; Columbus (1492), 296; Contarini, G. M., and Rosselli, F. (1506), 141–2, 301–6, Pl. VIII; Desliens,

N. (1541), 299 n.; Freire, João (1546), 308, 313–14, Fig. 5; Gemma Frisius (globe c. 1537), 158–9, 166–70, 279, 320–2, Pl. VII; La Cosa, Juan de (1500), 59–60, 65, 72–83, 107–9, 298–307, Pls. I, II, Figs. 2, 3, 4; Maggiolo, Vesconte (15.4), 308, 316; (1511), 301–6, 311; (1516), 308–10, 316–17, Pl. XIV; (1527), 308–9, 316; Martellus, Henricus, 8,, 296; Mercator (1538, 1541), 322; Münster, Sebastian, 322; Ptolemy, 5; Reinel, Pedro (Kunstmann I), 75, 140, 308–9, 312–14, Pl. XII; Ribeiro, Diogo (1525–30), 128–9, 308, 311–312, 316; Rosselli, Francesco, 296, 301–6; Ruysch, Johan (1507), 142–3, 301–6, Fig. 4; Verrazano, G. de (1529), 308, 311, 316; Viegas, Gaspar, 308; Waldseemüller, Martin, 143, 319–20, Pl. VI, Fig. 4
Marco Polo, 5–7, 46, 56, 87, 88, 223–4
Marcus, G. J., 13 n.
Markland, 11
Martins, Fernão, 7
Martyr, Peter, 97, 100–1, 147–9, 159, 266–8, 268–9, 269–70
Montecalunya, 39–40; see also John Cabot
Morison, S. E., cited, 117–18; 297, 311

Nansen, Fridtjof, 11, 311
Navarrete, Martin Fernandez de, 111
Newfoundland, 31, 83, 99, 298, 311–319
New Found Land, The, annexation of, 64; the summer scene (1497), 64–5, 210, 212–13; fishery, 88, 122, 136, 210, see also Baccalaos; Company Adventurers, 134, 161
North West Passage, 99, 119–20, 123, 124, 129, 143–4; in 1501–5, 130, 135, 148–9, 163–4, 165–70; project of 1521, 150, 166–7; Sebastian Cabot's claim, 151, 157–8, 272, 273, 274, 276, 277, 278, 279; in maps, 158, 166–70, 320–1

Index

Index